CONFESSIONS OF AN IRISH REBEL

Brendan Behan was born in Dublin in 1923. A member of the I.R.A., he was sentenced to three years in Borstal in 1939, and to fourteen years by a military court in Dublin in 1942.

He became a dominant literary figure almost overnight with the 1956 production of his play 'The Quare Fellow', based on his prison experiences. This recognition was reinforced by the success of BORSTAL BOY and his second play, 'The Hostage'.

Brendan Behan described his recreations in WHO'S WHO as 'drinking, talking, and swimming', but no factual description could do justice to his flamboyant, larger-than-life character. Generally regarded as irreverent and unpredictable if not actually dangerous, there was nonetheless no publicity which ever obscured his marked talents or his great understanding of human nature.

Brendan Behan died in 1964.

Borstal Boy

Brendan Behan

CONFESSIONS OF AN IRISH REBEL

ARROW

Arrow Books Limited
20 Vauxhall Bridge Road
London SW1V 2SA

An imprint of Random House UK Ltd

London Melbourne Sydney Auckland
Johannesburg and agencies throughout
the world

First published by Hutchinson & Co. 1965

Arena edition 1985

Reissued 1990

Arrow edition 1991

10 9 8 7 6

Printed and bound in Great Britain by
The Guernsey Press Co Ltd, Guernsey, C.I.

ISBN 0 09 936500 6

Do Rae — mar żan í
níor críocnocaḋ an leaḃar
seo ḋón Ġliaṅ 2000 a.ḋ. —
Roinnt Ġliaṅ żar. éis mo ḃáis

*A facsimile reproduction of Brendan Behan's
handwritten dedication, translated below*

TO REA
without whose help this book
would not have been written until
at least 2000 A.D. — many years
after my death

PREFACE

by Rae Jeffs

IT was in the spring of 1957, seven years before his death, that I first met Brendan Behan. He had come to the London offices of Hutchinson, his publishers, to deliver the manuscript of *Borstal Boy*.

I knew little about him, except that he was the Irish author of an extremely good play, *The Quare Fellow*, and that he was the star of one of the most talked-about television interviews of 1956.

When I met him, he was standing next to a table, a formidable figure, with his unruly hair cascading over his forehead and his clothes arrayed around him in the best fashion they could without the help of the wearer. His wife, Beatrice, sat in the corner at his side, and I was at once struck by the deep unspoken understanding that obviously existed between them.

We were introduced—Brendan's introductions to the opposite sex could hardly be described as formal—and I was asked to give a précis of my life up to that very moment. He listened quietly and was genuinely interested—an essential facet of his character which he lost only a few months before his death—interrupting only when he felt I had glossed over an important detail. When he learned that I came from Sussex, he was obviously delighted. Apparently he had been extremely well treated in the short time he had spent in a Sussex prison, and as a result he had a warm regard for anyone coming from that county.

The introductions over, Brendan, whose thirst took small account of licensing hours, called for a drink. With vicarage garden-party decorum, I enquired whether it would be tea or coffee?

'Do you call that a drink?' he roared, interpolating a stream of unbridled anglo-saxon words which would not normally be heard in a publishers' office.

And so began the first of my many lessons in nonconformity. Somehow I managed to get hold of a bottle of whiskey, and I returned triumphantly to the office, as much exhilarated by my feat as was the man himself on getting it.

For the rest of the afternoon, I was entertained by numerous stories which were not altogether easy to follow for the uninitiated, for Brendan had a most captivating way of unexpectedly breaking into song. He had an unlimited repertoire of folksongs and Dublin ballads which he would sing enchantingly by the hour in a light lilting brogue.

Suddenly, without word of warning, as if on castors, he glided to the door, Beatrice followed, and off down the passage shouting, '*Slán leat*', to the wide-eyed astonishment of the passers-by. I raced after him as I remembered the precious manuscript, still not delivered, only to receive the casually imparted information that he had 'left it at the BBC' and would 'go and get it'. I remember it was five-thirty by the clock in the street opposite, but the significance, in those early days, was lost on me. Some time later, I started out to look for him, but I did not have to go very far. I heard his voice coming from The George singing, somewhat more lustily than before, the same Dublin ballads.

Under the rumbustious bravado, Brendan was courteous, considerate and absurdly generous. Every person in the pub that evening was clustered round him as though drawn by a magnet, and it would have taken a bigger fool than myself not to discover the largeness of the heart that ticked behind the showman's mask. I had simply started out on a business mission, but in a matter of hours, I lived a lifetime. It was a most remarkable experience, and to those who poke the finger of scorn at objects of popular adulation, I can only say it was as though a five-hundred watt light had suddenly gone on. It wasn't necessarily that things were dull before, but that Brendan's presence produced an overwhelming current of electricity quite beyond the ordinary. He was not then a world-renowned figure, or the all-important copy for the morning's editions. He was a man being himself, more alive than the rest of us, and our batteries were charged with a vitality which, for me at any rate, changed the whole conception of life.

Throughout the following year, my connection with Brendan was mainly that of a public relations officer, and it was in this capacity that I began to pierce through his external ferocity, which is the life force of nearly all artists, and to discover the innocence, the tenderness and the sensitivity behind it.

Before any public appearance, he would assume a completely different personality. As we neared the television studios or the newspaper offices for an interview, I could almost see him building up the bricks of the wall that protected him from himself. Beads of perspiration would break out on his forehead, and he would be cruel, abusive and arrogant.

He knew he had to live up to his reputation as the tough I.R.A. rebel, the man who would assault not only others, but himself as well, rather than conform. He did not dare reveal that the ugliness of his experiences—death, bloodshed and prison routine—had not really touched the vital part of him. His essential being was strangely unaffected by the many painful events in his life, and this cloak of violence and abuse was necessary to hide his vulnerability. When the strain of impersonation became too much, a bout of drinking would follow—the best soporific of all. But when he realised this bulwark of self-protection was unnecessary, he became almost childlike in his frankness and candour.

With the publication of *Borstal Boy* in October 1958, Brendan's success was assured. My chief recollection of those days is the genuine pleasure which Brendan got from reading the reviews. It was almost as if he was no longer afraid to look in and recognise himself, and I think he was nearer at that time to establishing a real relationship with himself than he ever became again. Perhaps if he had managed it, the self-destructiveness that he carried within him would only have come to the surface spasmodically and certainly would not have killed him. I do not think that he wanted to die; only to stop living the life he had made for himself.

At any rate, at the time of which I am writing, he did not snatch for the whiskey bottle, nor impatiently throw the cuttings down, as I saw him do so many times afterwards. He sat in the chair quietly reading them, unafraid, and was both impressed and delighted with himself. Every now and again, he would point out a particularily good review and say, 'That's what so and so thinks of me,' and his head would lean a further two degrees towards his shoulder as the grin spread all over his face.

He was a natural writer—a fact he always accepted without any sense of conceit or shame. With the world-wide acclaim that greeted *The Hostage*, which had been produced by Theatre Workshop in the week preceding the publication of *Borstal Boy,* Brendan began to devote less of his time to writing. More and more did he set out to expose his spurious personality to the astonished public gaze, and while newspapers collected the valuable column inches, they somehow managed to convey, for the first time, that the end was as inevitable as the end of Dylan Thomas.

With Beatrice, always a patient and steadying influence, he stampeded through Paris, where *The Hostage,* chosen to represent Great Britain and later to win the award of best play of the year, was being presented at the *Theatre des Nations* Festival.

Still the column inches mounted with stories of boldness and flamboyance, and the hangers-on became more numerous, not so much on account of his undoubted talent, for which life meted out a cruel revenge, but because he was a character, a species of man distinctly rare.

Back in Dublin, it was hardly surprising that he found the city tedious and unconducive to work. *Borstal Boy* had been banned on account of the language, and if Dublin recognised his genius, like a mother with her child, she would not be a party to his extraordinary behaviour. Dublin knew her child—she had watched him grow up. Repeated demands from both publishers and agents to fulfill his contracts were ignored and, having an over-large conscience, when he saw the Hutchinson representative in the street he would quickly cross over to the other side.

Finally, I was asked to go over to Dublin and be, in Brendan's own words, his 'literary midwife.' Three weeks later I returned with *Brendan Behan's Island* and the slightly ravelled air of having myself been wound through the tape-recorder. Although the tapes were not captured entirely on soda-water, Brendan

10

took an extremely professional and serious view of his work. With very little prompting from me and without ever hearing the tapes, he would talk into the machine from ten minutes to two hours each day. In the end, of the forty-two thousand words, only two thousand were discarded as repetitive.

This decision to extract from Brendan, on tape, his text for the book on Ireland, was to be the start of my unique association with him, and one which only ended with his death. Although, at the time, I was unaware that the diversion from my role as publicity manager would be more than a temporary one, I was obviously happy in the knowledge that he had assumed I was the natural choice for the assignment, and that, by the end of it, he seemed so delighted with the partnership.

Shortly afterwards, he came to London, and a drinking bout took place, terminating in hospital. For the following nine months, Brendan, perhaps too acutely aware of his instability and emotional problems, struggled successfully to resist the temptation of drink. A new seed of hope sprang up inside him, and he began writing again—a third play—without any help or instigation.

But it was not to last. In America, where he was lionised, he began to drink again, and although he made repeated attempts to stop, he was fighting a losing battle as his physical being and will-power weakened. Although ashamed, he was now forced to admit, albeit to himself, that he could no longer write without help, but as he knew that working was essential to him— the only force stronger than his desire for drink—he asked that I should join him in New York and help him write the second part of his autobiography.

Confessions of an Irish Rebel was recorded on tape by Brendan during his last visit to America, and then put to one side to enable *Brendan Behan's New York* to be published in the same year as the World Fair. As a result, at the time of his death, the transcript of the tapes had not been edited in their entirety, and I have been left with the monumental task of producing the finished manuscript without his help. This I have done to the best of my ability, with the aid of additional material which he wrote at different times and anecdotes which he told me and which I have reproduced as nearly as possible in his own words.

I am extremely grateful to those people who have helped me, and particularly to Beatrice, whose cooperation has been of great value.

I am not a writer, and make no pretence to being one. It has occurred to me, however, that this fact, far from being a deterrent, has helped me considerably. Through the years of working in close collaboration with Brendan, I have been unhampered in remembering how he spoke by the interference of a style of my own. This does not mean, of course, that I have been able to emulate completely his inimitable style. There can only ever be one Brendan Behan. If I have been successful in producing only one small particle of his talent, I am more than satisfied. A faded print is better than none at all.

One final word. I think it is significant that never at any time did I have to ask Brendan for work; he would always ask me. And although the taping of *Brendan Behan's New York* was accomplished in less than four months before his death, when he was already a sick and dying man, he was the initiator of every recording session and obtained as much pleasure from it as life still held for him.

Perhaps nothing does greater credit to the magnitude of the man than that he chose to work with a person of totally opposing beliefs and politics, and who came from a country which he had fought against bitterly—both physically and mentally—at no small cost to himself.

Brendan never forgave my being English. In the final reckoning, he was too big a person to notice it.

UCKFIELD, SUSSEX

'YOU'RE for the Governor in the morning,' said this dreary red-headed little Welsh Methodist bastard of a screw.

'Thanks for telling me,' said I, in an almost English accent, as sarcastically as I politely could, 'but I'm not for 'im in the morning or any other bloody time, you little Welsh puff.'

'Bee-hann,' he screams, 'get in that cell.'

I had been in this Borstal Institution in England for I.R.A. activities for close on two years, and my treatment there, for which I have nothing but praise, had made me kind of cocky and sure of myself.

The lads stood by, looking at me with a fearful joy as I grinned and went in the cell.

In the morning I was opened up and slopped out as usual and then another Welsh orderly, not the ginger-headed Judas of the previous evening, brought me my breakfast and told me the incredible news.

'You're going out today, Paddy We've known it all week, but we wanted to keep it as a surprise for you so we could give you a proper cheer-off.'

Jesus, Joseph and Mary, Mother of God, I said in my mind, this is indeed a day for singing, but I would have liked to celebrate it in a more Christian fashion than drinking tea.

As we walked along the bare but friendly corridors to the Governor's office, I could not help wishing that it was my old Governor, C. A. Joyce, who would be shaking my hand, but he had been replaced recently by a new man, not a bad one at that, but in my opinion not so imaginative as Joyce, or his wife, who was a painter and a good one.

Afterwards, Joyce was to write to me, but he never wrote to me after he read *Borstal Boy,* although he wrote about me in a

13

book called *By Courtesy of the Criminal*.[1] I suspect he thought the language was too lurid.

I was put in the Governor's office and I stood to attention and said:

'Behan, Brendan Francis, 3501537662.'

The new Governor of His Majesty's Borstal Institution of the Day, as he elected to call it, shook my hand.

'*From the Sunday Telegraph, March 29th*, 1964.

Sir—Much has been written of Brendan Behan, his genius and his addiction to alcohol in particular—but as the governor of a Borstal Institution I had him in my charge and saw another side of his character that was positive and creditable. (Of course, I always saw the good in criminals and tried to use that positively.)

Would you be surprised to know that he was an intensely religious boy? He came to me as a member of the I.R.A. and as such was excommunicated. It worried him a great deal. He said to me one day: 'You must understand, sir, that the freedom of Ireland is me second religion. I was bred to believe in and work for it.' But very often he would come and say: 'Governor, couldn't you persuade the Father to let me go to Mass for I feel all lost without its consolation?'

I did ask the priest and he explained, so I told Brendan and he was very sad. Then I said: 'Listen, son. I'm not a Roman Catholic but I'd like to go to Mass with you. We'll sit together and I can't receive it for one reason and you for another but I shall say my prayers to the same God as you will.'

Sometimes we'd go into the R.C. chapel and I'd play the organ and we sang 'I'll Sing a Hymn to Mary' and 'Sweet Sacrament Divine' and he would talk about his mother. Then came the day when I was asked to report on his fitness for discharge. Now I wouldn't subject my countrymen to violence so I said: 'Brendan, I can't recommend your discharge unless you promise you won't go back trying to kill my countrymen when you know that we are already fighting one enemy. Do you see?'

The humour and wit of his character came up forthwith: 'Sure,' he said, 'I'll promise not to do anything until we've done with this bastard Hitler and after that I can always consider it again, can't I?'

He never lost touch with me over the years—often by telephone at 1 a.m., but never mind. *You* may think of him as the genius and the drunkard, but I remember him as a boy of 19 who wanted to serve God and who loved his mother and his country.

C. A. JOYCE,
Public Relations Office,
The Rainer Foundation,
Ryde, I.O.W.

The above letter is reproduced by kind permission of Mr. Joyce — R.J.

'Behan, you're being released this morning.'

'Thank you Sir,' I replied.

And he took me into an adjoining room where, together with another man, I saw my old friend Sergeant Sharpe of the Liverpool C.I.D.

'Hello, Brendan,' he said. 'It's come at last. At least they've made quite a man of you. When I pinched you in Liverpool, you were a skinny kid. Now, you're a fine man.'

'That, sergeant,' says I, 'is due to our vitaminised bread.'

So his colleague grunted, who was a young man of about twenty-three.

'Oh, you get vitaminised bread here, do you, while the people outside are starving. And some of the troops are not getting such good treatment as you fellows are.'

'For your information,' I answered, 'about twenty-five per cent of the population, of what you would call the criminal population, of this Institution fought on the beaches of France, more particularly at Dunkirk. I'm not aware that you ever did anything like that.'

'No,' he said, in his arrogant limey way, 'nor neither did you.'

'I never claimed to be an Englishman,' said I. 'I'm an Irish Republican.'

And I swear I would have knocked the fughing be-Jesus out of him had not Sergeant Sharpe intervened as he had on a previous occasion when I was first arrested in Liverpool in 1939. He had led the raid that had put me in this kip, and had stopped some of the younger, more enthusiastic members of the Force from doing a job on me and he had treated me rather like a father does a foolish child.

'Now take it easy Brendan. You're all right. You're going to get a nice little trip out of this.'

I was about to answer but he held up his hand in protest. 'Don't speak to me about these things, Brendan. I was on the Somme.'

'No doubt you were, Sergeant,' I said, 'and I'm sure you gave a good account of yourself.'

'Now I've a little document I've got to read to you.'

So he said—and it's a pity you can't hear my imitation of a Liverpool accent because I happen to be rather good at it.

'Prevention of Violence, Temporary Provisions Act 1939.

15

To Brendan Behan: Take notice that His Majesty's Secretary of State for Home Affairs has made an order requiring you to leave Great Britain forthwith until further notice of this order has been made, by reason of your instigation or preparation of acts of violence in Great Britain designed to influence goverment policy or public opinion with respect to Irish affairs.'

'Hear, hear,' I said.

'Shut up, you little bastard,' the Sergeant replied. 'I haven't finished reading it.'

'Go ahead,' I said, 'I'm listening.'

'Section 1 (2) of the Act empowers the Secretary of State to make an expulsion order if he is reasonably satisfied that a person is concerned in the preparation or instigation of acts of violence as described above, and that he is not a person who has been ordinarily resident in Great Britain throughout the last twenty years, or in the case of a person under the age of twenty years, throughout his life.

'If you object that there are no grounds, or no sufficient grounds for the making of the Expulsion Order against you, you may within forty-eight hours of the service of this Notice upon you send representations in writing to the Secretary of State stating the reason for your objection. If you make such representation, you will be detained in custody pending the reconsideration and disposal of your case.

'If you do not make representations within forty-eight hours of the service of this Notice upon you, you will as soon as may be thereafter be placed on board a ship about to leave Great Britain.'

Then he repeated: 'So take notice that you will be placed aboard a ship about to leave Great Britain . . .'

'Twice,' I said with a grin.

'Shut up, you little git. Within forty-eight hours. Now,' said the Sergeant, 'do you accept service of this Order?'

'I most certainly do,' I answered.

He put his arm around me, smiling gently as he did so.

'In next to no time, we'll have you as smart as paint so that even your mother won't know you after this long time. Run up to the Part-Worn stores and fix yourself up with some decent clothes for the trip.'

As I faced the officer-in-charge of the store, I had the inclination for the last time to stand to the mat, state my registered number, name, age and religious denomination, but he was a good man and was only doing his job like the rest of them. He looked every inch the Englishman and I felt he would ride a horse if he had one.

'Paddy,' he said, 'we're not going to give you an ordinary discharge suit. We couldn't get your measure in time. This came on us all of a sudden. The Home Secretary seems to have made up his mind very fast. We're going to give you a sports coat and flannels and a couple of shirts, some ties, shoes and socks.'

I went up and for the first time in over two years I put on long trousers. They felt very awkward as if I was wearing two blankets round my legs, but smart enough I'm sure. The only trouble was that the flannels were a bit tight and I had it in mind that I might come in them. Certainly the Borstal boy assisting the Part-Worn screw had seemed a bit anxious about it.

On my way back to the Governor's office, I met some of my old chinas, and I felt a kind of sadness that I would no longer rib them, nor they me, as we had done over so many months.

For a moment we were all united in our sadness, and then I left.

The Governor was waiting for me and I asked him if I could say goodbye to a few special friends and in particular to the Matron, whom I still picture today as the eternal creator of half knitted socks.

But he was adamant. 'I'm afraid not,' he said. 'You'll only say goodbye to me.'

And Sergeant Sharpe, who was to be my escort, coughed fiercely in the doorway to give me the nod to mind what I was about.

'Goodbye,' I said civilly enough, 'and a soldier's farewell to you.'

He shook my hand again.

'Thank you, Behan. That's very kind of you.'

Being Anglo-Indian, he didn't understand that this meant: 'Hello, how are you and fugh you,' but Sergeant Sharpe understood and he laughed heartily when we came out the door.

We went down the steps into the car and I just caught a glimpse out of the corner of my eye of Matron frantically waving a half-knitted sock at me. It wasn't a bad picture, at that, to carry away with me.

The only other person who saw me going off was an agricultural officer, a cockney who was called, for some strange reason, Pony Moore. He waved his hand at me.

'Good luck, Paddy.'

'Good luck, Pony,' and then I remembered that the Governor would be listening so I shouted 'Goodbye Mr. Moore,' very respectfully, because you were not supposed to call officers by their Christian names, first names or nicknames.

This was the last I saw of Borstal.

The fresh cold wind that was blowing as we left turned into a blizzard as we stood on Woodbridge station waiting to get on the train for London. I don't know why it is, but whoever designs these stations should be made by law to stand on them on cold wintry mornings so that they get the full benefit of their own cleverality.

I reflected on the excellence of my condition.

'The wicked,' I thought happily, 'prosper in a wicked world.'

But my good humour changed, for didn't I have to share a carriage with some half-idiot from East Jesus Kansas or Balham's Ass or some such, who was giving out the pay about the hardships endured by the British. I could have told him about the hardships of his compatriots back in the Institution, but with Sergeant Sharpe listening I didn't like to push my luck. Instead I sat back in the corner of the carriage putting the day through my thoughts. It was all very good.

When we reached Euston there was an air raid. I had heard the sirens many times back in Borstal and seen the planes, but somehow this was different and I was strangely afraid. I had been at Euston Station before on my way to Feltham Boys' Prison and the architecture wasn't exactly conducive to confidence with all that glass overhead. And I'd learnt about building, all my people being in that industry, so I knew what to expect when the big bang came.

But all the people I saw had the appearance of hard work and walked methodically, saving their energy for the crucial moment. I gave a good imitation, I think.

'Come on,' said Sharpe, 'look alive there. You know I'm supposed to put the handcuffs on you.'

'Oh,' I said, 'put them on if you like.'

The sergeant grinned. 'I don't think you're worth it. Instead, we'll go and find something to eat.'

'How about something to drink?'

'Well,' he said, 'we may see about that too.'

So we went into the station restaurant and we ate a large feed, and being eighteen years old I was able to do the meal more than justice because, by God, it was a terrible meal. It finished up with a thing called Victory Duff which was the most awful muck. I think Hitler must have sent it to the English. But, however, they were surrounded by U-boats at the time and they were doing the best they could under difficult circumstances.

After the meal we made an odd adjournment here and there and, having plenty of the right stuff inside us, we caught the train for Liverpool.

I struck out a bar of a song and withdrew it immediately. Sitting opposite me was a red-faced man with an ugly strong face, and he was caressing not one bottle of malt but two.

I nudged the sergeant.

'Get an eyeful of that,' I whispered. 'How about you and me getting in on the act? And furthermore,' says I, 'I'll mark your card for you. I see by the label on the case that he's a cop and even if I've nothing in common with this whore's melt, I'm not beyond hunker-sliding to screw-bastards when it suits me.'

'O.K. Brendan,' he replied. 'Go ahead and see what you can do.'

In the matter of alcohol, principles are few so I got up and stretched myself lazily and eased myself down in the spare seat next door to my new-found friend. We got into conversation easily about the price of things, the black-out, race-tracks and greyhound tracks, women and the looks of girls in Liverpool. I told him I was on my way to Liverpool with my uncle, pointing to Sergeant Sharpe as I did so, to join the Navy.

Being a particularly thick cop, he didn't ask why I didn't join the Navy in London. I will in my bollocks, I thought to myself.

'Oh,' he said, 'with your uncle, is that right?'

'Yes,' I replied. 'Actually, to tell the truth, I'm only telling you confidentially, for you seem a respectable man, my uncle is a detective officer.' And I raised my eyes as I spoke as though butter wouldn't ever melt in my mouth.

'Jesus, that's a funny thing. I'm a Jack myself,' he said.

And hypocrite that I am, I even looked surprised.

'Ask your uncle, would he care for a drink with me?'

I leaned over to Sharpe and gave him the wink as I spoke. 'Uncle Hughie, I was telling this bloke we're going up for me to join the Navy in Liverpool.'

The other old one interrupted. 'Good luck to you lad,' and to Sharpe, 'Would you like a drop of Scotch with me? We're in the same line of business I understand from your nephew here. It calls for a celebration.'

'Certainly,' said Sharpe. 'Actually I'm a Sergeant in the Liverpool C.I.D.'

'Very pleased to meet you,' said the other guy. 'I'm with the Blackpool C.I.D.' And he turned lovingly to me and I was grateful for the growing dusk so he couldn't see the shame in my eyes as he said: 'So this young man is going away to fight for King and Country. I think we should give him a drink too.'

'Well,' said Sharpe, 'I know he'd be able for it.'

We all drank and smoked merrily into the dark. There was a blue pilot light at the top of the carriage and I could just see the outlines of the face of the Blackpool cop drawing with great pleasure on his cigarette.

After a little while I got a bit tired but I wanted to piss and I knew I would not be allowed to walk along the corridor alone. I equally did not want to spoil our story at this stage of the game even though we had had the message. All the same I badly wanted one and Sharpe must have sensed it for he said, 'Want a walk, Paddy?' and he got up and took me to the toilet.

'You first,' I said, 'age before ignorance,' although by this time I was breaking my neck.

Sharpe made way for me at the door. 'Right there, Brendan,' he said, 'in you go and no funny business trying to jump out of the window and scarper.'

I was grateful to him and left the door open, or rather slightly open so he would understand, and when I came out we walked slowly with a great peace back to the carriage.

I looked at them both and thought that in a way they would

have made good drinking companions in any other walk of life and reflected with sadness on the change that must come over them when they were on a job. I am not fond of police anywhere.

At Liverpool we were supposed to go straight to the jail, where I was to be kept for the night to wait to go to the boat—not at Liverpool for some reason but at Holyhead—in the morning. But we called in to pay our respects to the local publicans on the way, and never being one to miss whatever drop might be stirring, I got so fughing drunk that they wouldn't let me into the prison. That's the first time I was ever refused admittance to the nick.

'What do you want me to do with him?' remarked Sharpe sarcastically. 'Register him at the Adelphi Hotel?' Which is about the largest and smartest hotel in Liverpool and is frequented by all the racegoers to Aintree—a four star kip, whatever that means.

Sharpe then handed the station sergeant my deportation papers and after a whispered conversation I was taken in. I waved goodbye to Sharpe and he told me he would see me in the morning, and I was escorted along a dark corridor by the station sergeant and a screw—a Scottish bastard—and down a flight of stairs to an open door.

Being in the humour, I sang them a few bars of the songs about the Invincibles and was just about to break into the sad but lovely Kevin Barry when the Scottish screw said:

'Shut up, you sloppy Irish mick, and get in the cell. And if I hear any more of your bloody row in the night, I'll come down personally and attend to the matter myself.'

They banged out the door and I could hear their footsteps retreating in the distance.

I looked round the room. Bare concrete walls and floor again and the same wooden bench for a bed and a pillow of the same material. I coiled myself up, put my jacket behind my head, pulled the coarse blankets over me, contemplated committing a mortal sin, realised I was too drunk and fell into a deep sleep.

Waking, I didn't wonder where I was. There were noises of key-jangling and slopping out. A face looked in the spy-hole. I knew him, and I'd know the tenth generation of him for he was a miserable whore's get of a screw whom I'd known from two years previously.

He turned the key in the lock and stood facing me. 'Come on Bee-hann. Down to the wash-house. You're going home. If I had my way, I would do in the lot of you I.R.A. men.'

'You did your best in the Troubles,' I replied. 'But I've a better home to go to than you have, be Jaysus.'

Jesus look down on you, I said in my own mind, if I ever get you in a place where I can give you a kick in the bollocks, but I said nothing more. I had a hang-over this high. As high as St. George's Hall or the Liver Building in Liverpool.

He took me to the day-room, where Sergeant Sharpe was waiting and I was given back my cigarettes and matches which had been lifted from me the night before. Apologetically, Sharpe put the handcuffs on me, for the sake of propriety, he whispered, and we caught the train to Holyhead.

As soon as we arrived, he let me off the hook and introduced me to a lot of cops and we began discussing rugby football—a favourite pastime of mine—in the bar of the Ship Hotel. We had so many glasses of chat that these cops were nearly getting sacked, because they could have been letting tribes of Nazis into the bloody place for all they cared by the time they'd got a few stiffeners into themselves and us. And we had plenty of Scotch because they were well in with the stewards of the place.

I was the last up the gangplank, roaring and singing and I fell in with a whole crowd of Irishmen. They were curious to know why I was the last on board.

'Because,' says I, 'I'm a deportee. I've just served a sentence of nearly three years in England.'

'Oh, Jesus,' said a well-dressed man of about thirty-six in a Cork accent, 'that must have been terrible.'

'Well,' I answered truthfully, 'it was mixed-middling. At the beginning it wasn't so hot, but after that I was better treated than I ever was in my life before.'

So some of them liked this, but more of them didn't. But they all agreed that I was a hero and a patriot and threw buckets of drink into me. And we arrived at Dún Laoire, commonly known as Dunleary, but known to some as Kingstown, and it was good to see the waves lash up and over the East Pier on this wintry morning. The sun was in mind to come out but having a look at the weather it was in lost heart and went back again.

Through the haze I could not see 'the fair hills of Holy Ireland' but I could smell the tang of generations of me and I choked back the tears that were now pressing and anxious to be free. All the familiar landmarks were there as if I'd never left them and I had them all counted in my mind as surely as if they were paraded in front of me.

'Where is your travel permit?' said an immigration man.

'Here it is,' I said, handing him my deportation order.

'What in the name of Jesus is that?'

'That's the only kind of travel permit I have got, you good for nothing civil servant bastard.'

He read it, looked at it and handed it back to me.

'Are you Irish?'

'No' I said, 'as a matter of a fact, I'm a Yemenite Arab.'

Two detectives came forward who were evidently there to meet me.

'Apparently he *is* Brendan Behan,' they said.

The immigration officer shook my hand and his hard face softened.

'Céad míle fáilte romhat abhaile.' (A hundred thousand welcomes home to you.)

I could not answer. There are no words and it would be impertinence to try. I walked down the gangway. I was free.

I MUST have got on the dirtiest train in Ireland because most of them are excellent and quite clean. But this one that took me from Dún Laoire to Dublin was a filthy looking yoke. I pulled down the window and poked out my head. Though the ground was frosty it was going to be a beautiful day and the sun had taken more heart now and began to shine. I could see familiar houses and people busying themselves with the moments of the day and I marvelled at the greenness of the fields and the trees in regular rows that seemed to stretch for miles. They had lost their leaves in readiness for the winter.

There was a hatchet-faced oul' strap in the carriage with me with a young clean looking youth with a pile of papers on his knee, and two Dublin men in the corner who were moaning their lot throughout the entire trip. I swear that if you put some people down at the Ritz with a million nicker and Gina Lollobrigida thrown in to boot, they would still find something to crap about.

As the train pulled in to Dublin station I opened the east side carriage door and was over the barrier as quick as you please.

It seemed like a century since I had walked up the road to my home in Crumlin, a Dublin Corporation housing estate. There were gleams of sun coming through the trees and the frosty air had a great smell of smoke in it. For fifteen minutes or so I walked around but the clock was not made that could measure time at that moment.

My father and mother were there to greet me and they embraced me and so did my little sister Carmel, who is now married to a Scottish carpenter and lives in England.

I had thought many times of home and my family when I was in Borstal and I pictured them, when the frost was crisp under foot, sitting round the fire in Dublin where there were hearths that would welcome me when I did get out. Now I marvelled how three years could be concertinaed as if I had never been away. My mother cried a little and told me about Nancy at the Morning Star, what Craigavad said to the Mendicity man when he brought round the porridge and I wouldn't have minded so much but he was using that old walking-stick to stir it with, and how about Mick, avic, who only came there to sell his breakfast for the price of a glass of chat? And amongst it all she slipped it in.

'Maureen is dying from consumption.'

Hell and heaven and despair and presumption and hope. We had talked together, laughed together, done the things that young boys and girls do together. I had been in this girl's house and I knew her father, her mother and her brothers. I'd fought alongside her brothers and we had shared the same battlefields of the poor.

How could death come to one so young?

I went over to her home which was a vegetable shop in Benburb Street buildings, down near Guinness's Brewery in the heart of Dublin. When I got there, Maureen was selling a cabbage by the head to an oul' one and, to tell the honest truth, for a moment I wasn't sure whether it was her or her sister, ten years older, that I was seeing, for when I left home Maureen was little more than a child, and now she was a tall brown-haired blue-eyed woman.

'Hello, Brendan,' she said, 'and how are you?'

'Not so bad, kid,' I replied as I walked through the shop into the kitchen beyond.

There was no one at home but she followed me through and asked me what I would like for my dinner, it being Friday. She was never sure, she said, what religion I was, although all belonging to me were Catholics since 432 A.D. But I knew fish was scarce, so I said I was a Protestant and she gave me a steak. Later she discovered I was not a Protestant, whatever else I was, but a Catholic, and she said I had sold Jesus Christ for a pound of beef. She apologised for the state of the rooms, explaining that her two brothers, Eddie and Paddy, the male adult members of the family, were interned and as her father was an invalid there was no one that could do wall-papering. As this was my trade at the time, she asked me if I would ever sling the joint—as the saying has it in Dublin—or, in other words, paper the walls.

'Sure,' I said, 'sure I will, Maureen.'

But we fell into talking about this and that and me telling her stories of great bravery for the cause in England and her sitting there and taking it all in. And then she tells me of the confessions of an I.R.A. Chief of Staff, which her father swore were Gospel truth and which to me were absolutely nonsensical.

'Brendan,' she said, 'I object to your views and your bad language. I've a mind to ask you to go.'

In fact when a friend of hers arrived, Maureen asked him to put me out.

'Get out, Brendan Behan,' the friend said.

'Jesus,' I replied, 'I've not opened my fughing mouth.'

But I didn't go and over the days I slung the joint and I was happy to be with her. We talked quietly while I worked and I was delighted to find that the last three years had not diminished my skill. The rooms looked neat and trim and a peace descended that I had not known.

Shortly after this, Maureen was sent to Crooksling sanatorium in the Dublin mountains and I went up to see this girl with whom I had a very pure relationship.

I am a cowardly man by nature, and to go there I had to take a couple of drinks and when I saw her so small and lonely in that stark, ether-smelling ward of the hospital, I knew that I loved her very deeply. I brought her some flowers and I sang a couple of songs and she seemed extremely happy. Which in some ways implies that the Catholic religion might be the true one. I had been extra religious as a kid myself but later I had had difficulties with myself and sex and had seen my friends excommunicated and heard about my father being excommunicated with thousands of others. Now I had been excommunicated myself but I suppose at heart I am a daylight atheist for I would not like to die without a priest.

I kissed Maureen very chastely on the lips.

'Goodbye,' I said, 'goodbye,' because I knew I would not see her again. I'm not an amateur doctor, for Jesus sake, but I knew I was in the presence of death, and in one so young, with whom I was in love.

I left the sanatorium and with such money as I had—which wasn't a lot—I went to the Embankments' Bar beside the sanatorium. I reflected sadly on the words of Shakespeare, a very great Englishman, who said: 'Play the man.' He didn't say, 'Be a man,' he only said, 'Play the man.'

Oh God, Oh Sacred Heart, the Lord have mercy on her, I tried to 'play the man,' for I could not be one now. I sat in the snug of the bar putting on a brave face and there was a young fellow there passing the time of day with no harm to anyone. But I was not able for him and I left to come out into the daylight with a heart as black as night.

I had decided to walk awhile, but to crown me didn't I see Mrs. Jones from the Wren's Nest, out in the Strawberry Beds, coming my way with her scrawny face and her red Anti-Christ pig's eyes. At the best of times I would not go within an ass's roar of her.

Like the hammers of hell, I was on the Blessington bus for Dublin, changing there onto the number 21 for Watling Street.

Maureen's grandmother was at the door of her little house as I walked the steps up.

'How is my grand-daughter?'

The directness of her question was something I was not prepared for, and I knew Maureen was not going so well, but I replied in my lying fashion:

'She's okay, she's all right,' and I looked at her face to see if she believed me and she nodded her head in grateful acknowledgement.

'Would you ever come in, Brendan,' she said, 'and have a cup of coffee? Paddy will be home soon and he's been asking for you.'

Paddy was her son and the father of Maureen but to tell the truth, I was not in the humour to talk to anyone apart from the fact that coffee is a drink I particularly detest and tea was rationed at the time, yet it was not in me to refuse. It is great to be on your own for a bit, in the sun, for this is something you never are in any prison for all their solitary confinements and I had had my share of those. The fughpigs watched you every moment and even at such times when the worst of us would give a dog privacy. I was not that much of a sinner to refuse the old one, though, and I followed her into the house.

Paddy O'Reilly was nicknamed the 'Man of Blood' because he worked at the slaughter house and was usually covered with the blood of animals rather than the blood of human beings, although I have a rather soft spot for animals and do not like to see them killed.

I have never been able to talk about things that mean a deal to me, and I'm not implying by this that anything I may have to say would cause Christ to come down off His cross or anything to that effect, but I'm just not able for it and that's all there is to it. So I was glad when Mrs. O'Reilly asked me about my days in Borstal. I told her about the West Belfast I.R.A. man who had asked to see me, though I didn't tell her that I was arsing round the Stations of the Cross at the time.

Her sons and grandsons were all in the I.R.A. along with my own family, so she was more than interested when I told her that this Belfast man knew I was trained in Killiney Castle with Seumas MacIlhenna and Tommy Gunn. Tommy was smashing at a party or a ceilidh and I had shared both with him many a time. And we fell to remembering what great gas Tommy was.

Just then Paddy walked in, still wearing his blood-stained apron and as he shook my hand he said:

'Céad míle fáilte romhat abhaile.'

I thanked him and said, *'Go raibh maith agat.'*

He had a strong but sad face and he was a good man. The Lord have mercy on him. He is no longer with us.

'How's Maureen?' he asked for he knew I would not be sitting there for the good of my health.

I had acquired a certain amount of British slang, some of it from Borstal and some from brothers and cousins of mine who had fought in the British Army and in the Royal Air Force—a most honourable organization, despite the fact that I am supposedly against it.

'Paddy,' I whispered out of the old one's hearing, 'I think Maureen has bought it,' meaning that I thought she was dying and Paddy answered very sadly:

'We will go down to the corner and we will have a jar.'

For in times of great trouble, I am sorry to say an Irishman will have a drink for to drown his sorrows and Mrs. O'Reilly had overheard us.

'Brendan,' she said, 'you told me Maureen was well.'

'Yes, sure, so she is. Of course she's well,' I lied.

'I don't think so. You and Paddy O'Reilly are not going down to have a drink for nothing.'

'Look,' I said, 'maybe she is not so well.'

It was not for me to tell her that her grand-daughter was dying, but she was.

And the poor frail, but lovely old woman, who had been through the times of The Troubles and whose grandson I'd seen on a murder charge—a very honourable one if I might say so—broke down and wept.

Paddy and I went out and left her to her grief which I suppose was not very courageous of us.

'Brendan,' he said, 'do you believe this?'

'Yes,' I answered, 'I've seen people dying before, Paddy, and she is definitely on the way out.'

So he wept and I wept and we drank. And I sang a verse of a song which had been taught to me by my mother:

'With rue my heart is laden, for golden friends I had,
Bright youth and rose-lipped maiden, and many a light-foot
lad,
By brooks too broad for leaping, the lightfoot boys are laid,
And the rose-lipped girls are sleeping, in fields where the
roses fade.'

I did not see Maureen again and that is all I want to say about it. But I wish to God she was with me today.

And if these are the confessions of an Irish rebel, they are indeed confessions.

L IK E Séan O'Casey, the greatest playwright living in my opinion, my family's land was all in window-boxes and the only time I ever dug a field was with my father the time of the strike, when the Dublin Corporation gave the men plots of one-eighth of an acre out on Dean Swift's in Glasnevin.

And it was to Glasnevin Cemetery that I went this Easter Sunday 1942, but not to dig a field. I had gone there with the rest of the Irish Republican Army, or what was left of it, to take part in the Easter Rising Commemoration parade, which is held at the graveside of the men who died for the freedom of Ireland in 1916.

There were a couple of thousand at the Commemoration, not all of them active members of the I.R.A. Some of them indeed were British soldiers on leave, but in mufti.

I reflected sadly on my two I.R.A. comrades now lying in the clay who had been sentenced to death in England by so-called British justice. They were two innocent but very brave men. One of them was arrested in London within half an hour of the explosion which took place in Coventry. There had been protest meetings and demonstrations all over Ireland and America. They would not, so soon, be forgotten.

Still and all, I was here with thousands of others, thinking of them.

'God save Ireland,' cried the heroes,
'God save Ireland,' cry we all,
'Whether on the scaffold high or the battlefield we die,
Sure, no matter when for Ireland dear we fall.''

I fell in with Cafferty, a young bricklayer of about seventeen summers.

'Brendan,' he said, 'I think the police are following us.'

I looked round and saw the squad cars and inside them sets of fugh-faced bastards intent on nothing less than grievous bodily harm. I don't think they were very much interested in me, but they were interested in Andrew, Lasarian and Joseph, three Irish Republican Army officers who were just in front of us. I was never an officer of anything.

It was good to feel the thousands of free people about me, a freedom to which I was not yet entirely accustomed.

Get stuffed, you old bastards, or we'll have a few words on the way back.

Cafferty was kicking the sods of green-topped turf apprehensively so I put the word about that if the cops tried to molest the three fellows, we would beat them up. They couldn't possibly shoot the lot of us. With function and capernosity, we'd have riveted them with digs in the old mincepies.

I have a sense of humour that would nearly cause me to laugh at a funeral, providing it wasn't my own. But when I am dealing with ignorant swine of police my humour deserts me and all I want to do is to needle them as best I can according to their particular brand of insolence. I started singing Gaelic songs, very rebel ones at that, and soon a lot of the other blokes joined in too.

The fracas started on our way back from the Cemetery. It was short and sweet like an ass's gallop but in those few moments I lived a full life's span, and in the years that followed I was never to forget them.

Ah, Mother of Jesus, it was a fughing disgrace. The hungry-faced police jumped out of their cars and went to arrest Andrew, Lasarian and Joseph. They gathered around them and looked as if they were going to go mad any minute. My stomach was trying to get rid of my dinner and a cold sweat broke out on me. All at once I threw off my overcoat and went to attack them with my fists.

'Come on, we'll fix this bloody shower,' I said to Cafferty.

Everyone was shouting and saying things and one big ugly-faced policeman going mad with the temper, and shouting himself to tell them to shut up, when all of a sudden somebody screamed, 'That man has a gun,' and I looked round and saw the steel glint of a revolver in one of the I.R.A. officers' hand and he was altogether hysterical.

"I'll use it, I'll use it,' he screamed.

Christ, said I in my own mind, why wasn't I back in Borstal, or Feltham Boys' Prison, in solitary? At least I would be there in peace and on my own instead of here with my guts twisted up inside me.

As I snatched the revolver out of the officer's hand, the police opened fire. I didn't, and not until they opened fire did I fire back at them and, still firing, Cafferty and I made a desperate run for it.

We jumped over the wall of the nearest house, a little sub-urban petit-bourgeois home, and crouched in the shrubbery at the back of the wall trying to get back into breathing practice. A cold clammy sweat now broke out on my forehead in delayed action for the fright I hadn't had time to have during the shooting. My hands were trembling and I would have liked to see if my voice was still with me but I knew the effort of holding my breath to stop my stammer would have made me nearly pass out in a weakness.

It was about one o'clock in the afternoon and today winter had made way for spring.

I nudged Cafferty for the door of the house opened and I could see a middle-aged woman bent in haggard fashion over a bowl of milk which she carried in her hand. She spotted the pair of us immediately and let out a cry that would freeze the heart of the hangman, and she shook the bowl of milk so much with fright that she nearly churned it. You could almost see the butter appearing on the top. But it wasn't the poor soul's fault. Not every day in the week would you see two light youths of nineteen and seventeen years of age appearing over your garden wall. In fear and trembling she turned back towards the door shouting as she did so, 'Jack, Jack! There's two fellows coming in here with guns!' Because by this time Cafferty and I, half bent up so as not to be too conspicuous from the road, had made for her door.

We heard footsteps coming from the back parlour and a deep burly voice, 'Be Jaysus, and they're not coming in here.'

And I thought I'd see a guy of about six foot with shoulders on him like King Kong's. I'd seen the film when I was a young boy of about twelve or thirteen and he was the most terrifying gorilla you could possibly imagine. Dracula and Frankenstein were a wedding night in comparison.

Instead of which a little man smaller than myself came out.

He looked defiantly at us, but I could tell he was as nervous as us with our eyes going over every inch of him and every feature of his face and figure.

"You can't come in here,' he said.

'I'm sorry,' says I, 'but we've got to,' and then I smiled and slipped in 'sir' because he was a decent enough old skin and only trying to protect his own. Though his mouth was firm and angry, I knew, relieved, that his heart was softening.

'But there's little children in the house.'

I felt like crying for the first time in years. I would rather cut off an arm than harm a hair of a child's head, but I could not blame him for thinking differently. All at once, I felt my groin stiffen in fear and the cold clammy sweat danced a jig on my forehead. Time is, time was, time is no more, I said in my own mind. We can't stand here arguing the moments away.

'We don't want to frighten any little children, but there are people out there,' I said, nodding my head in the direction of the road, 'who mean us no good.' For we could hear the shouting of the police and the noises of the approaching army lorries. I clenched my teeth—and I had a good set in those days—and Cafferty and I pushed the poor old bastard back into his own home at gunpoint. His only crime was being there when he could have been over at Michael's giving out the pay about the big race in England over a glass or two of porter. His oul' one gathered the children around her muttering words to the Virgin Mary as she did so. On the wall was a picture of Our Lord carrying a lamp and underneath, carved in wood, the words 'Stand Firm.'

We did and the divil take the begrudgers.

'If you are going to stop here,' said the brave man, 'hand me over the barker,' meaning the skit, the revolver.

'In my bollocks,' says I, 'Nobody gets my revolver, that's for sure. Use your bloody sense. We've got to defend ourselves. We're not going to interfere with you or yours. If there's a fight here, you can go upstairs.'

His wattles flamed in anger and for a moment I thought he was going to cut up rough and I felt more in the humour for the religion of my fathers than I had done since I was excommunicated. Oh, Sacred Heart, no more violence!

But he only said: 'Listen till I tell you. I won't be ordered around in my own house by a pup like you,' which I think was very courageous and furthermore very sensible of him.

I sat beside Cafferty on the stairs which led straight out of the front room of the place and faced the door so that we were nice and handy for anything that might be coming our way from that direction. I wiped the sweat off too and wished that my sick bilious headache would give my other thoughts a break. Better than a dozen of stout that break would be.

We heard footsteps coming to the door. My Jesus, my heart fell into my boots and in my defenceless misery I wished I could wake up and find out that I had been dreaming all this and say that's how it would be if you were wanted by the police. But it seemed very likely that that's how things were going to be as the knock came on the door. Up like a shot I was, with my revolver steady in my hand.

'Holy Mary, don't fire,' the poor man shouted out. 'That's my daughter returning from Mass,' and sure enough the door opened and a very attractive girl of about my own age, or maybe a few months younger, came in. She banged out the door behind her and put the missal on the table, pushing aside the dirty dishes from the half-eaten dinner as she did so. I hid the skit in my right-hand trouser pocket as best I could, but without a coat the butt was easily seen. I needn't have minded for you could tell she was a sensitive soul and would have seen the hunted look in our eyes anyway.

She turned as she spoke. 'Are you the boys that were in the fighting up in Glasnevin Cemetery?'

'Yes, I am—we are,' I replied, and Cafferty elbowed me not to be saying too much, but not too strongly for on account of my having been pinched in England doing my bit for the cause, he had great *meas** for me.

She asked me what I knew about it and I told her what had taken place, at the same time giving good account of ourselves. I was always hot in the heels for admiration.

'I can tell you,' she said, 'that there's a cordon of military and police all round the place,' and fearless rebel that I am, I desperately wanted to shit and so I did in double quick time out the back and wiped myself and back again as trim as you

1. Respect.

34

like and she still standing there as if I had never left. Fear can do this to a man and no mistake.

She smiled and touched my arm.

'I think I can get you out.' Words sweet to my ear, may I never tire of hearing them.

'Can you?' I said.

Hard on her heels we followed and I had it in mind to have the old barker a little more to hand than in the trouser pocket, so I fingered it and felt the warmth come back into my crotch after the cold fear and decided I would push my luck and leave it where it was: the revolver, I mean.

There was no one around, but I could hear voices shouting in the distance, and as the day had not yet begun to feel its age there was still plenty of time for the rozzers to do a good job on us.

The girl brought us across by a side entrance to Glasnevin Cemetery formerly unknown to me, although I'd known the cemetery all my life and all my deaths, because practically all my ancestors are buried there. And though they say the air is healthy there, I wasn't in mind to be sampling it this day or the next.

We followed her across the cemetery to the side exit, and there we were free. God is all right and His mother as well, I thought to myself.

'*Go raibh míle maith agat* (that you may have a thousand thanks),' I said and with sincerity as I shook her hand.

'That's all right, *tá fáilte romhat* (you are welcome),' said she looking at both of us, '*slán libh* (goodbye).'

'*Slán a't.*'

And I nearly fell out of my standing, for this girl then handed us two packets of Sweet Afton cigarettes, a box of matches and several bars of chocolate which shows a kindness and an understanding that you'd not be meeting every day. I felt the lump come up in my throat, swallowed back hard, for I am not a hard man and these things touch me. And I had not seen her take any of these things from the house.

We made for Moibhi road, out towards the north side of Dublin, and I could hear the trams far away in the distance and imagined the old ones up there, after Mass and a sup or two of the plain porter and glad of a few minutes' chat as they rode the distance home, a bit jarred and singing.

Turning the corners heavily now, the trams gathered speed for the hills and the church bells banged more heavily as the day began to get more gloomy with the fading light of the afternoon.

In misery I discovered that such money as I had, which wasn't a terrible lot, but enough for a few drinks, I'd left in my overcoat which I had thrown off at the start of the shooting, and Cafferty didn't have any money whatsoever.

We sat down behind a hedge in a cornfield and lit up our cigarettes not wishing to search our hearts to find our voices. I drew the smoke deeply into my lungs, felt it circle around and up and out and stared straight at it as it billowed in front of me. We had to have money for no matter how we rationed the bars of chocolate, they couldn't last for more than a day or two. Which made me do the meanest thing I have ever done in my life, or at any rate, one of the meanest. We were forced to hold up a pitch-and-toss school—what the Australians call a two-up. They were innocent people enjoying a game of a Sunday afternoon and were utterly bewildered by the sudden appearance of two slight youths demanding the loot at the point of a gun. One old fellow, braver than the rest, went for to hit me in the face, 'Fughing swine, bloody bastard. I'll teach you young puppies how to behave. By Christ, I haven't done with you,' as we grabbed the money and disappeared into the near darkness again, thank Jesus and still breathing, and devil a much the matter with us, thanks be to God and His Blessed Mother.

The bells out in the city rang a quarter past seven, and I knew the pubs would be closing soon for the day, such were the licensing laws in Ireland at the time. However we felt our standard of living had gone up with a bang and we had another smoke and finished off the chocolate when I remembered some relations of mine who were living nearby and might be persuaded to help us, to the tune of some clothing at any rate.

I hadn't noticed the sharp frost in the air until then, and besides an overcoat was essential for another reason. A man who is carrying a revolver in his trouser pocket doesn't exactly encourage friendship and the thing was so noticeable that you'd hardly be needing a fanfare of the President's trumpets to announce it.

We decided to push our luck and up at the door and knocking

on it, but in terror now, for I was not one of the wrap-the-green-flag-round-me juniors that came into the I.R.A. from the Gaelic League, well ready to die for the honour of Ireland. I was ready to die for an overcoat and probably would from the perishing cold if the D.M.P's (Dublin Metropolitan Police) didn't make a meat ball of me first.

Jesus, wasn't that little enough to ask? What harm would I be doing them? At least, they could only refuse and wouldn't make a dinner of us.

The door opened.

Then the smile faded and the gentleness receded and anger came from the pit of my stomach and I twisted the palm round in my hand. You poxy-faced bastard of a whore's melt, I said in my own mind, and prepared to give him a belt; but when all is said and done, it would have been to no effect. They were not kindly disposed towards us and I put it to myself that one day I would give them the rub over it.

I caught Cafferty looking at me in a kind of sad but friendly way that cheered me up a bit and I looked back at him as if to say, 'It'll be O.K. kid,' and I felt ten feet tall and responsible but wishing all the same I was in bed at home in Russell Street with my mother telling me, half-laughing in spite of herself, that I was a good-for-nothing Irish Mick and her sending me out for the message with the hard day's earnings and the jug to put a drop in, and she waiting on the stuff to no avail.

A man needed all his strength in the times that were in it, and I turned on my heel, touching Cafferty on the arm as I did so.

'Come on,' I said, 'I know where to go.'

We went to a house in a terrible slum place, God forgive me for saying so because I don't want to sound ungrateful, but it consisted of converted coachmen's houses, which didn't look as nice as the old London mews before they became fashionable. In one of them lived a kindly woman who had known my family many a long year and had been a companion of my mother's at school. She would give us a chance, I knew.

'Connie,' I said, 'we're on the run,'

'Yes,' she answered, 'and you don't want to be standing out there. You're identified, the both of you. I heard the news on the wireless. You had better come in before the likes of them see you.'

The blessings of Jaysus on you and on everyone like you and it's my praise that I'm giving you, but aloud I said:

'See, can you do anything for us?'

'Certainly, Brendan,' she said, 'I'll do the same for you as I did for all the boys in 1920, 1921, 1922 and 1923. I'll fix you up.'

And she took us in and gives us this plate of bacon and cabbage, which was her own dinner for sure, as she would hardly be likely to have food enough for herself, let alone to spare, and a glass of porter, and I felt the warmth embrace me like a blanket after the cold and Jesus, Mary and Joseph wasn't she apologising for the sparsity of it all?

'Connie,' I said, 'didn't you take us in and feed us and clothe us, and for the rest, I'll take the will for the deed, and dark and black as things are for us they are no longer as dark and black as they were before.'

She fixed us up with some rugs and cushions on the floor which was the best the poor soul could do, and lying down I started to read the Sunday Independent, but it was cold with my arms outside the rug, so I put the paper down and my arms inside and I must have fallen asleep for the next thing I knew was Cafferty shaking me and telling me that we should be away before daylight.

I left the house as a blind man leaves his dog and all thoughts went past me and jumped out of the queue ahead of me, I was that unable for them.

We turned the corner and into the dawn.

This jewel that houses our hopes and our fears
Was knocked up from the swamp in the last hundred years;
But the last shall be first and the first shall be last:
May the Lord in his mercy be kind to Belfast.

THIS poem is called, 'Ballad to a Traditional Refrain,' and was written by the Belfast poet, Maurice Craig, who has now left his native city. I include it here for the simple reason that Cafferty and I had to leave our native city and make for the border before the sun had the heart to get up that Monday morning.

Now everyone knows about the border between the North and South of Ireland—the Six Counties as they are called—but it is not very real in everyday life. Like millions of others, I believe in the freedom of Ireland and to me the border is completely nonsensical. In one place it actually partitions a farmhouse and you could be having a shit in the South and your breakfast in the North by simply walking a few steps. By the same token you'd be mad not to cross the street and have a gill of the plain porter on the southern side for the sufficient reason that the drink here is cheaper, not being subject to British tax laws.

But I wasn't much troubled by these things today. My political thinking was directed only to our own safety. In the half-light of the dawn, I recognised Eddie, Maureen's brother and an old and trusted friend of mine in the I.R.A., running up the street towards me. He pulled us into a doorway away from the light of the street lamp and told me he had had instructions to take the gun off me. He had been looking for us all night and I could tell he was weary of the load of it. I would have liked to have helped him for he was a good skin and I knew his mother and father, brothers and sisters as well as I knew my own and we fought the same battles together, on the playground and elsewhere, with great function and capernosity.

'I'll give you the barker, Eddie,' I said, 'if you will hand me over yours in return,' for he was standing that close to me that you would have to be an eejit to miss it.

But he refused and it wasn't until many years later that he told me that the heroes of officialdom had given him a completely useless weapon to exchange with mine, which I must say was very sporting of them. In my bollocks and to hell with you. Up the Republic!

We shook hands in sadness.

'*Slán leat,* Eddie,' I said.

'*Slán a't* and mind yourself,' he said as he put his arm round me in a tender, smiling, approving sort of way.

The bells in the city rang a quarter to five and the air of the early spring morning was frosty and blunt as metal.

Nothing of any consequence happened on our way to the border apart from a few little shootings here and there, which I would prefer to forget, for I am not a killer myself and if I did kill I only killed in war and I am very sorry for it. I wish, I very sincerely wish, that I could be heard saying this, because it is not any boast. I never killed anyone for land or for anything that could be described as plentifying myself. If I killed, it was a soldier, as a member of the Irish Republican Army, of which I was proud to be a member.

In Belfast, we went to the house of a young girl on whom I was trying to make an impression while Cafferty was giving out the pay on the enormous wages being earned by the workers in the factories and the shipyards in the north. He mentioned one friend in particular, and while I wasn't trying to give this girl the idea that I was a millionaire or anything like that, I didn't expect Cafferty to spell it out that before the war this man had been like ourselves, now—penniless. Now there's a friend for you.

The next day I was at a wedding of a woman of the *Cumann na mBhan*—the League of Women—which is the female opposite number of the Irish Republican Army. She was marrying an I.R.A. man so it was all in the family.

40

The centre of these bridal festivities in the Falls Road area, which is the main Catholic area, was a small red-bricked house in the ghetto of Belfast, and it stood in a line of other red-bricked houses that might be found anywhere in either the north of England, or the north of Ireland, in Liverpool or in Belfast.

The house was surrounded by gunmen, some of them carrying Thompson sub-machine guns, while others had long Webleys and Colt automatics, in case the Royal Ulster Constabulary might make a surprise raid, which knowing the cowardice of the bastards of the police, north or south, they wouldn't have the guts to do.

But honest to Jesus you'd have to laugh for inside the house everyone was dancing and singing as if every day of the week you'd be marrying your mot under armed guard.

It was a great night and put me in mind of my father and mother and he getting up to take the floor in 'Haste to the Wedding', and the two of them singing:

> Says herself to meself, 'We're as good as the rest,'
> Says herself to meself, 'Sure we're better nor gold,'
> Says herself to meself, 'You're as wild as the rest of them,'
> 'Kathy,' says I, 'sure we're time enough old . . .'

There was plenty of drink, plenty of Guinness and whiskey and by the time we had a few jars in us, the Royal Ulster Constabulary could have raided the joint and taken us along for good measure. I'm happy to say, however, that the guards were more conscientious, even though we were handing them the odd pint from out the window.

I noticed one fellow had a long spring, which is used by plumbers and fitters to bend a pipe, but he had it up his sleeve, and if you got a belt of it it certainly wouldn't improve your health.

I did not let on that I had seen it but I was shaken all the same and was glad when Ambush, an old friend of mine, handed me the gargle and asked for a stave or two on the mouth-organ, at which I am fairly adept. I played the tune of the 'Internationale' and Ambush joined in with the words and then sang a merry song about a hunger strike.

'Let me carry your cross for Ireland, Lord,
　　The time of our trial draws near,
And the pangs and the pains of the sacrifices
　　Must be borne by loved ones dear.
But Lord take me from the offering throng,
　　There are others less prepared,
Though anxious and all as we are to die
　　That Ireland may be spared.'

Among the guests at the wedding was the bridegroom's rejected suitoress, who was also an Irish Republican armyess, if I may be so disrespectful of the movement, and not wishing to be left out of the proceedings, she sang:

'I will wear a smile tonight, my dear,
　　Though the false one may be there,
The gems they hang around you
　　Still linger in my hair.'

Someone at the back of the room signalled to me for to stop her, but she wasn't done yet, and without further warning, a most blood-curdling moan went through the place as she threw back her shawl for further utterance:

'And even he who's left me,
　　Will think my heart is light
Though I'll cry my bit tomorrow
　　I'll wear a smile tonight.'

Don't ask me the meaning, for this is Belfast language, but in matters of sentiment there can be nothing but nonsensicality.

We were all a good way gone by now in the process of liquidation, and an old one stood up and sang a song about her late husband, who was a gunner and had met some quicker gunner in action at the Dardanelles. The quicker gunner was on the cousin's side which is an example to people not to be getting mixed up in family quarrels.

Then Ambush gave another bar, not on the European disturbances, but on rebel ones, 'Here comes our Fenian blade.' He had a good voice which is a thing I admire in a citizen, being no mean performer on the gargle trap myself.

'Give us a stave, Brendan,' he said when he finished, so I sang to the assembled Orangemen 'God save the King' backwards, which is something I had picked up from a china in Borstal. My family would be shocked out of their boots and the present company did not at all relish England or anything to do with it, but the day was so far gone that discretion was no longer the better part of valour.

But to show there was no favouritism, cute Christian that I am, I sang with an ever-increasing voice that could be heard all over Belfast:

> Come out and rattle your bin,
> Tiddy-fol-loll, tiddy-fol-lay.

In the pogroms the people used to warn one another of the approach of the murder gang, from street to street, by rattling the tops of the dustbins and this was the song they sang. It is a good song, as most Northern songs are.

'Encore!' they shouted in jovial humour, 'give us the one you sang at the wake!'

I had to give three encores, and if I say so myself, I was in fine voice.

Cafferty and I remained in Belfast until the heat blew off a little, for we heard on the wireless that a most intensive search was being carried on for the pair of us and I got a kind of pleasure thinking of the uniformed men going mad from dreaming of the stripe they'd fall in for if they got us

We saw no signs of police activity till we reached a village on the Dublin County border. Some of them were sitting in their cars while other uniformed police were standing around. We went into a tiny public house that I knew, and where they knew me, and we were shown immediately into a little room at the back. There was a slide in the wall communicating with the bar and having plenty of the readies, I shouted through it.

'A pint of stout myself. A pint of stout?' Cafferty nodded. So we had the stout and a crubeen each and a plate of bread and butter, and the steaming hot pig's foot warmed us up for the road and what we might have to face out there.

We shoved the empty plates back through the hatch, had a piss for good measure and went back out into the road.

All was quiet outside now except for the birds who were getting up over our heads and the spring making way for the summer and I took in the air and the sun and the smell of the fresh earth.

When we reached the outskirts of the city, Cafferty and I separated as we had heard that there was an order out for me to be shot on sight, as I having fired the gun, was considered the more dangerous. In my bollocks, I said in my own mind and not in the sight of God who is there to see us all.

But it wouldn't be doing Cafferty any good, for at this stage of the game, he could only be termed an accessory or whatever the be Jaysus they call it.

The order for me to be shot was issued by Chief Superintendent Gantley, a whore's melt of a man, and another ex-Free State Army guttersnipe, neither of whom were ever in the Irish Republican Army, at least as active members. Afterwards Gantley, Séan of that ilk, was shot by one of his own men when he was leading a bravado raid on two criminals—if they can be so called for it is not very often I use the word—who were hiding in the Hammond Lane Foundry in Dublin. Although Gantley is dead, I am happy to relate I am still here.

With a mutter of encouragement, for I was sorry to see him go, Cafferty went off down the street until the sun and the light enveloped him and he was gone.

When my mother was still at school, she had a friend, Chrissie Richardson, who lived in an orphanage in Dublin. Later, when my mother was the caretaker of an organisation called the Irish White Cross in Harcourt Street, Chrissie brought her boy-friend Alf, a Geordie, a man from Newcastle and a very delightful one in my opinion, up to my mother's house, and he was on the run, not for the fact that he was an Irish Republican soldier, but because he was a deserter from the British Army. My mother put him up and she put Chrissie up until they got married and then we all lived in the same street.

To tell the truth, when I first heard Alf speak I thought he was a foreigner, though in some parts of England he'd probably be taken for an Irishman on account of his accent.

I went now to Alf and Chrissie's house and I hid there, in the home of an ex-soldier of the British army with the very proud

44

distinction of having deserted, and they gave me a bed and enough of food and treated me like one of their own.

I joined in with the Dublin Brigade of the Irish Republican Army and we held up a number of pawn shops and at one of them forcibly bagged for the cause some £2,000 to £3,000. Somebody said that we should have got a medal for finding the place, seeing as how it had changed its address.

Cafferty also raided pawn shops and was arrested and released under these circumstances. He and two other Republican men had gone into one of the biggest pawn offices in Dublin, and while the two of them had held up the clerks at the counter, Cafferty stuck his revolver against the back of the neck of a carpenter who had the misfortune to be mending the floor that very morning.

'Keep on hitting that floor, Mac, and nothing bad will happen you, but if you attempt to raise your head, I'll blow it off you.'

'All right,' says the carpenter, 'I was through the Troubled Times,' and he kept on hitting the floor, while Cafferty and the other two scarpered with the money.

Several days later the three of them were arrested by the Broy Harriers, by Gantley and his merry men, and wherever Gantley is planted I don't think he looks all that merry now, having been shot as I said by one of his own squad. They were great men at shooting because they were usually half drunk when they came out of the Castle (which is where the Specials have their Headquarters) on a job.

The carpenter was called upon to identify them.

'Certainly,' says he, 'I'll identify them. Just show me their feet.'

So the policeman thought this was the most extraordinary request, but at the same time he was glad to get a witness, because the clerks in the pawn office just announced they didn't want to have anything to do with it. They marched the carpenter along where all these guys' feet were, and when he came to Cafferty's he said:

'That's the man!'

'How the hell?' said Cafferty. 'Are you mad or what? To make an identification you must place your hand on the person's shoulder and look into his face.'

'You're the man that put the gun at the back of my neck at

the pawn office on such a date, 1942, this year of Our Lord.'

'Look, you haven't even seen my face until this moment.'

'No,' says the carpenter, 'but I saw your shoes and if you were looking at somebody's shoes for five minutes with a ·45 at the back of your neck you would know every wrinkle in those shoes, as well as you know the wrinkles in your own face when you are shaving it.'

Cafferty was charged and the carpenter was called upon to give evidence, which he agreed to do. And the police said he was a great man and a good citizen and they gave him plenty of whiskey, plenty of good entertainment and all the rest of it.

But before he came to give evidence, he received at his house, a shoe box with a dirty old shoe in it and attached to the shoe was a Mass card and in the box was a bullet. On the Mass card was written the carpenter's name and the day of the forthcoming trial. 'In Memoriam of his dear soul. Will those who think of him today, a little prayer to Jesus say. Hang his picture on the wall. Gone but not forgotten.'

The carpenter took this as a strong hint and desisted from his efforts to become a state witness.

'How the hell could I identify a man from his shoes?' he said to the police.

And Cafferty was released.

OUTSIDE the sun was just beginning on a feeble attempt to come out on this summer's day, 1942, and while others were getting ready to go about their business I sat down this morning after a kipper, some mushrooms, tea with bread and marmalade and butter and reflected on my condition.

Even if I had no money there were people who would give me the odd pint of porter or a glass of malt betimes in return for the old chat or a piece of my impertinence.

I was at Jack Corr's residence in number 15, Blessington Street, Dublin, near to where my great-grandmother and my grandfather lived. I had decided that a bit of light and air would be more to my taste and light and air I got for the asking without moving a muscle.

The door flew open as if the devil himself was behind it, and a lot of mean-faced bastards grabbed me as I made for the window. I was treated to a piece of verbal abuse by Gantley and his minions, but I was not physically assaulted as I had been in Liverpool when I was last arrested. One of the detective officers slipped me a packet of cigarettes and a box of matches, some would say tor to soften me up to give information, but I am always prepared to look upon these things as manifestations of human charity. They searched me, putting their hands along the seams of my trousers where they found the gun.

'You wouldn't have come in here so shagging easy,' I said, 'if I had had the time to use it. You'll never drive the Irish out of Ireland, and that's for fughing sure.'

Gantley looked at me and sighed, as if he had heard nothing, and with a younger, dark-haired one put the handcuffs on me.

I was taken out to a waiting car where a crowd had now gathered and one of them made a half-hearted attempt to speak to me.

'Come on,' said the dark-haired one, 'move off out of that.

47

There's nothing to see here. Come on, get a move on with you.'

We drove to station headquarters where the sergeant wrote down my name and my particulars, and I was put in one of the cells looking out towards the flats, to await trial in the morning.

I sat on the side of the bed and lit up a choker, staring into it as if mesmerised, watching the ash falling to the floor, and remained sitting long after. Jesus Christ, even now I was locked up only three hours and this time it would be for ever.

I lay back on the mattress trying to put my mind on other things and settled myself more comfortably by putting the end of my blanket on the wooden pillow to soften it. Afterwards I lay half-eating the sleep until I was deep in it.

When I awoke there was silence but for the chimes of Christ Church, lonely in the night, from the top of the hill. I wanted to use the lavatory and by lighting a match I found it in the corner from the door. I stood over it in cold and loneliness and my despair marked time while I used it.

Bloody shit-houses. I'd give them pushing and shoving and roaring and bawling if I ever met them outside. But I'd never be outside again and I gave a long, long sniff and was turning it into a sneeze when the clanking of keys in the lock of the door interrupted me. The warder was carrying a tray with aluminium cans on it. It was my dinner avic and you wouldn't want to be disturbing a sinner in his sleep and like Lanna Machree's dog what harm is there going a bit of the road with everyone? He put the tray down as he spoke, giving me the wink as he did so.

In one of the cans there was a thick soup while the other held potatoes, and before the warder had banged out the door I had made good account of my appetite and felt the better for it.

I lay back on my bed and wondered if they would take me to court in the morning and knew the desperate fear of the condemned man waking up the morning of his execution. It wasn't even possible that morning should come, when at least I would not be in solitude. Fighting is better than loneliness even if they were distributing nothing better than thumps and verbal abuse.

At last I heard footsteps coming and the key turning in the lock.

'Right, follow me. Down for a wash.' A big lump of a fellow and friendly with it all and I went down to the wash house with him, feeling more alive.

Puffed, powdered and shaved, I was taken in a squad car to Collins' Barracks, where I saw Andrew, Lasarian and Joseph who were being charged with me for their part in the shooting at Glasnevin. I had not seen them since and now for a moment we all stood together united in sadness. We were charged with attempted murder and being in possession of arms and remanded to Bridewell Prison to await trial.

The previous day there had been a long debate in the Cabinet, I understand, as to whether my case should be heard at the Special Military Court or the Special Criminal Court. Although the same shower of bastards sat at both Courts, the Special Military one, under the Special Powers Act, could only find you guilty and sentence you to death, or find you not guilty and discharge you. They had no other alternative. At the Special Criminal Court, where there was a sketchy idea of normal law procedure, they could sentence you to death or to imprisonment, but they could only sentence you to capital punishment in the case of a capital charge, if you had killed somebody.

For two weeks, Andrew Lasarian, Joseph and myself were all in 'C' wing awaiting trial. We were in separate cells, two, three and one, and although we had to do our own chores and clean up our cells, we did not have to slop out our chamber pots as there was a proper 'jacks' in the corner. The chain however was outside the door as these shower of bastards were taking nothing to chance. The cleaners would come around each morning and pull them. On the second morning I sat on my bed listening to the old ones flushing all the lavatories until this one arrives at my door.

'Will I pull your chain, sir?' she asked.

'Yes please, ma'm.'

'What are you in for, son?'

'Shooting at the fughing police.'

'Ah, Jesus,' she wailed, 'what will they do to you for that?'

'They'll fughing well hang me, that's what they'll do.'

'Jesus, Mary and Joseph,' and now she was nearly crying with it. 'God help your poor mother.'

'Screw my mother,' I said. 'It's not her they'll be hanging, it's me.'

She went off down the landing muttering to herself.

Being on remand we could smoke, and I was grateful not to have to ration myself with the reading. But the waiting battered my bared nerves and all I could do with the sickness in my stomach was to lean over the side of the bed and wish that the waiting would end. Except, God look down on you, it could be the end.

Until this day when the warder unlocks us earlier than usual and tells us to stand to our doors and wait for our escort as we were to appear before the Special Criminal Court that day. We were taken down to the prison yard where a police tender was waiting. Each one of us was handcuffed to a screw, who was armed, and we all piled in the tender, team-handed. Three other 'Harriers,' carrying Thompson sub-machine guns, climbed in alongside with us to ensure we did not run away with the escort.

The doors banged out and the engine started and we sat there looking at the floor wondering at the times we were in.

When we arrived at Collins' Barracks we were brought into a waiting room and our handcuffs were removed. Our names were shouted and we went into the Tribunal to face Colonel John Joyce and several other uniformed men. As we were soldiers of the Irish Republican Army we refused to recognise the Court and the Court entered pleas of 'Not Guilty' after it had been established that we were of right mind.

More right-minded than you'll ever be, you brown-arsed bollockses, I said in my own mind.

Andrew, Lasarian and Joseph were charged with possessing firearms and having incriminating documents and being members of an illegal organisation, while I was charged with the attempted murder of Patrick Kirwan and Martin Hanrahan, or Martin Kirwan and Patrick Hanrahan, who gives a fugh which, and for being also in illegal possession of firearms.

Colonel John Joyce and the officers sat in front of us on a slightly raised counter of sorts, their caps and their swords in front of them and our military escort told us quite civilly to go into the dock and stop there.

The police told their story and, with one exception, told it without any venom, and I reflected on the sadness of Irishmen fighting Irishmen or indeed, I'm ashamed even now to say, of men fighting men, or men fighting women or women fighting women anywhere, because I suppose at heart I'm a pacifist.

The colonel asked us had we anything to say and I decided to use the same statement that had put the Judge at Liverpool in a vicious and unjudicial temper before sentencing me to three years Borstal Detention.

After I had said, 'Gentlemen' and all to that effect, I continued: 'But there is but the one settlement to the Irish Question, and until the thirty-two-county Republic of Ireland is once more functioning, Ireland unfree shall never be at peace. God save Ireland!' and I shouted 'Up the Republic!' across the room and into the faces as they settled themselves to sentence us.

Andrew and Lasarian got seven years and Joseph, on account of his youth I suppose, eighteen months.

My guts twisted up inside of me and I could feel the stomach muscles snarl and stiffen. Fourteen years penal servitude. You fugh-faced bastard, tight-lipped screw-shit. That the devil may choke you and the Republic, but leave me out of the shouting for the cause all on my own. A kick up the bollocks is what I'd like to give you.

It was over and there's an end on it. I got the heaviest sentence despite the fact that I was the least guilty of the four in the eyes of the Irish Republic. Later I had the satisfaction of reading in our Republican Underground Journal, which is printed in Belfast, that 'Volunteer Behan displayed great courage in the face of the officers of the Special Criminal Court.' I read this with rather an ironical smile.

Following us at the trial were some light youths who had been arrested for a bank hold-up in a border town, and I knew from experience that this is a job that gives one no glory if you are caught because, despite the fact that you are robbing in the name of the Republic and for the cause, you are specifically forbidden by general orders of the I.R.A. to refuse to recognise the court; you cannot claim political protection and you face your sentence as an ordinary criminal. I have nothing against criminals except every criminal I know is a Tory and a bore, and in Ireland votes, when he is out of the nick and has a vote, for the people who were shoving some of my friends against the wall

51

and sending me and others to fourteen years, seven years and eighteen months' penal servitude.

I admired these fellows so much on this day, for they were coming up smiling all over their plaques, and with the example of their courage in my mind, I went down smiling too and in good humour, for as somebody said, 'Any man who shoots at a policeman at fourteen yards and misses him deserves a year for every yard he missed him by!'

I met my mother outside the room and the mothers of some of the other boys, and my mother was in tears and I gave her my hand and struggled for the breath to speak and, in doing so, knew it would not come.

I ran down the steps and into the police van for Mountjoy Jail. There were already quite a few blokes in there and I climbed inside next to Andrew. There was a boy sitting on the other side and although there was plenty of room, he only moved an inch or two. Lasarian was sitting near the door and I handed him a lighted cigarette which he put in his mouth, hung on to it and drew smoke, gazing on the end of it. The guard slammed the door dividing the driver's compartment from us and we moved off.

There were slits at the top for ventilation and I stood up to look out and saw the back of the Central Criminal Court and thought wistfully about Robert Emmet, a doctor's son and a great leader of the fight for Irish Independence, who was tried there for his pains.

I commented on the district we passed through. 'We're going past the Plaza now, the picture house.'

'I go to it every Sunday. Never miss it,' said the boy and smacked his lips as if in anticipation of the next Sunday's outing.

'Well, you're going to miss it next Sunday,' said Lasarian sharply.

The boy worked his mouth a little but said nothing. I tried to console him telling him he was bound to have his sentence reduced for good behaviour and that it was his first offence and all to that effect, but after a while I could see it was no good, so I gave up.

Up Blessington Street we went, round Berkeley Road, down the North Circular, down and around and up the avenue to the main gate. There were shouts from the Guard to the warders at the gate, the gate opened and the van moved forward.

'We're going in,' I said as I turned my head from the ventilation slit, and sat down by Andrew. We all drew our breath in unison as the van drove slowly in and stopped opposite the steps leading to the prison. There was a man on the inner gate and he banged the side of the van with his fist.

'Put out them cigarettes and hurry up, get out.'

We filed out and stood in a line in the yard and looked around, and the screw did too, at other prisoners nodding to each other while they weeded round a grass verge. They didn't nod to us but only to each other.

A screw shouted impatiently. 'Look sharp there, you bastards, I want this verge tidied up before you go to bed.'

Some of the prisoners wore heavy frieze suits, dark grey with a broad stripe, and caps of the same colour with a large button on top. Others wore no jackets but cotton shirts and a heavy piece of cloth round the neck to represent a tie.

A bullet-headed coal-block of a man, with a face good for hardness but bad for colour, came down the steps, followed by a warder with a silver band round his cap. The guard stiffened to attention.

'All receptions correct, sir.'

Bullet-head nodded and indicated for us to follow him and we were taken to a place that resembled the accident ward of a hospital. Here eighty other I.R.A. men were waiting to give their names to a warder writing in a large book. In the corner were bath cubicles.

'Breandán Ó Beacháin,' I said to the warder, who up to this moment was carrying on a love affair with the book and his mouth eating out the ink as he wrote, he was that close to it.

He snuffled something to himself and raised his head, 'Ah, you're one of the fellows who was in gaol over in England.'

'Yes,' I answered, and what's it to you, you lousebound, deskbound bastard leaving the Republic to look after itself, but quietly to myself.

'You're a tough guy.' And his beady little eyes became brave with governors, chiefs, principals, clerks and Jaysus knows who around to protect him.

'I'll show you whether I fughing am or not,' and at that time, if I say so myself, I was pretty tough.

Two warders grabbed me by the arm. 'Come on, Brendan,' the grey-haired one said, 'there's no sense in villainy here. He didn't mean you any harm.'

They took me over to the bath cubicles where I refused to be searched before taking off my clothes and Andrew and Lasarian did the same.

We were given nine inches of water apiece, 'in case we bloody well drink it,' I shouted in at the fellow in the next cubicle.

I felt good after the bath and holding the towel away, I looked down at myself. Jesus, it must be a terrible thing to get old, I thought, with bent old legs and twisted buniony toes, and the crinkle in my belly would straighten out in this kip without the aid of much porter, for it was the drink that did the most damage.

Another prisoner unlocked the cubicle and handed me my prison clothes and I rapped into the young boy, Joseph, who was standing with some other prisoners and Andrew and Lasarian.

We were marched in single file through the main corridor and into the prison.

'Stand here in the centre,' said the warder when we got to what seemed to be the main street of the prison. It was at the junction of the four wings; 'A' leading straight west; 'B' and 'C' at angles in the middle and 'D' the continuation of 'A' going east. There were steel galleries all round, three of them in each wing, and steel stairs joining them. Beside 'A' wing was the shaft to the kitchen, and beside them, in the centre of the circle, was a stone pillar with a triangle hanging on it.

> 'A hungry feeling
> Came o'er me stealing
> And the mice were squealing in my prison cell,
> And that old triangle
> Went jingle jangle,
> Along the banks of the Royal Canal.
>
> To begin the morning
> The warder bawling

"Get out of bed and clean up your cell,"
And that old triangle
Went jingle jangle,
Along the banks of the Royal Canal.'

Towards the bottom of 'D' wing, there was a red metal door with a barred gate painted aluminium over it. It was the door of the hang-house.

Andrew, Lasarian, Joseph and I were in 'B' wing and one of the fellows that had held up the bank on a border town whose trial followed ours.

'Stand to a cell door, each one of you,' rasped a warder, and to me, 'Come on, you, get a move on yourself there.'

I moved slowly around a bit and was glad that I was giving the needle to this fugh-faced, desiccated old bastard. His gills wattled in anger as he pushed me towards the cell door, handing me my kit—pillowcases containing sheets and a towel—as he did so.

He opened the door and my Jesus, my heart fell into my boots. It was like the black hole of Calcutta only the walls were white-washed, otherwise you wouldn't have seen them at all, as half the window was below the level of the ground. In the dim light I could see the usual inscriptions on the walls. There were hearts and flowers and names that I couldn't decipher too well.

The warder slammed the door behind me, lifted the cover over in the little spy-hole in the door, knocked it down again and was off across the corridor, his footsteps fading as he did so. I walked the ten paces down from the door to the apology for a window, and reflected in misery the amount of exercise I would be getting if I did this every day of the fourteen year stretch.

In the morning I was opened up, having accomplished the usual prison formalities of doing my cell, eating my breakfast, using the chamber-pot and slopping it out with the others.

Nobody spoke of it of course, but there was an air of tension about the place as we heard that a prisoner in 'D' wing, Bernard Kirwan by name, was due to be topped shortly, but as he is not here to defend himself, I'll say no more about him, except that he had a very gay personality.

55

Being summer, I had come in late from the exercising yard after a game of hand-ball with a young fellow from Limerick called Hickey. He was a decent lad and known throughout the nick for this reason. Our shirts were washed each week by the ladies on the female side of the prison and they would hang them out in the exercise yard. It would relieve the monotony of the times, us standing at the window keeping an eye out for them and they stretching and reaching off chairs to hang them on the line. But sometimes the shirts were so badly done, that you wouldn't be knowing whether they had been washed at all. Hickey got fed up with this one time, and he wrote on the collar of his shirt, which was as limp as the wire from the morning's pull, 'More starch here,' and he got it back with a note pinned to the tail of it, 'Less shit here.'

But on this day as Hickey and I came in together, Bernard Kirwan was with his visitors and two warders, and shoving aside the two warders who stood aghast at the idea of a condemned man having contact with anybody, he dashed out from the cell and he embraced us both.

'Tomorrow,' he said, 'at ten past eight, I'll be praying for you in heaven.'

The Lord have mercy on him. I hope his prayers were heard.

The next morning as he was taken out to be executed, he put a cup of water on the back of his right hand and turned to the warder and said: 'You see, that's the hand of a man that's going to be hanged in ten minutes,' and his hand never shook.

Somebody said to me he was very brave. 'No,' says I, 'he was very mad.' For he didn't know a lot about execution by hanging, which is a very painful method of dying according to reports I've heard from the various gaols I was in.

Years later I based my play 'The Quare Fellow' on the last few weeks of this man's life.

The only other execution in the 'Joy' while I was there was of a boy from the County Kerry, who had fired a shot at the police, which was one of the charges that had got me my stretch. But the inscrutable ways of the Lord being what they are, he was thought to be more important than I was, and he was shot. I would like to put it on record that he was executed, not by the British and not by the Northern Ireland authorities, but by Mister Eamon de Valera's Republican Government, which proves that statements like 'your own looking after you' are complete nonsense.

The prison routine at Mountjoy was similar to the gaol at Liverpool with the exception that most of my comrades here were engaged in various handicraft classes such as embroidery and basket-work. They sat on their chairs in silent rows embroidering mostly fughing monuments to misery, 'In Memory of Our Lord Jesus Christ,' and 'the Sacred Heart,' and 'To the soldiers of the Republic executed from 1939 to 1942,' and one more ambitious hungry-faced little bastard gave a list of those who were hanged or shot or killed.

Jesus, Mary and Joseph, it put years on me, and there wasn't man or boy among us who didn't make these Celtic crosses from matches in memory of some bloody thing or another. After a while some of the fellows became really handy at it, and they would stick together pieces of used matchsticks and make them into all sorts of things. I was never able for it and my fingers were scarred like the hands of drug addicts with the needle marks from sewing mail-bags up in Walton gaol in England. But I used to collect their rejects and send them out to friends of mine who would say: 'Brendan Behan made this up in Mountjoy Prison.'

Now the days began to shorten and the autumn got weaker and weaker and then beaten into winter and an awful east wind that was up around the gaol and we on our way to Christmas.

The embroidery classes had given way to a great plethora of Christmas cards, but I didn't have anything to do with it as I was too busy reading and smoking and having an occasional drink, by the courtesy of a warder, who made a few ha'pence shopping in drink and cigarettes and shopping out letters, until he was caught and given his cards.

But one of the fellows, who is since dead, the Lord have mercy on him, designed a Christmas card in the shape of a tombstone, in memory of a soldier of the Republic who had been executed during that year, and he intended to send it to this young man's parents. The front of the card gave an account of his life and his death and inside was written: 'In loving memory of Jimmy McSherry, died for the Republic of Ireland, November, 1942. Will those who think of him today, A little prayer to Jesus say. Wishing his father and mother a very happy

Christmas and a bright and prosperous New Year, signed, Yours sincerely, Jimmy Stokes.'

On February the ninth, I was twenty and on St. Patrick's Day, Andrew, Lasarian, Joseph and I were in the exercise yard with shamrocks in our lapels, though I had never gone a bundle on St. Patrick's Day or on shamrock, but it reminded us of Easter and the Republican Feast and the march to Glasnevin cemetery.

There was a certain amount of monotony in our spring and summer days, though you'd get that in any nick, only more so. But time passed well and I was getting used to it, and you could always have a bit of sport during the day.

That night I had a bit of a read till they put the lights out, and then thinking that a year of the fourteen year stretch had passed, went asleep.

If you go to the Curragh camp, just ask for number nine,
You'll see three swaddies standing there and the best looking
one is mine.

W E W E R E slopped out earlier than usual this morning
and the warder told me to put a tie on when I had
finished my breakfast.

'I will in my bollocks,' I told him.

As I had my visit at the beginning of the month and hadn't
put in for a special one, I didn't think it could be that, unless
it was some good-for-nothing-do-good man from the Society
for the Rehabilitation of Recidivist Prisoners or the Department
of Lick-your-arse Reformers. I had no intention of jazzing
myself up for the likes of them. I had one of them to visit me
previously and he spoke in terms of the royal 'we,' as if he was
not above doing a job himself, casing a joint for some rocks.
Stealing a penny from a blind man's plate would have been
more in his line.

There was great excitement among the blokes because they'd
seen an empty coach drawn up in the yard and no new receptions
to account for it. They kept looking up at the screw in charge of
the landing as if they were going to learn anything by getting
a look at him. At last a screw read from a list: 'The following
will be transferred to the military prison at Arbour Hill,' and I
looked at Andrew who looked at me and Lasarian looked at
us both because there was little chance of us not being included
in this lot.

I wasn't out of my mind about this transaction because I
had heard that the cells there were only about sixteen feet by
eight and that a prisoner in solitary confinement could only

59

walk five paces each way. But I also knew that beyond the boundary wall of the exercise yard were the graves of the men who had been executed in Easter Week, 1916: Thomas J. Clarke, Pádraig H. Pearse, Thomas MacDonagh and the rest. I knew their names and all belonging to them as well as I knew my own.

Eamon de Valera would have been executed too, had it not been for Bernard Shaw's letter printed in an English paper, which proved that the spirit of these brave men had awakened chords throughout the world. 'My own view is that the men who were shot in cold blood after capture or surrender,' wrote Bernard Shaw, 'were prisoners of war and it was therefore entirely incorrect to slaughter them . . . I cannot regard as a traitor any Irishman taken in a fight for Irish Independence against the British Government, which was a fair fight in everything except the enormous odds my countrymen had to face.'

At Westminster, John Dillon appealed to Asquith. 'It is not murderers who are being executed, but men who fought a clean fight, a brave fight.'

De Valera's sentence was commuted to penal servitude for life, 'Convict 95' in Dartmoor.

'Twas in Kilmainham prison yard our fifteen martyrs died,
And cold and still in Arbour Hill they are lying side by side,
But we will yet pay back the debt for the spirit is still alive
In men who stood thro' fire and blood with Convict 95.

In the heels of the hunt, our names were called and ah, I said to myself, a change is as good as a rest, and we ran upstairs in great jubilation to collect our small kit. We were handcuffed in pairs and the cuffs were attached to two long chains, one for each side of the coach. I got handcuffed to Hickey, and Andrew and Lasarian were on the chain beside. We stood in line for the start, shipshape and Bristol fashion and as quick as an ass's gallop we were up and in the coach moving out of the exercise yard and speeding on the open road for the five minutes run to Arbour Hill.

I'd not have believed a person if they'd told me that summer would ever end as I looked over the Dublin mountains, the moors and the marshes, and smelt again the sea, and I sang out for myself; 'The sea, oh, the sea, *a ghrádh gheal mo chroidhe.*' Everyone looked at me in surprise but in great humour and there were shouts for the old songs I knew. Some I had heard in my own home from my mother, although a few of her generation were made ashamed of the old tunes that kept up the hearts of the people for years. I was always curious to find out what they used to sing in the times before herself and made a point of listening to the old ones on pension day in the pub.

I sang, 'Get up, says Skin-the-Goat,' and 'James Carey with his son,' and everyone joined in, screws and all, with the sad and lovely 'Kevin Barry,' known the two sides of the Atlantic.

Until the coach stops in the yard of the prison. The handcuffs and chains were taken off and we were lined up in the yard. One screw went into the building to get receipts for our safe delivery, while the principal screw took us through another door to get our kit.

We began to take off our clothes and most of us by now didn't give a God damn, one way or another, about our nakedness, but a new fellow, Thomas Magaretty, was standing in the corner of the room with his right hand over his crotch and lower too. He reddened up and his face went over every inch of me as I sang, 'I've got a lovely bunch of coconuts,' and I could have bitten the tongue back into my throat when he whispered under his breath that he'd only one bollock. How anyone would know the difference I do not know, but apparently he seemed to think they did.

The same fellow used to receive letters from his wife addressed to 'Thomas Magaretty, Political Poisoner,' and, be Jaysus, say it as one who shouldn't, he certainly looked like one. He had hair as white as snow and a skin that was tired from the stretching, and the effort he took to go last in the showers on account of his having only one bollock would go through you. He could take a joke if it was two feet from his nose.

One time, in the half-light of a November's evening, I attired myself in the shower with a towel round my middle and stretched out my arms as if I was an apparition from Salvador Dali's 'Crucifixion,' and when Magaretty saw me, the poor little bugger fled screaming, 'Oh, Jesus, the place is haunted!'

It's a queer world but the best we've got to be going on with.

After Christmas we were shifted again, this time about thirty miles, to the Curragh Internment camp, and glad that we were here, for we had been through the mill together, though none of us spoke of it, and I was surprised to find I knew a great many of the prisoners, including my friend, Cafferty. But it wasn't only members of the I.R.A. who were interned in the camp, for there were a number of British, Canadian, American and German fliers there too, although they were in separate camps to us.

Now I have never been one to give out the pay about the lack of bravery in others, being a natural coward myself, but in the case of the British, American and Canadian fliers, they were rather cowardly to give themselves up, because they could have got back from Free State territory if they had repaired their aeroplanes inside twenty-four hours and flown them to Northern Ireland. For the matter of that, they could have left their wrecked aircraft and even walked across the border or taken a bus. I heard there was plenty who did.

Some of these internees, no doubt sensible men, preferred to spend the rest of the war as heroes amongst the racing ladies of the Curragh rather than face further horrors, for they all got parole, as far as I could see, for about twenty-four hours a day. The Germans, on the other hand, had no alternative, but they too had their supporters amongst some of the Irish bourgeoisie and indeed amongst some of the British.

In the Curragh, there were from thirty to forty of us sleeping in huts together, and although Andrew was in a different hut further up, Lasarian and Joseph, who was with us again now, were in beds next door to mine, while Cafferty was under the window near the door. Opposite me was a Tyrone man, six feet three inches in his stockinged feet, with a mass of blond curly hair.

He came across to me and Cafferty introduced us.

'You should apply for admittance to the hospital,' said the Tyrone man.

I will in my bollocks, I said in my own mind. 'Why? There's nothing wrong with me.' Neither there wasn't. I was as perfect a specimen of Irish youth as you would have found anywhere. I had nice teeth, good hair, good complexion, no stomach and altogether was God's gift to the feminine race if I could have found any of them around.

But this Tyrone man had a point, for the hospital got the best of the meat that came into the prison and the cooks the best of the meat that came into the hospital; for as the saying has it, first up is the best dressed, and he was pretty friendly with the cooks.

There was another reason as well. Whatever may be said against the Free State Army, they do not starve you and every tubercular patient in the hospital got two bottles of stout a day and twelve ounces of chicken. Against their arrival in the hospital, some of the fellows stole new chamber-pots from the stores, so when they were first admitted and not able for the stout, they'd be pouring it into the chamber pots, each of which held approximately one gallon, and each day they would return the empty bottles as the screws insisted.

On my first evening in the Curragh, one or two of the blokes had arranged a party for me in the hospital as it was nearly my twenty-first birthday. They had saved up sufficient of stout and chicken for to enable us to carry on until at least three in the morning. A happier hospital I've never seen in my life. The singing got well under way, and us throwing out from the roots, our rich tenor voices increasing in volume with the intake of stout.

The sergeants of the 'Linseed Lancers,' as we called the Medical Corps, came in to sing an aria from *Lucia di Lammermoor*, and one from Gounod's *Faust,* and I contributed a couple of numbers myself. It is said that we were drinking a toast to ourselves, the felons of our land.

'Let tyrants mock and traitors sneer, little do we care,
A felon's cap is the noblest crown an Irish head can wear.
And every Gael in Inisfail who scorns the serf's vile brand,
From Lee to Boyne, would gladly join the felons of our land.'

I was in the process of celebrating this song with a toast, drinking from a chamber pot, when one of the guards passed by the window. Hearing the noise, he looked in and promptly fainted when he saw me raising a chamber pot to my lips and eagerly drinking from it.

As I lay, warm and jarred in my bed that night, I looked across at Lasarian, his face lit in the glow of a dog-end.

63

'Count your bloody sheep,' I said. 'This is a good kip.'

The Curragh camp was divided politically into three divisions: those who supported the official I.R.A., those who, like myself, supported the unofficial I.R.A., and those who didn't agree with either side and formed a group of their own.

I had sympathy with all of them and on all sides I had friends, but I was tempted to join the first division in which there was Cathal Goulding, a very dear friend of mine whom I had known since childhood. We had known each other almost from the time we were born. We had been in the Fianna Boy Scout Organisation together and joined the I.R.A. together, had been thrown out of it together, and been taken back in it together.

He was doing a stretch in the Curragh for an armed raid. As a matter of fact, I did join his division for a while but whichever side you favoured, you were forbidden to patronise the others. You could not even talk to them. Now I am the most inconsistent person in the world and I could never keep up things like this for long, not out of any sense of decency but because I would forget to keep it up.

After having warned me several times about talking to the other groups, the official I.R.A. got fed up with Brendan Francis Behan, and I was thrown out. Cathal gave me a packet of cigarettes as a leaving present. Jesus, you'd be thinking I was going to America, instead of across a concrete path. I then joined those who supported the less official I.R.A., some of whom were also very dear friends of mine, and still are, and to whom I would look for succour, rather than to perhaps any other persons in Ireland.

Outside the camp, it was popularly supposed that the three divisions were for those who supported the Allies, those who supported the Germans and those who supported the Left Wing. But such was not so.

Cut it any way you like, we were a mixed bag, nationally, politically and socially and you'd be needing a medal not to be affected by the many cross-currents at work. In every prisoner-of-war camp there is a barbed-wire pyschosis which makes outside judgments truly ridiculous, and there's an end on it.

But none of us were badly treated in my time there, although I did hear that when the so-called purge was on in 1940 some of the blokes got an extremely rough time indeed. One of them was Rory Brugha. His father, Cathal Brugha, was a former Minister for Defence in the Irish Republican Cabinet and a martyr of the Civil War. Incidentally, he was one of the last men to be killed in it. He regarded the acceptance of the Treaty document as 'national suicide.' I believe his ancestors were from Yorkshire and, if I may say so and the Brughas will excuse me, when he rose to deliver his final condemnation of the Treaty, he said with a typical Yorkshire stubbornness:

'England's position is weak; Ireland's position is strong. Why, if instead of being so strong, our last cartridge had been fired, our last shilling had been spent, and our last man were lying on the ground, and his enemies howling round him and their bayonets raised ready to plunge them into his body, that man should say—true to the tradition handed down—if they said to him: "Now will you come into the Empire?"— he should say, and he would say: "No, I will not".'

At the risk of being accused of favouritism, I must mention another Yorkshire man, Rudge Hathaway, who was also one of the last to die in the Civil War. He was killed in the Clashmealcon caves in the County Kerry, where the Free State soldiers, I'm ashamed to say, and the fughing rotten bastards of the Dublin guards put down barrels of blazing tar for to smoke him out.

But Brugha's son was ordered to run the gauntlet and get his meals like anyone else and to do this he had to go between a file of Free State Army police shit who beat him with batons on his way to and from the kitchen, which is one of the most disgusting stories I have ever heard, but I know it to be true, because friends of mine, whom I trust, told me so and it was common conversation in the camp at the time.

By the time the year 1943 was over, we knew everyone and and everyone knew us and we were glad to be together even in a familiar routine. Then early in the New Year, the snow came—which is not very common in Ireland—and it was hard to believe that we were ever warm. Still and all, we lived through the winter and the devil wouldn't kill us in summer.

It was Cathal Goulding made the bet. One hundred cigarettes that I wouldn't run round the camp starko-bollocko in the snow.

'Sure thing, Cathal,' said I. 'Of course I will,' and I'm up early the next morning in the dark and cold and the snow starting to come down again but melting over me, and round the camp like a shot with me, for I was slim and light on my feet as a feather, though if you were to see me now and see me then I suppose you'd notice a difference.

I ran naked round the place, warm and in great delight, slashing and smacking the snow with my bare feet, then down in it, rolling over and over and biting it like candy-floss at the fair. By the time I was back at the hut, the real genuine undiluted stuff was coming down in soft flakes, mild and gentle. My body was glowing from the snow and my hairs were curling from the damp of it and I felt the heat come back into my crotch as I put on my clothes and thought of the hundred snout I would be getting. They would be somebody's rations for a time to come.

Afterwards, I was sitting in the john, the lavatory, which we called 'Bolands,' in honour of the Minister for Justice of the day whose name it was, and I had the privilege of listening to two young fellows discussing the affair. 'For a boy so slim,' one said, 'Behan is a pretty tough guy.'

The blessing of Jesus on you and all belonging to you.

I do not recommend that anyone should drink potheen by choice, for it stands to common sense that the fine old drop of moonshine made with all sorts of improvised utensils cannot improve the health. But for want of a better alternative, we did make it in the Curragh camp. It was a very united demonstration, for it incorporated all three divisions.

The official side gave us the piping for to make a worm and from the less official side, less official even than ourselves, we obtained a supply of sugar, while we ourselves supplied the cereal and the skill of Gerrity and Gallagher and Jack Lynch to manufacture the finished product.

One man, Black Dan O'Toole, who was really a cook in the kitchen and gave us the best meat and, if I may say so, was as fine a soldier as ever the Republican Army produced, and these three, Gerrity, Gallagher, a Mayo man from the west of Ireland, and Jack Lynch from west Cork, supervised the preparation of the mixture in readiness for the Easter celebrations of 1945.

Potheen is made as a result of grain of some description being first of all fermented and then boiled and then distilled and finally forced through a worm by steam pressure, where it comes out at the other end in tiny drops.

Most of us agreed that under no circumstances were the first three drops to be drunk, but that they had to be given to the fairies.

'Oh, fugh the fairies,' said Dan O'Toole. 'I don't believe in that bloody nonsense.'

'Oh, no,' we insisted. 'You have to throw them out,' and throw them out we did. Afterwards a doctor told me that we weren't so foolish as we looked, because roughly the first three drops of the distilled spirit contain a lot of fusel oil which is likely to blind you if you drink it.

It was four o'clock in the afternoon before we finished distilling the potheen and, although Spring hadn't the mind to know what it was at, in the sun it was quite warm.

Then Jack Lynch roared out that the Easter concert went on in three hours' time and we'd better get the chamber pots and fill them up ready for the ding-dong later on.

The concert put years on me, not for that it was bad—I gave them a big hand when they finished—but I was suspended that much with the waiting for the fruits of the afternoon labours that I didn't give a fugh, one way or another, whether it was Bizet's *Carmen* or *The Wearing of the Green* or, for the matter of that, *Ol' King Cole* they were playing. Some of the others, I noticed, went for it like fresh bread however.

That night, and a better drunk I hope never to enjoy for the rest of my life, we were joined by a great many military police, one at least of whom was in an advanced state of intoxication due to his being rather more paternal with his captives than he should have been. He asked me to sing him some Gaelic songs and right rebel ones at that, and the more insulting at that, the better this bloke liked them, and I being full of potheen and full of goodwill towards one and all was in good voice, though I say so myself.

The night ended with a bit of a song, *My Dark Rosaleen*.

> 'O! the Erne shall run red
> With redundance of blood,
> The earth shall rock beneath our tread,
> And flames wrap hill and wood,

And gun-peal and slogan cry
Wake many a glen serene,
Eer you shall fade, eer you shall die,
My Dark Rosaleen,
My own Rosaleen!
The Judgement Hour must first be nigh,
Eer you can fade, eer you can die,
My Dark Rosaleen!'

Which is by James Joyce's favourite poet, James Clarence Mangan, who died of the cholera fever in the great famine of 1847, and who also wrote:

'Roll forth my song, like the rushing river,
That sweeps along to the mighty sea;
God will inspire me while I deliver
 My soul of thee!
Tell thou the world, when my bones lie whitening
Amid the last homes of youth and eld,
That there was once one whose veins ran lightening
No eye beheld.'

Get up the cutting, you Kerry bastard from Limerick. Up the Republic!

These songs were sung as never before or since by myself on Easter Sunday, 1945, very well full of home distilled potheen fresh from the Curragh camp and from which the late Daniel O'Toole, Donal Dubh or Black Dan as we called him, from the colour of his hair and not from the colour of his heart, the Lord have mercy on him, was prevented from drinking the first three drops.

Shortly after this, Hitler's death was announced over the wireless to the widespread cheers of the majority of both the internees and the prisoners. But I had two friends whose views on Hitler were so different and whose hatred of each other was so intense that they'd be nearly coming to blows every time they met.

Eamonn was a Dublin ex-civil servant and he seemed to think that Hitler wasn't as black as he was painted, while Gerry, who was a Cork man of five foot nothing, detested Hitler and all his works and pomps. He was the most aggresive man in Munster and the toughest I've ever seen in my life. In the camp, he'd be doing physical exercises and all to that effect each morning, while the rest of us were taking it easy and doing sod all except improving the shining hour by the bit of chat. But this geezer had fought in the International Brigade at Madrid and on the Ebro Front, as had some of the other fellows in the camp —quite a good number as a matter of fact.

At tea time that day, Cafferty, Cathal, Eamonn and I were talking about Hitler.

'Gerry must be pleased with the news,' said Eamonn, 'but Hitler wasn't a bad old skin for all that.'

'Well,' I said, 'Gerry at this moment thinks in the time of the Fuhrer's death that you should meet each other and shake hands on it.'

For the stir-about-spoon and sheer villainy, I'd be hard to equal and I winked across the table at Cathal as I spoke.

'Is that right?' said Eamonn. 'And I wouldn't think the less of him for that.'

But at the same time, he pretended not to be too much interested. The moment he had his scoff eaten, he went out. After tea, the kitchen orderlies cleared us all out and Cathal, Cafferty and I rambled round talking and smoking and stopping every now and then to get a fresh light, when who should I see out of the corner of my right eye but Eamonn walking across to Gerry.

'I believe,' he said, 'that you are showing some sympathy for the Fuhrer at last, now that he is dead.'

And Gerry took one look at him, his teeth clenched like something in a dog show.

'Fugh you and the Fuhrer, you fughing fascist ba stard,' he said jumping straight at him.

I caught the two of them by the scruffs of their necks and separated them for I thought they would have killed each other.

'Up! Out of it, you dirty pair of bloody savages.' The Military Policeman came across the yard towards us. Sweetest voice in the land of Erin, me life on you, said I in my own mind, for I could see by the looks on their faces that this is where Brendan is in for a bundle too.

'The bloody idea. If you want a fight, do it on my labour

69

party, and I'll soon show you before you're very much older that you're on the wrong ship.' And he turned to me. 'What's it all about, Behan?'

I said I knew nothing. I heard shouting, ran over and separated them. Begod, I had it, and the Father of Lies, God bless him and the Mother of Lies, too.

The corporal stood looking at me doubtfully, drew a deep breath, nodded and walked away. Honest to God, I was sorry and a bit ashamed of being sorry instead of laughing myself sick over a bit of a gag to relieve the monotony of the times we were in. Eamonn and Gerry rambled off in the direction of their huts and I thought we might all live to have worse ailments than shagging over Hitler and he lying dead with his mot.

T HAT night, warm in my bed, I lay in the half-light and rolled up a tiny dog-end. Every tinker has his way of dancing and every cripple his way of walking and even if all of us were the kids that our mothers had warned us about we were not a bad crowd at that, and the part of North Dublin that I came from was as tough as any. I sat looking round me in the dark. Lasarian, Cafferty and Joseph were all asleep, and where the blue light in the hut lit their faces, innocent they looked.

I read a few extra pages of a book by Arthur Koestler and as much as I could before I too went to sleep.

As a rule I didn't take much interest in what fughing British convoy had gone where or how far the Allied armies were stretching themselves in occupied territory, but since Hitler snuffed there was a great tension and impatience amongst some of the fellows and particularly amongst the internees, wondering when they were going to get out. It didn't bother me a load. There was little chance for me going out, whatever chance there was for the others.

This morning a lot of military police were talking in groups by the scoff house and it didn't take long before word got around that all the internees were to be released immediately and a great number of the prisoners too.

Andrew, Lasarian and Joseph went out and I thought Cafferty would die from excitement, his hand shaking while he shook mine to tell me he'd go and see my family before the day was 'bet'.

I watched them into the lorry and waved and turned away over to the exercise yard with Cathal. All the internees were in the yard being marshalled by the Sergeant-Major in pairs for the collecting base, an ass's roar from where we stood, to wait for buses to take them home. Only twenty-two of us, supposed to be the hard core of the Irish Republican Army, in which I was proud to be included, were selected to remain behind in the camp.

The Sergeant-Major ordered that there was to be no demonstration or cheering or anything, because I suppose he thought it would be unfair to us, and in a way he was right. But God never closes one door but he opens another, and if He takes away with His right hand He gives back with His left and more besides, for we were in a camp normally for thousands which was now completely empty; we could have slept in a hut for ourselves if we liked and eaten the rations of six men because, as I remarked previously, the Free State Army was never stingy with food.

Cathal and I did sod all for a week, except eat sea-pie, which is a kind of Irish stew with suet instead of potatoes in it, and great food at that, and play games of handball.

It was summer and the sun was high up and the leaves strong and green, and the days were the kind you'd know Christ died for you, though I envied the others seeing the mountains again in the weather we were in, for you can see them any side of you, even from the middle of Dublin.

This morning I was still in bed.

'Beehann!'

I fughing near jumped out of my skin. Now what, you louse-bound military bastard, said I to myself, putting down my book.

The guard burst open the door of the hut and was on top of me.

'Right,' he said, 'pack up your stuff and don't take all night over it.'

'What's up? Are the rest of us for home now?'

'You'll see,' standing over me as he spoke.

I jumped out of bed and got dressed quickly and collected my kit and the guard hurried me across the yard to the Reception. Cathal was already there and we nodded to each other and smiled.

'Looks as though we're off.'

'Sure thing kid,' Cathal replied and the other prisoners who had now joined us laughed and joked and pretended to belt into each other with their fists. We were told to stand in a line and there wasn't a man in the line but that he'd be thinking of his discharge and the next thing we knew was the guards coming over with long chains and handcuffs.

Lord Jesus, Holy Mary, Mother of God, I would like to die just here, weary of the struggle, to slip out of it, and if I never saw disappointment fall like a cloak over every inch of the others I experienced it now.

We were handcuffed two by two and the cuffs attached to the two long chains as they had been from Arbour Hill, but this time the chains were not for the coach but for two fughing guards at the end of the line, for we were only being shifted a few yards up the road to a smaller gaol, known as the glass-house. Cathal and I got ourselves handcuffed together and stood in the middle of the do-it-yourself shaft like a bloody pair of drays pulling a coach and twenty-two, and off we went, the next best to anything you might be seeing at the Dublin Horse Show out in Ballsbridge.

The principal officer in our military escort was a small and dangerous looking bastard who made up for his smallness by aggressiveness. He ran up and down the line, telling every one to get a move on and waving his baton as he did so and shoving it into the faces of the more innocent looking of us. Yes, and you shove it into my face, you puffed up belly-bastard with your shrivelled up Jesus, and you won't know what's hit you until you meet it coming back.

'Don't mind him,' Cathal said, 'he's only trying to give us the needle.'

I was not afraid of him, for if I was afraid of the engine driver I was not afraid of the oil rag, and I had his measure. He was the type to go sucking round after big bullying bollocks and liked to hear himself described in the pubs locally as a 'great little bit of stuff.'

'There's only one bloke around here who reckons he's entitled to do any needling and that's himself,' I said and no sooner said than this party of Germans and Canadians from the collecting base start insulting us. For a moment or so we all stopped in honest amazement for here were two so-called bitter enemies, united in venom against the natives of the State whose hospitality they were enjoying, and united only in their common hatred of us, the Irish Republican Army, while three weeks previously the likes of them were killing one another, chalking it up on the wall or on the wings of their aircraft or whatever they did.

I caught one German by the scruff of his neck.

'Come here,' said I, 'you skinny-looking hun bastard. I've only one hand but I've two plates of meat and I swear if I don't break you with that one hand for a beginning, I'll give you a kick up in the balls that you won't be forgetting, not this day nor tomorrow.'

What we call in the slums at home 'a Ringsend uppercut,' and I would have done so, only the military police drew their revolvers at these heroes of the Second World War and told them to buggar off out of it and leave us alone. A fughing good job they did, because with or without the chains we'd have given a fair account of ourselves.

The reason they attacked us, I suppose, was that the Canadians believed we were neutral or in favour of the Germans and the Germans believed we were neutral or in favour of the allies, whereas in actual fact we were in favour of one side only: that was our own.

> Hillside and valley, prison wall and cave,
> Trumpet the story of the gallant fight they made,
> Weary, outnumbered, undaunted, unafraid,
> Proud marched the soldiers of the rearguard.

By the time we reached the glasshouse up the bloody big hill I was tired and hungry and out of humour and was glad that there were no people around to stop and stare at us in our misery—two lines of prisoners on two chains. We trudged into a doorway at the side of the building and up a flight of stairs where a sergeant unmanacled us and another younger one took our names and went off to report our safe arrival. We were taken to our cells, but not locked in and we left our kit and went to the dining hall where there was a very good meal prepared for us of ham and potatoes and cabbage which we ate with considerable enjoyment.

The cooking was now done by professional Free State Army cooks, rather than by our own boys who had sketchy ideas about what constituted cooking.

74

We were the only blokes in the glasshouse and we led a very tolerable existence, but there were another eight I.R.A. prisoners up in Port Laoise, or Maryborough prison as we usually call the State Penitentiary, who were living under vile conditions and all of them were wearing only blankets because they had refused to wear prison clothes. For the matter of that, one of them, Séan McCaughey, was to die during my time in the glasshouse. He died on a hunger and thirst strike in May 1946. Now I knew a number of things about this young man and one of them was that when he was lying in his bed after ten or twelve days with neither a bite to eat nor a sup to drink, the warder came into his cell and threw buckets of water over him saying: 'Now, you bastard, if you won't take water one way, you'll bloody well take it another.'

On the day of his death, Cathal and I sang all sorts of rebel songs, including one about the coronation:

> It was on July the twenty-eighth,
> In the year of thirty-seven,
> That a fire was lit without e'er a grate
> And the flames leapt up to Heaven.
>
> The King and Queen came sailing down
> The loch in the best of order,
> And we welcomed them to Belfast town
> With a bonfire on the border.
>
> The King walked up and down the deck
> Surrounded by his G-Men,
> The Queen put a muffler round her neck
> Assisted by her weemen.
>
> When asked, 'What glare is that I see?'
> The reply was there in order,
> ' 'T's Ireland united in loyalty
> With a bonfire on the border.'
>
> Some said the flames were Ulster's own,
> And more they were extraneous,
> But a Down man swore they lit their lone,
> That combustion was spontaneous.

A man that loves his King and Queen,
And stands for law and order,
Said the flames were orange, white and green,
In the bonfire on the border.

With an ever-increasing din that could be heard all over the
glasshouse, we united our voices in:

'Down by the glenside I met an old woman
A-plucking young nettles, nor saw I was coming,
I listened awhile to the song she was humming:
Glory O! Glory O! to the Bold Fenian Men!

Some died by the glenside, some died 'mid the stranger,
And wise men have told us their cause was a failure,
But they stood by old Ireland an' never feared danger,
Glory O! Glory O! to the Bold Fenian Men!

I passed on my way, God be praised that I met her,
Be life long or short, I shall never forget her,
We may have great men—but we'll never have better,
Glory O! Glory O! to the Bold Fenian Men!

which was written by my uncle, Peadar Kearney, and has been
glory-ohed from the national throat so often that it might be
thought it grew there.

My uncle wrote it to an air he got from an old woman in
the Coombe. He died in 1942 and left after him, besides his
sons and grandchildren, his loyal and great-hearted sweet-
heart, comrade and wife, Eva. Neither of them expected anything for what they did. The cause was their life and they lived
it. And it's a good job for his widow that she expected nothing,
for that, precisely, is what she got.

The firing party for Séan McCaughey was held in Dublin and
the Guard of Honour fired revolvers over his coffin.

'From you holster, withdraw. Fire! fire! fire.'

Funnily enough, the Guard of Honour in the Free State
Army only use rifles, but in the I.R.A. we never use anything
but revolvers. There are six men in our Guard of Honour and
eight in the Free State Army who, strangely, give their shooting

orders in Irish, whereas ours are given in English. We also have the distinction of using live ammunition.

After the ceremony, Séan's body was taken by special train to Belfast for the burial at Milltown cemetery. He and the likes of him were brave men. I sat on my bed in the cell and fell to remembering Yeat's poem, *Sixteen Dead Men*.

> O but we talked at large before
>   The sixteen men were shot,
> But who can talk of give and take,
>   What should be and what not
> While those dead men are loitering there
>   To stir the boiling pot?

The last time I had heard this poem, I was with Rory, my step-brother, in the snug of the Shaky Man's and an old one had remarked that to take as a headquarters the most prominent target in the whole city was ridiculous strategy and Rory said: 'But what sense of theatre—what marvellous sense of theatre.'

I knew what he meant. Hadn't I stood in the Queen's Theatre in Dublin with the frenzied Saturday night crowd for the 'Transformation Scene: Burning G.P.O.' while the very amplifiers carrying Pearse's oration over the grave of Rossa were deafened in a mad roar of cheering that went on till the darkness came down and we had till the end of the next act to compose our features and look at our neighbours without embarrassment?

In my childhood I could remember the whole week a damn sight better than I can now, for I have learned enough arithmetic to know that I could not possibly have taken part in the Rising which happened seven years before I was born.

And I reflected on the funeral service in Belfast. At the best of times, to get into the company of Ulster-born people is to be bored within an inch of your life with dialect stories of Northern wit. Usually the Protestants tell stories of pawky Papists and funny Fenians and their Catholic confederates return the compliment with desperate amusing remarks of larky Lutherans and witty Wesleyans. The unfortunate Dublin man, usually terrified out of his wits, for they are tough kiddies up there, has to grin and bear it and swallow it with their other guff about some 'dacent man' giving another 'dacent man' a glass of water after he was taken from under a two-ton truck, the 'dacent men' being of different religion.

However, Séan McCaughey was getting a good send off and he wouldn't be bothered much about that.

In the glasshouse we were allowed to wear our own clothes and were indeed supplied by the Free State Army with a certain type of civilian clothing called Martin Henrys when our own wore out.

We all went out to exercise together, marching round behind each other and managing to get in the few words of conversation in the passageway between the exercise yard and the hospital. After a while we discovered that practically anybody, by saying to the doctor that they felt they were suffering from tuberculosis, could get the usual two bottles of stout and twelve ounces of chicken per day.

At one time, there was a guy in a prison who stayed in his cell all day refusing to mix with the others and he got his two of stout and chicken carried to him on account of his nerves, for he said Lord Goddard kept appearing to him in his sleep to welcome him back to dear old blighty. But that wasn't this day nor yesterday, and the doctor rejected me, though I am happy to say he accepted a lot of the other guys, so there was always a bottle of Guinness lying around the place which is very welcome after a game of handball played in an old shed round at the back of the exercise yard.

The Nuremburg trials started towards the end of 1945 and we, perhaps extraordinarily enough for prisoners, were universally on the side, not of the prisoners, but of the prosecutors. When you are pinched you don't expect anyone to lay down the red carpet for you and you'd be a soft eejit to expect anything at all, even though the judge would say to the jury that all prejudice must be put out of your mind. I could see the logic of this hypocrisy for everyone has their own way of looking at things: you can be a patriot in the one breath and a murderer in the other.

I regret to say that I favoured capital punishment at the time to a limited extent, even for a woman, and I felt that justice was being meted out to these people. I am not very proud of these sentiments today.

During the trial, Cathal and I were coming in to take a shower after playing a game of handball and there was this military corporal, a nice decent little round ball of a fellow, an innocent creature from the midlands of Ireland, waiting to see us in. He nodded to us, his face open in a smile.

'Hello,' said I and I was trying to be clever, I was, 'how is the beast of Belsen?'

I did not think it was possible to hurt the feelings of a Redcap (as we commonly called a military policeman) but this good little fellow was extremely hurt and I had to apologise to him. And be Jaysus, not the first nor last of many apologies I've had to make subsequently.

We had visits on Saturday afternoons when we sat in compartments like those of a discreet pawnshop and talked across a counter to our relatives and friends in the opposite compartment. A military policeman supervised the proceedings, walking up and down and warning us the time was up, with relief on my part, for I always felt like an ass at a Horse Show.

Our days in the compound, as we called the glasshouse, were much the same and each day past is like a bank balance growing to a prisoner, but I wasn't thinking of discharge now though some of the other blokes were.

There was one mad Republican amongst us who I think would have preferred to stay in chokey for the rest of his life and deaths if this would help the Republican movement, not alone in the thirty-two counties of Ireland, but in Bangkok, Hangchow, and Alaska as well. He was from the North and I knew the place well not only from my own visits there but there was something else as well. As a kid I had sat at the feet of the oul' ones, listening to their talk on my I.R.A. relatives who were stationed near there or in prison during the First World War, and my younger brother, a regular soldier in the Royal Irish Fusiliers, was also stationed near there in the Second.

But this geezer's Republican wrath put years on me and the dreadful military songs of the Irish Republican Army which he sang with a stirring scream—'Let me carry your cross for Ireland, Lord, the time of our trial draws near'—but, except for the fact that he was always singing it, I would have enjoyed the song about the County Down. 'There's a rocky old road I would follow.'

My experiences in the line of boxing are mostly confined to

the lane running alongside the railway end of Croke Park in Dublin, where as a kid, I'd meet my opponents from the more profitable parts and engage them pugilistically. But one or two of the fellows were pretty smart at it, and in one case professionally so.

On the night that Martin Thornton fought Bruce Woodcock in Dublin these fellows were giving out the pay on the science of boxing, and Jack Doyle's coming home from Chicago after the big fight and people out along Gardiner Street and a banner the width of Waterford Street with Saint Patrick in green whiskers playing a harp on it.

I wasn't much interested in the science of boxing, but I was interested in the science of knocking the head off two dozen of stout and I got so stocious that I had to be carried back to my cell.

Except for the absence of women to which I was accustomed, I did not really suffer any terrible pains, and if there wasn't a deal to be doing, I've never had much difficulty in passing the time, even if it meant just looking out of the window. As Cathal said we were all being left in it together, team-handed.

The blizzard started late in the Autumn and though the cold was sharp, I would have been a lot colder if I'd had to get out and about in it, and because my mind was gone numb from the cold, I couldn't think myself away any more this morning. I began putting an air to the I.R.A. song to keep things going some way.

> And when the war is over,
>   And dear old Ireland's free,
> I'll take her to a Church to wed,
>   And a rebel's wife she'll be.
> We're off to Dublin in the Green, the Green,
>   Where the helmets glister in the sun,
> Where the bayonets flash and the rifles crash,
>   To the echo of a Thompson gun.

Though devil a fughing helmet I ever saw, and wasn't I the half-pay of an idiot to be singing it at all? And I was opened up to be told the incredible news. The government had made an order releasing me at once. There was an amnesty, an amnesty for us all.

When I knew I was going to be free again, I knew I was going to be free again to hunger and to poverty and to no kind of pyjamas, not even Free State Army ones. But I knew also I was free to the lights of my native city, which are very large and welcoming, and oh! I don't know—I was young at the time for Jesus' sake. Winter didn't bother me as it does now. It is always winter in Dublin.

I ONCE heard a Neo-Old I.R.A. man shout up to a well-known public figure who was trying to address a meeting. 'You have the best of men in your jails.' I may not, nor no one belonging to me, have agreed with his opinions, but be Jaysus, I felt the best of men today, like Shaggy Lad the liveliest day he ever saw.

The blizzard was still blowing, lashing up and over the buildings, and by the time I was out of the compound it began spitting snow-water and I, for all of that, was reminded of the beautiful days of high summer, the excitement I was in.

I was met by a girl who is married to a friend of mine, the secretary of a greyhound course in Dublin. 'Céad míle fáilte, Breandán,' and she put her arms around me and kissed me on the two cheeks.

'Go raibh maith agat go deo, a ghrá, mar gheall ar an bhfáilte lách sin' (Thank you for ever, love, for that kind of welcome), I answered, happy that somebody was anxious that I should come back.

So away we went up to Dublin with a good few places to visit and I was bought numerous pints, meeting this one and that, getting credit of my sufferings and not a one missing but a little more beside, and I responded forth by swilling the pints and by singing innumerable rebel songs, most of which, alas, such is the depravity of the times, contained bollockses of the Roman Emperors.

In the Shaky Man's was a rugged-faced middle-aged man in tweed clothes, as befitted his rank of Englishman, and one would be hard put to tell the man from the horse out in the hunting field, except be Jaysus, any decent horse would drop dead from the shame if he managed to get up on its back.

'I was at the Isle of Man for my honeymoon,' he said, and I thought I was going to be treated to one of those God-damned talks, the likes of which you hear on the BBC third programme.

'How did that go?' I answered, not caring a fiddler's fugh one way or another.

'Well, we had a great reception leaving it.'

I heard subsequently that he became secretary to the British Home Office or something of State, Sir Anthony Bollockshop or Jockstrap or some such name.

We went out of the Shaky Man's and with an adjournment here and there at The Blue Lion, O'Meara's and Davy Byrne's, we arrived up in Crumlin and I was so maggoty drunk that I can remember nothing more. Till that evening when my father took me out through the city to a big suburban public house known as the Floating Ballroom, where I was warmly greeted by everybody in the place and they piled up loads of Guinness's stout which I was well able to contend with.

Later on we went to a friend's house where they had a piano and a daughter Mary that was able to play it. My father was a great fiddler, and so was my uncle who had a fiddle presented him for writing the Irish National Anthem, and my father played it this night, standing beside the piano, and Mary playing the piano. Then my father sang a song about the potato famine:

Oh, the praties they were small over there,
Oh, the praties they were small over here,
Oh, the praties they were small, but we ate them skin and all,
They were better than fugh-all, over here.

We all laughed despite the shame and disgrace of the terrible starvation, for honest to Jesus you'd have to laugh at the old fellow, and he'd be nearly putting bits like that into the hymns, only he was never very near where they'd be singing them.

Then Jack, the printer, sang a stave. He was a short, plump and very cheerful man, a Protestant, working for a Protestant newspaper, the Dublin *Evening Mail*, now unhappily defunct. Whether Protestant or Catholic, it was a paper of the native Dubliner and had existed since 1823 and was the only Irish newspaper that ever wrote an editorial in my favour. This was when I was in the extraordinary position of receiving very high honours in France and Sweden and England and America and various other little places, while so far as the Irish bourgeoisie

83

was concerned and the Irish amateur intelligentsia, I was the back of the neck. This did not concern me, because first of all if you had a play on for two weeks in Dublin that would be quite a run. But they resented my success in little villages like Paris and Stockholm and London and New York and they attributed this success to the fact that I ridiculed my Faith and my Fatherland.

I have never ridiculed my Faith, but as regards my Fatherland the first duty of a writer is to let his Fatherland down, otherwise he is no writer. In the name of Jesus, how the hell can a writer attack any one else's Fatherland if he doesn't attack his own?

The editorial in the *Evening Mail* was headed simply, BRENDAN BEHAN. 'Behan has brought great honour to his native city. We don't say his native country, because we don't circulate very much outside the area of the city of Dublin.'

The song Jack sang, oddly enough, was from the Jacobite wars and favoured King James against King William.

> Do you remember, long ago,
>   Kathleen?
> When your lover whispered low,
> 'Shall I stay or shall I go,
>   Kathleen?'
> And you answered proudly, 'Go!
> And join King James and strike a blow
> For the Green!'

Kathleen is my mother's name and maybe Jack thought the song was about her.

Mary was a lovely girl, about my own age and weight in fact, but I hadn't the courage to try. So myself and herself, we sang duets mostly of the songs of Thomas Moore, a man for whom I have a great affection. He was a friend of Robert Emmet's and it was said that he used to reduce George IV to tears by singing songs about Robert Emmet's sad life, and execution and love affair with Sarah Curran who cared so much about him that she married a Highland officer the year after he was dead. C'est la vie.

Mary must have been warmed by these songs, for afterwards

we got quite friendly and I brought her out a couple of times during the next week, and if I say so myself, I was not quite so awkward as an ex-Borstal, ex-convict might be expected to be with a girl.

For days following, I drank everything that was to be found in the line of porter, though I kept off the hard stuff, until my mother suggested I go out and do a bit of a job and knock out something for herself and the family. I looked out of the window and shuddered but she was adamant and, alas, not the worst of us is free from the improving influence of a good woman.

I gave my union card to the surly looking individual in charge and when he read my name, by the looks on his face, I think he would have liked to give the twenty-six counties back to the English, as long as I was in on the deal, but he gave me a job.

I was to go down to Caherdaniel in the South of Ireland to repair and restore the home of Daniel O'Connor, known as 'The Liberator,' because he's supposed to have given us Catholic emancipation, but he was also the man who called out the British troops against the Irish workers when he was Lord Mayor of the city in 1843. Jesus, Mary and Joseph, it was a terrible job, but I was more frightened of the curses of my mother that I was of refusing the job, so I took it.

I was practically born in the pot, for my father and my grandfathers were painters and my earliest recollections would be of my father in overalls, carrying brushes and paint and sometimes glazing tools. I was a fourth-year apprentice to the painting trade myself and I'd been two years in the Day Apprentice School in Dublin so I was given the job of painter-in-charge.

They were a good bunch of fellows on the whole and we all called each other by nicknames out of the painter's bible, *The Ragged Trousered Philanthropists* by Robert Tressall, although a lot of them had never read the book, or any other book, either.

However, there was one tight-lipped mean scab-bastard who would have shopped his mother for the inch she stood on, and for the first time in my life I sacked a man and I sacked him for this reason. I'd a thirst on me and was repairing it in a public house not an ass's bawl from O'Connell's house when this man comes up to me and says: 'Mr. Behan, are you the painter-in-charge here?'

'Yes,' I says.

'Well, I'll tell you one thing and that's not two, there are a number of your painters and other workers drinking across the street.'

'And I'll tell you what you can do,' I said. 'You can take your three cards, unemployment insurance, National Health insurance, and wet time (for everyone in the building trade receives compensation when the weather is too bad for work), and one is to go away, the second to stop away and the third not to come back.'

I'd have been glad to give him a lesson, and maybe the knee, too, up into his marriage prospects, but he didn't hang around long enough.

With me at the time was the O.C. of the London I.R.A. who'd got a sentence of twenty years in England but was let out after ten.

'I sacked that fellow,' I said.

'How the hell did you come to sack anybody, Brendan?'

'Well, if he grassed on his mates even, what's he going to do about us?'

We had a few more rounds and were joined by some other blokes who were now on their dinner break and we fell to discussing the funds for the restoration of the Liberator's home and how they were obtained from all over the world. A young girl, who happened to be Jewish, mentioned the Pope.

'Oh, fugh the Pope,' I said, and most of them laughed at this, but one old man, a sharp-featured shop-keeper by the looks of him, glared at me in Nationalistic fashion, his countenance, if it ever can be so described, assuming an indignant expression.

'I'll have you know, young puppy,' he said, 'that the Pope has subscribed £5,000 for the restoration of Daniel O'Connell's old home.'

Just as well, I said in my own mind, for I don't notice the likes of you putting your hands in your pockets to keep the place from falling into rack and ruin. Instead, we all agreed that the Pope was a good man, the Pope was a beautiful fellow and the Jewish girl searched every inch of our faces to be sure we weren't codding her.

That Sunday, at Mass, I saw her and she was looking up in ecstasy at the altar and at the priest and I thought to myself that converts make the best Catholics by times.

The priest who was taking the service was a namesake of mine, Father Behan, and it has been indicated that I was popularly believed to be his son which, so far as I know I'm not. But he was a very dear friend of mine. I remember one day being in the sacristy with him. He showed me the monstrance and where the precious stones had been prised out of it.

'Would you look at that, Brendan?' he said.

Jesus, could you leave anything out of your hands after that, with the robbers that are going nowadays?

He had been a Chaplain in the First World War and had gone to see Lord Kitchener because the priests were being hindered in attending to the Irish soldiers.

'What part of Ireland do you come from?' asked Kitchener.

'I come from Kerry,' Father Behan replied.

'I'm a Kerry man, the same as you are. I come from the south of Kerry. Do you know how I became Secretary for War?'

'No,' says Father Behan. 'I suppose you wanted to.'

'There was nothing I wanted less. There was a time in my life when I would have shot the Secretary for War quite willingly and died for Ireland in the process,' and he then explained to Father Behan how it had happened. In South Kerry when he was a boy, all the youth in the district were Fenians; that is to say they were members of the Irish Republican Brotherhood which had as its object the execution of a few landlords and the overthrow of the British Government.

'The Fenian Movement,' as it came to be known generally, was founded in New York by John O'Mahony on Saint Patrick's Day in 1858. He was an Irish speaker and familiar with the legends of the Fenians of old and he had fled from Ireland, first to Paris and then to America to escape arrest after the Insurrection of 1848, as did several others. The reason it was founded on Saint Patrick's Day is of no historical significance other than the fact that it was the only day that most Irishmen, of which there were many, were free from work. And they refused to work, not because they wanted to get drunk but because they wanted to attend the church of their calling.

Most of the members of 'The Fenian Movement' in Ireland in Kitchener's youth were ex-officers of either the Union or the Confederate Forces of the American Civil War who had slipped into the country to train the young men against the British forces. Kitchener joined them, but when the local district inspector of the Royal Irish Constabulary informed his aunt of this—he was reared by an aunt—she promptly sent him to Woolwich, where he became a cadet and eventually Secretary for War. I remember, as a boy, a real 'pukka' Englishman whose bristling moustache covered his face in the front parlour window as I went down the street, and who hid Séan Treacy from the Tans. He looked like the poster of Kitchener—'Your king and country need you'—and pointing a finger and showing an eye that would drive the most timid into the armed forces of the Crown or into the I.R.A. or into something.

His name was Sergeant-Major House and he was the only man in our street to remember my father as a boy. I believe he had fought in the Crimean war and had met his wife, an Irishwoman, when he was drilling the Militia, as it was called before the First World War. The Militia was made up of people from the country—tramps and layabouts. They would be brought to the Curragh to do a month's training, given some feeding and a bit of campaigning and then they would run around the flat plains of the County Kildare like madmen, trying to get to the first pub. At the conclusion of their service, they were presented with one pound, and the Sergeant-Major would roar: 'Militia, to your workhouses, poor-houses, doss-houses and gaols, disperse!'

Father Behan laughed when I told him this story. He was a good and very loyal priest. In his diocese, at one part of a very lonely road nearby where we were restoring the house, there was a shooting of an old man who'd given Ireland no service but a wrong one. The police came down in droves, but couldn't find out anything about it, for the Irish, for all their peculiarities, are not a nation of shoppers.

A little while later, after I had kipped in for the night, Father Behan came to see me.

'Would you ever come out and give me a hand?' he said.

Now I am a very easily terrified man and I'd seen nothing in England or in Ireland to prepare me for this. I saw a woman who'd hanged herself and it was said that she died because she knew the murderer of the old man.

Father Behan, his boy and I, we cut down this poor, poor

and still lovely woman, and the priest breathed a few words of the Catholic religion, as it would be, over her on this and the last day. At that point I fainted.

When I recovered, we gently lifted the dead woman and placed her in the ponytrap, and Father Behan leant over her and very lovingly gave her the last rites as well as he could. I don't know what happens when people commit suicide, but I do know that they are not altogether out of the church.

I was at this poor woman's funeral later and these things to me are like blood to the eyes. She was attended by her family and her relations. During the service, Father Behan stood up. 'This woman,' he said, 'I think she did not know what she was doing. I think she was mad.'

We took her at dead of night to her grave in consecrated ground, over the Kerry mountains and under the Kerry sky and looking far away over the Atlantic, watched by the Blasket Islands lying out in the bay. Afterwards I asked Father Behan if it was right to give her the last sacraments.

'Brendan,' he answered,' 'who are we to judge? Maybe it was an accident.'

I was never so proud of the Catholic clergy before as I was this day, for my early experiences in gaol in England had given me the idea that religion of any description had nothing to do with mercy or pity or love.

The English Catholics had no time for the Irish and some of the priests were very dour, and they all of course excommunicated members of the Irish Republican Army, being anxious to show that despite the fact that they were Catholics they were devils incarnate; they were not Italian. 'The Englishman Italianate is the Devil Incarnate,' is the Elizabethan saying and by Jesus, they lived up to it.

The Church of England chaplains, however, were universally liked and they were liked for the simple reason that they were very solid men for their church. The Church of England chaplain in the Borstal Institution of which I am the second most famous member (the first being Neville George Heath, who murdered about five women and expiated his crimes on the gallows, and was the first Borstal boy to get a commission in the R.A.F. and the first from our Institution to pay the supreme penalty for his après-Borstal activities) had a custom of giving a special breakfast for his Holy Communion, which was called 'Agape,' the Greek word for a love feast.

I was often asked along, not to the service of course, but to the gathering afterwards, on account of the Padre being highly delighted with the way I had flatted the ceiling of the C. of E. chapel. The breakfast consisted of our ordinary rations but it was always served in cups and saucers brought in by the ladies of the Parish, and the Padre would give us a cigarette afterwards. These weekly meetings were famous, but the Padre was more famous for a row he'd had with a warder.

There was this negro boy, Malcolm Ring, which is not his real name, but I'm so fed up with libel actions that I'm afraid to mention the name of God Almighty in case He might take an action against me, and he's from Tiger Bay in Cardiff and he's doing a stretch for chopping off the right arm of a Norwegian sailor and is a very devout communicant of the Church of England. But this warder thinks he only puts his name down for Holy Communion for the buns and the snout.

So next Sunday, because of this warder, Darkie as we familiarly and ignorantly called him, doesn't turn up, and the Chaplain goes to see him and asks him why was this? After a great deal of questioning, Darkie tells the Chaplain the reason although he said it was the only time in his life he'd spoken to a minister.

The Padre went to this warder and said: 'If you don't apologise to this boy, I will resign and I will tell the whole world the reason why.'

So the minister goes to the Governor, who was also a very strong Church of England man, and up till that time, I did not realise that the Church of England took their religion seriously at all, one way or another, but apparently they do, and the Governor tells the screw that the minister doesn't have to resign, but the screw does, unless he apologises. So, in the heels of the hunt, the screw has to apologise to Darkie, and the Padre was well-known amongst the boys for it.

The other parallel to this I discovered in San Francisco, where I met the priest who was attending the Catholic clients for the gas chamber in San Quentin. Chessman was there at the time and the priest went to see him on many occasions, although

Chessman was not of the same Faith. The warden of the gaol objected to these visits and he sent for the priest.

'Father,' he said, 'I understand that you have been seeing Chessman.'

'Yes,' replied the priest. 'Why not? He's a child of God like anybody else.'

'Well, it so happens Chessman is not one of your persuasion.'

'No, nor anyone else's, is he?'

'No,' said the warden, 'and I don't want you to be seeing him.'

'I'll see him any time I damn well like. I'm entitled to see him for ours is a prophetic Faith and we try to take the brand from out the fire. I see hopes that Chessman might eventually become a Catholic.'

Which the priest said to me, was the biggest lie he ever told in his life, because there was a bigger chance of Chessman converting him than there ever was of him converting Chessman.

W E LEFT Caherdaniel early in the morning and drove back up to Dublin. It had been a hard job and towards the end we had worked over the time and at great speed, almost throwing the paint on with four-inch flat brushes.

Now it was all over and having the energy to spare for it, we sang a bit of a song:

With your left right, right about turn, this is the way we go,
Charging with fixed bayonets, the terror of every foe,
The glory of ould Ireland and a thousand buccaneers,
And a terror to creation are the Dublin Fusiliers.

While the other blokes sang another verse, I fell to wondering how it was that in a couple of generations, the Dublin Fusiliers had been forgotten, for by Christ they were fair enough to shed their blood in countless thousands.

I had an uncle in the Royal Dublin Fusiliers who was killed at Menin in the first World War, and each year the Belgian Army has rather a polite custom of sounding the last post at the Menin Gate. I was over for it once, blood being thicker than water I suppose. My father stole his rifle, but he used it against the British Army instead of using it in the British Army. But when my uncle was knocked off, my grandmother had a pension for him from His Majesty's government of the time.

We sang and drank our way for several hours, till the sun went down and us in Dublin in the dark.

There was an elderly woman in the snug of the Shaky Man and having got a pint in my hand, I went across to her, more in the mind of civility than for any other reason.

'Good evening, Maria,' I said, 'and how's yourself?'

She lifted her face from out her shawl. 'Not too bad, Brendan,' she said.

'And how's the oul fellow?' meaning her husband.

'Oh, he's working in London in an ammunition works down in Woolwich. He's not getting a whole lot, around £10 a week.'

'How's Séan?'

'Ah, Séan is doing a bit better than that. The oul fellow gets £10 a week, sends me home £6 and drinks £4. Séan now is a grand lad. He's in an aeronautical works and he's making aeroplanes and he sends home £4 a week.'

'Tell me, how about Mary?'

'Don't mention that whore to me. She's in the chapel praying we'll never have another war.'

The next morning I am walking up Grafton Street, minding my own business, when Michael O'Flaherty, a house-painter friend of mine, stops me.

'Would you ever do an unofficial job, Brendan?'

'Well,' says I, 'I've never been notorious for doing anything except unofficial jobs. There is only one thing I like better than an unofficial job, and that's an unofficial strike, and there's only one thing I like better than an unofficial strike and that's an unofficial lightning strike.'

'Do you remember Dick Timmons?'

'Aye, sure and I do.'

'He's serving a long sentence over in England.'

'Tut, tut,' I said, 'we must do something about that.'

'There's a fellow there, over in England, who wants to take him out of gaol.'

I started laughing thinking of it.

'There are a lot of people who want to be taken out of gaol,' I said.

Michael thought I was taking him for a right eejit and it didn't altogether please him.

'This man happens to be a fellow citizen of yours, a Dublin man, born in Capel Street.'

Now I was reared a strict Dubliner and my mother was born in Capel Street so I felt a bit ashamed for having laughed.

'Okay,' I said, 'surely I'll help.'

I went up to my home and collected a few things and arranged to meet Barry O'Sullivan, an Irish American who was a very good soldier and a very good Irish Patriot, who was to give me his passport for the trip over. Michael had fixed up for me to have a revolver and for an R.A.F. bloke to give me his identity card and Service paybook and we were all to meet on the hour in Donal's pub.

Donal himself was behind the counter this morning, and muttering to himself in Waterford Irish, which was a habit of his when he was off the gargle. He was a man of 56 or 57 and I sometimes joined in his muttering. When he was in the withdrawal stages from a bash at the bottle, I could even say his part of the dialogue and make him say things he had no intention of saying, such as giving me a round of drinks on credit, which he might normally not wish to do. But today he had not reached the withdrawal stage and I paid for my pint when Michael and Barry arrived in with the necessary documents.

We stayed awhile having a jar and me rather enjoying the thoughts of visiting England, after an enforced absence of nearly six years, to give a fellow what we call in I.R.A. slang a tug, a pull out, which was a great piece of impertinence on my part and some would say very foolhardy.

Outside Donal's we gripped hands and I was given the revolver and we talked for a few moments, shook hands again and then parted, me to go to Belfast and the others about their business.

I had a good few places to visit on the way up to the border, and with an odd adjournment, I had been the best part of five days travelling before I got to Belfast. As my delay was not exactly what you might call in the line of business, I looked through my pockets to make sure I still had the necessary documents.

Barry had on his passport, one artificial eye, which I had not noticed when I met him, and I hoped the same would go for me. The doctrinaire stated that my wife was expecting a baby, and at that time I'd no wife and no baby, both of which malefactions I have made up for since. I did not concentrate on the fact that I was a day later than this document allowed for embarkation.

I handed over the papers to a seedy-looking official who asked me why had I a civilian suit on and why was I a day late? In those days anyone travelling on service permits was usually expected to wear the uniform of whatever service he was in, but I made out I'd been on compassionate leave and had to stay the extra day because of the wife's pregnancy.

Eventually I was allowed to board the ship, the Ulster Monarch, for Liverpool, which was full of service men and I got exceedingly drunk on the journey for I have discovered no better way of doing your work as a soldier of the Irish Republic than by getting drunk.

Standing at the bar next to me was a Jewish fellow of about 48, small but comfortably furnished with brown hair.

'What's your number?' he said. 'When do you get out?' meaning when would I return to civvy street.

'My number is 70,' says I, which is the number of my parent's house in Dublin, and I explained I was in the R.A.F. just back from leave.

'Look, Behan, I know you and you're not in the Royal Air Force. If your number is 70, you should have been let out with the Royal Flying Corps in 1919.'

But he smiled as he said this and was friendly with it.

'Well, so what,' I said. 'What number should I say?'

'Say any fughing number you like, but for Jesus' sake don't say a low number,' and he paused for to give the matter great thought. 'Say 1970.'

'Okay,' I said, 'suits me,' and we picked up our pints on the counter beside us and pulled on them with great satisfaction.

We stayed at the bar for the rest of the journey with your man there speaking with ardour about his services to King and Empire, though I couldn't discover what these were, the element of secrecy was so vital.

After we docked at Liverpool all the service men were marched out in file for inspection and I noticed an ugly-looking sergeant who was paying me particular attention. Jesus, and I nearly having an accident for wondering how I was going to get out of this little situation, carrying a revolver.

I went over to this fellow, whose name I would give except for the fear of the Federal Bureau of Investigation and Scotland Yard, and I clicked my heels smartly and said: 'Sergeant.'

'Yeh, what do you want?'

'I would like to go to the lavatory.'

'What you want is a bottle of gin for your kidneys,' but he said okay all the same and I fell out the ranks and got on a tram.

Fugh you and the R.A.F. I said in my own mind.

I went straight away to see Eddie the Dublin guy, who gave

me the information as to where we might pick up the contacts for to get Dick out of the shovel and pick, the nick, and we went down to a place in Gloucestershire and successfully gave him the tug.

Even at this stage of the game, it would not do to go into details as to how this was done. It was a highly organised operation and one that required a deal of planning and I would not like to spoil the game for others by shooting my mouth off now. We borrowed a lorry belonging to the Royal Army Service Corps, commonly known as the strawberry jam robbers, and brought Dick back from Gloucestershire to Liverpool, avoiding hundreds of horrible looking police dogs which I for one didn't care to see. By God, we were good men in those days.

There was a car waiting for us at Liverpool, an old Austin which belonged to Eddie's brother—he had bought it out of his gratuity when he left the R.A.F.—and it was all fixed that we would drive to Bradford to the house of an Englishman where we would sleep the night. Travel is a great inducer of gloom for man is not made for so much running around and by the time we arrived we were all kind of upset blokes. Though people think it's the terrors that go scarpering, it's mostly not and we were in the torment of our thoughts.

The front door opened before we were out the car, and a small man of about forty summers beckoned to Eddie, who was driving, to take the car a little way up the road behind a hedge, and he called to Dick and myself to go on in the house.

Charlie, for that was his name, had been given a life sentence but had only done a stretch of six years. I was curious to know what he'd done for so heavy a sentence, so I asked Eddie who said that he'd found a soldier with his mother and he'd hacked the soldier up. But there were extenuating circumstances and considerable leniency was shown and quite rightly so in my opinion.

I never saw such a night for rain. As I lay warm, dry and well-fed in bed, I felt we were making out all right, at least for the moment.

Dick whispered across at me, 'There'll be some screws out tonight looking for me.'

'I'd sooner them than me, kid,' I said as I listened to the rain pelting off the windows.

'Shower of fughing sods.'

We fell asleep thinking of them all out there, cold and miserable and drenching. But it would roll off them, I said to myself. They'd get rusty before they'd get pneumonia.

From Bradford we drove to Manchester to the home of the parents of a friend of mine who'd been in the same block as me in Mountjoy gaol. The father had been a compositor on the *Irish Press*, which is de Valera's newspaper, and he took the tape of the telex about his own son's death and fainted at the machine. This unfortunate boy was cycling up Holles Street, past the hospital where I was born, when a police car shot out of a turning and one of the brave and very drunken gunmen of the Irish Special Branch shoved a machine gun out of the side of the car and shot him in the back.

The parents gave us a very warm welcome, took us in without questions and that night I shared the bed with Gerry, another son, who was a clerical student. We had been lying there some time and everyone in the house was settled down for the night and I could see Gerry's face mostly hidden in the blankets and lit in the glow of his cigarette. He reached over and I caught it from his fingers and put it in my mouth. I blew into the dark above me and whispered, 'Do you remember your brother?'

He did not answer at once, and then said, more softly still, 'Yes, a little bit.'

So I sang a song for him;

> Oft times I sit by my lone and ponder
>   On the times we had in the days now gone,
> When I see a smile on your picture yonder,
>   I hear your voice in a well-loved song.
> But now you're lying where the breeze is sighing
>   Through the cold wet grass that is growing o'er
> The lonely grave where yourself is laid,
>   My friend has left me and my heart is sore.
> No more we'll argue the high thought of ages,
>   Or join his voice in a roaring song,
> For one is but half a pair of sages,
>   And the bass is dumb when the tenor's gone.
> He'll not confound me, with wise words drown me,
>   In discourse down me, for he's no more.
> Our speech is lonely with one voice only,
>   My friend has left me and my heart is sore.

I whispered good night to him, and drew softly and invisibly on my cigarette, listening to the wind outside and thinking of the bastards of the police murdering an innocent young boy. But it was not all harshness I had in mind.

I was at school at the Irish Christian Brothers from whom I parted by mutual consent in 1936. But I was informed by them during a lesson that during the Troubles the women of the working class areas in Dublin made cans of tea and sandwiches for the British troops. Not that the sandwiches would have been very sumptuous, but they consisted of bread, margarine and tinned beef, which is all the people had. I rushed home to tell my grandmother as quick as an ass's gallop.

'You'd four sons fighting on the barricades in the Easter week rising,' I said. 'Is it really true that the women of Dublin, and in the slums in particular, that they fed the British Army?'

'Certainly,' she said, 'I fed them myself.'

'In the name of Jaysus, how would you allow for that?'

'Brendan,' she said, 'there were some mothers reared them and God help them, they didn't know whether they were in Holland or Iceland. They only knew one thing. That they were there to fight and they were wearing khaki uniforms and had rifles and at the end of it all they were only bits of chaps.'

And I lay on my bed that night and reflected on these things and felt, in my opinion, that that is what happens to make a woman. I shut my eyes and let on to myself to be asleep, when I did go to sleep.

We left early in the morning and drove to Leeds. It was one of those days that you'd feel like coming back to life, to be open and in the air, with the green grass and the trees. I was fed up with the swings, travelling from Lancashire to Yorkshire, but when you're on the move, you're on the move and the brightness of the sun can only improve things.

By the time we reached the outskirts of Leeds, we were in the height of good humour and we stopped for a rosiner. It was at a place called Cross Flatts Park which is in a suburb somewhere on the tram-line past Armley Prison. I remember it (the park, not the shovel-and-pick) because there was a kiosk in the middle which had tables for games and chairs where old men and women sat round and talked or played shove ha'-penny. The three of us stood with the people outside looking in, for there was a notice which read, 'No admittance, except by special invitation, to anyone under sixty-five years old.'

Needless to say I got a special invitation (voice from Crumlin: Leave it to you, no show without Punch) and took the others in with me. In the middle of the room, which was crowded, there was a gentleman like Wilfred Pickles leading choruses of old songs with an accordian. Nothing loth, as the man said, first removing a jockey of Tullamore tobacco from his jaw, I got up and sang an Irish song, 'In Glendalough Lived an Ould Saint', and received much boolaboss. Amidst the Yorkshire talk, 'Good lad Paddy,' and so forth, I heard one aged gurrier distinctly use the words: *'Maith an bhuachaill thú.'*

God bless my soul, said I, or words to that effect, looking around for the source of this salutation. I saw an old man smiling beside me and he said, *'Cé'n caoi 'bhfuil tú*, Paddy?'

'Táimse go maith, go raibh maith agat,' said I in some wonder.

'That's as far as I can, lad,' said he and told me a bit about himself. He was from Leeds, had been born and raised there and, except for the First World War, had never been outside of it. But his parents were from the Joyce country, and he said: 'Fifty years ago round York Road, with all the old people on Saturday nights and Sunday mornings when they met together it was always Irish they used. We young ones couldn't help picking up a bit here and there listening to them.'

For the matter of that, the great Irish preacher and missioner of the Gaeltacht, an tAthair O Conghaile, whose father, brothers, relatives and in-laws are old friends of my own, I'm proud to say, conducts a retreat in Irish in Huddersfield every year, for the Connemara workers there.

We left the kiosk like early Christian martyrs and got back into the car. People have gone into gaol with less reluctance but we didn't want to push our luck too far. In the centre of the city we stopped at Albert Cowling's Wine Lodge, which I heartily recommend for a good sup and a bite. Whatever else ails me it is a bar I shall never forget, for on the walls of the lavatory were written many things.

'What do you think of our pub here?' Mr. Cowling asked me.

'I think it is excellent,' I said.

'And what about the writing on the walls down there?' he said, pointing in the direction of the 'jacks'.

'Well,' said I, being a very hypocritical man, 'I think it is pretty disgusting. Do you not want it taken off? You should have your walls washed.'

'Have them washed?' he exclaimed. 'I'm going to have them varnished.'

That night we slept in a barn with a horse that was making so much row I thought he must have been mending his own shoes. Jaysus, all the sins of his past life must have passed in front of him that night.

I was thankful to see the dawn until I noticed a man looking across at us through the window, and I was nearly going to put one through him with the revolver when Dick shouts out, 'Don't shoot for God's sake. He's only a taxidermist.' Apparently he was quite a famous person and Dick had met him before, so he was able to recognise him.

Sure enough, the old fellow was holding up at the window stuffed dogs, cats and other animals. I think he must have thought that we were down and outs or something and maybe would like the job of stitching them up for the price of a pint. We shook our heads at him and after a little while he went away.

This day, Eddie, Dick and myself drove down the town instead of moving off, for we were waiting information as to when to drive to Liverpool to get a boat across, and there was a man in Leeds who had served a life sentence and who we thought might help us. We parked the car in the centre of the town and walked the rest of the distance.

Leeds is not what you'd expect at all (this is getting into a back-handed class of a compliment) but a clean, bright and pleasant city, in which I remember the Swinegate, bluntly named as befits a street in the capital of Yorkshire, with an old bridge over a little river at the end of it. On the way up to the house, we passed some policemen smoking and chatting and having an easy time for themselves. They drew to one side to let us pass.

'I wonder who they think we are?' I said.

'Probably the blokes that would call round the back for the pig-feeding,' said Dick.

'Fair enough,' I said, laughing at the thought, 'but if they wondered at all, they'd probably only think we're three Irish boys out for a walk.' Which I suppose in a way is exactly what we were.

At the house we learned we were to go back to Manchester to the house of an Irish woman who owned a public house. The blessings of Jesus on you, I said in my own mind. I was beginning to enjoy the swings.

Many years later, when I was the guest of honour at a literary luncheon, I was to meet again one or two of the people who had helped me when I was on the run. Although at that time I was in hiding I found them very loyal, even though they did not entirely agree with the I.R.A. They hid me, fed me and gave me ammunition—money, not bullets.

This Literary Luncheon at Harrogate was a marvellous affair and was one of the few pure pleasures of my life. I met Frank Swinnerton, for whom I've a great affection, and I was treated very nicely by Lord Boothby and the Countess of Harewood in the charming way that only the English have, when they like and if they like. The Irish charm is rather facile and also we have a tendency to say sometimes, not what we believe but what we think we are wanted to believe. The English, however, are even more subtle liars in a sense than we are.

At the time of the signing of the Treaty negotiations in 1921 between England and Ireland, the Earl of Birkenhead, who by all accounts was a very charming man and an alcoholic like myself, and Winston Churchill, who apparently could be a charmer when he liked, took Michael Collins to one side from the Delegation and they flattered him in all sorts of ways which he fell for with disastrous results for Ireland. God be good to Michael Collins though, because he subscribed to me before I was born. He gave my mother £20 when he was Commander-in-Chief of the Irish Free State Army and my father was fighting against him down in the country.

There is a tendency on my part to be anti-English to the extent that I dislike the Tories, but I could never say I was badly treated in England. I was badly treated in Liverpool, ironically enough by the Liverpool-Irish, who were in the police there. But I don't feel, and a person can only feel as he feels, that the ordinary English cop treated me badly, and if somebody wants to make something out of that, I suppose they could, but I can't. I'm not alone too weary but I don't feel that way, and in this instance I cannot tell lies.

You'd think 'twas a crime to be human,
To sometimes get scared in the Park,
When a copper sneaks up there behind you,
And flashes his light in the dark.
To regard savage dogs with suspicion,
In case that the bastards would bite,
To be hauled off to jail on suspicion,
And scared of a scream in the night.

'LISTEN now, and for Jaysus sake, Brendan, stop shouting there at the top of your bloody voice. I suppose you want the pair of us to get run in, to get pitched out of this place,' said Dick savagely as we drove on the journey from Leeds to Manchester. I could see he was a kind of upset man so I muttered, 'I'm sorry,' in a low solemn voice, rather like a Sinn Fein speaker after saying 'nineteen-sixteen'. For the rest of the drive we did sod all, except smoke and I listening to Dick telling both Eddie and me what he was done for and how he was done, and not minding a word of what he was saying for I was thinking of the pull I would be getting at the public house the other end. And there was no shortage of ammunition either.

It's a queer world, God knows, but I have discovered that there are money-raising funds for practically every kind of organisation. I knew of a fund in Ireland for giving money to distressed Protestants, but not many of the natives would say they were Protestants to qualify for the grant. I think I would get converted if they would give me a lump sum and finish it up and then I'd get back to being a Catholic. I mean it is a dangerous way of getting a few quid, from a spiritual point of view. I might get run over by a motor car or something and die in heresy.

102

On the strength of these thoughts, I persuaded Eddie to stop the car, as we were nearly at the Irishwoman's home, for me to give myself a stiff glass of malt. The place was empty except for two elderly ladies, a pensioner from the Indian army and a silver merchant up at the counter, and before the hour had passed we knew all belonging to each other since the Ark. The famed British reserve is as much a myth as the idea of the Broth-of-a-boy Irishman. We left the place and got back into the car.

Our mot in Manchester was an extremely nice woman and I left Dick and Eddie with her because I had to contact a sailor by the name of William Scurrie, a very noble fellow who is since dead. But to get in touch with William Scurrie, I had to go to the home of Stephen Lally who lived in Manchester. He had been in the Connaught Rangers which was one of the Irish regiments that was disbanded in 1921 after the signing of the Treaty with England, and Stephen was in India with the regiment when they revolted after hearing the news of the Black-and-Tan atrocities against the Irish people. James Daley, from the County Westmeath, led the mutiny, and William Scurrie was present in a prison cell for his part in the revolt when James Daley was shot for this so-called crime. I like to put these things on record, because in America and in England, and indeed in Ireland, there are a great number of people who claim that they fought for the cause of Ireland and they did not.

There is a song written about James Daley:

The grey clouds had crept o'er the stillness of morning,
The dewdrop was clinging with icicles health,
The note of the bugle had sounded its warning,
A brave Irish soldier they sentenced to death.

Lay him away on the hillsides,
Along with the brave and the bold,
Inscribe his name on the roll of fame,
In letters of purest gold.

'My conscience shall never convict me,'
He said with his last dying breath,
'But God bless the cause of freedom,
For which I am sentenced to death.'

103

Lay him away on the hillsides
Along with the brave and the bold,
Inscribe his name on the roll of fame
In letters of purest gold.

To the cold barrack square the young hero they brought him,
A bandage they put round, they put round his head,
The smoke of the rifles, it sounded no warning,
When the blast fell away, our young hero lay dead.

Lay him away on the hillsides
Along with the brave and the bold,
Inscribe his name on the roll of fame
In letters of purest gold.

Stephen Lally was a brave soldier of England and a very
brave soldier of Ireland and a good tempered example to anyone
of how to give a knock and take one without doing your nut
over it. I am inclined to lose my temper sometimes and on this
occasion when I had to contact Stephen for to get in touch with
William Scurrie, I won't forget his example.

We had to make a telephone call to Rory Brugha in Ireland
and, under the circumstances, a private house in Manchester
was not exactly the best place from which to make it. Although
I believed that soldiers, police and warders were for the most
part an ignorant body of men, I did not want to make it too
easy for any old John Bull's bastard of a copper to find me.
A cousin of mine, who is in the Irish Guards, was stationed in
London at the time so we decided to scarper to the Smoke,
make the telephone call and come back to Manchester immediately afterwards.

You may find it hard to believe that I ever had relations in the
army since I don't think I ever took any organisations of a
military nature seriously, other than the I.R.A., but the fact
remains that this cousin of mine got the Military Medal in the
last war which was not given away with the rations. At the risk
of losing my visa to visit the States, I may say that every time
an American crosses the Atlantic he seems to get a medal,
upon which grounds I should be entitled to about twenty of
them.

However, at this stage of the game, both Stephen and myself were short of money for the fare, but into Thy Hands I commended my spirit, Lord Jesus, for didn't Stephen have a lodger who'd kept some money for to visit his sister who was a nurse in London? He lent us £10 and as quick as an ass's gallop we were on the train. There was a lovely girl in our carriage, but she wasn't having any just then, and I have a stammer, and it made me worse and more nervous and not very able to speak to anyone by the time we reached London.

'That will teach you not to act like a registered ponce,' said Stephen.

We went and saw the cousin and asked him if I could make a telephone call over to Ireland without anyone hearing me.

'Sure,' he said, 'we'll go up to Chelsea Barracks.'

Now there was a young boy sitting at the telephone in the Barracks which was the one I wanted to use, because it was in a recess away from everyone else. The poor little bugger had probably waited all day to speak to his mot in Poplar or Balham with no one else around to jeer, and he was reluctant to give up his place to a strange Mick.

'Look,' I said, 'you bloody little short-arsed ——t, get off that fughing chair,' for I really had my spike up now and I aimed a kick at him when I let on to be aiming at the chair.

'Surprised at you, Brendan,' Stephen said quietly and I did not forget it.

However, I made the call to Rory Brugha who, despite the fact that he is a capitalist, is a very good friend of mine, and to make a call of this nature from Chelsea Barracks might sound extraordinary to anybody who doesn't understand Ireland and England, but the way you have to look at it is this:

Who made you lance-corporal?
Who made you lance-corporal?
Who made you lance-corporal,
When you couldn't do orderly man?

When I was young, I used to be,
As fine a man as ever you'd see,
And the Prince of Wales, he says to me,
'Come, join the British Army.'

105

Toora loora loora loo,
They're looking for monkeys up in the Zoo.
And if I had a face like you,
I'd join the British Army.

Sarah Curley baked the cake;
'Twas all for poor Kate Condon's sake,
I threw meself into the lake,
Pretending I was barmy.

Toora loora loora loo,
'Twas the only thing that I could do,
To work me ticket home to you,
And leave the British Army.

It was late when we came out of the Barracks and too late
for the train to Manchester.

'What a lovely night,' said my cousin, and yes, said I in my
own mind, if I had anything to go with it. But it was a good
night and even warm, except for a breeze springing up. We
walked slowly along the King's Road and then my cousin
remembered a girl he had once met who worked in a night club
somewhere off the Edgware Road.

'She's a smasher, Brendan,' he said, 'and half Irish too.'

In normal circumstances I'd have said I don't give a fish's tit
what she is as long as she is ready for *that*, but my cousin is a
decent skin, and in any event he was taking me for a rosiner
and I didn't want to offend him, so I just said, 'A lot of people
I've met in England seem to be of Irish descent, particularly
in the various gaols I was in. And to prove that they were as
British as anyone else, they were worse to me than anyone else.'

We got on a bus to Marble Arch and walked the short
distance down the Edgware Road to the club, when my cousin
spots the girl sitting at a table by herself. When all fruit fails,
welcome haws.

'This is Frankie Mahoney,' said the cousin, giving me the
nod as he did so, 'and he is over here on a few days holiday,
having spent most of his time fighting for the cause of good
old Ireland, he and all belonging to him.'

'Ah,' she said with an Irish country accent which she tried to overload with imitation cockney, 'my heart is always with the boys. Long live the Republicans is what I always say. Where were you in gaol sir? My father was in Dartmoor. Mr. de Valera was there, too. Real high class you know. Look at de Valera now—twenty two thousand a year and a palace above in the Phoenix Park. And he started in Dartmoor with my poor old father. That's what I always say, if you want to get on you have to go in. I was in the 'Joy' myself often enough to be President of Ireland three times over.'

By now I was in good humour and the night was fine and I began doing the big shot, the sophisticate who had been in most of the goals.

'In New York,' I said, 'the gaol is called *Sing Sing*, and in Rome it is called *Regina Coeli*, which means Queen of Heaven, while in Paris it is called *La Sante*, which means Health.'

She was obviously impressed. 'Can you speak French?' she said.

'A little. I have a great interest in French life, in the French language and in French letters.'

'How dare you! How dare you mention such things! You dirty bastard,' she said, 'A dog has more manners.'

'It's all equal to me whether you fancy her or not,' said Stephen interrupting, 'but you can fancy her without passing remarks on the girl of the like and she good enough to be sitting amongst us.'

'Oh, kip in sometime, for Christ's sake,' said I.

'He's a fughing sex machanic, I reckon,' said my cousin, laughing, and he began telling us about his judies and debating whether a man could ponce on more than one judy at once. Which, I suppose is mostly what any geezer talks about, but Stephen was bored. We left the joint and walked the distance to Euston to catch the early morning train back to Manchester.

I suffer from a weakness of character that I can't keep up indignation for long, and although I was sorry because I was beginning to fancy a bit of fruit again, I wasn't bitter. When I am in good humour, I could not be bitter about anything. In the train, I began telling Stephen about the pictures I'd seen, because I went to two shows a week since I was four for nothing, as my uncle owned a cine-variety house in Dublin and a picture house in Ringsend. And then I fell to remembering my grandmother who lived in the next house to ours, where she occupied the back top room with her son, Paddy, the Lord have mercy on him, for he is now dead. He was a stepbrother of my father, because my grandmother, like my mother, married twice.

In the back parlour of this house lived a very old lady called Mrs. Mary Murphy. This was her real name actually and I'm not inventing it for effect. I'm not working for the *Irish Echo* in America, which recorded that fourteen thousand ex-I.R.A. men swept down State Street in Chicago wearing I.R.A. sashes. As an ex-member of the I.R.A. I must say that I've never seen an I.R.A. sash, but if there had been that number of men really in the I.R.A. we would have taken back the Isle of Man, not to mention the Six Counties.

Mrs. Murphy had a cat called Minnie and I could never eat quaker oats for years because she used to feed Minnie on these oats. She used to get money out of the Church of Ireland, which is the Protestant Church, and out of the Roman Catholic Church, because, alternatively, she claimed to be a member of both. She also had a picture of Daniel O'Connell, the Catholic fountainhead of Irish independence, and of Queen Victoria. When she sent for the Protestant minister, who was a Salvation Army officer, she would tell me to climb up and take down the picture of Daniel O'Connell and put up Queen Victoria.

'I could die happy,' she would tell the poor unfortunate man, 'if you gave me a few shillings here and there,' and the minister would hand her a donation of ten shillings.

When the priest would come, she'd tell me to take down Queen Victoria and put up Dan O'Connell.

'I could die happy, Father, if only I had the few shillings that I owe the neighbours,' she would say.

Afterwards, she would immediately turn to me. 'Run over across to the corner, son, and order a dozen of Guinness stout,' which we call 'the product.' However, she got so sick that my grandmother, who was a master of ceremonies at these affairs, took matters into her own hands.

'Mrs. Murphy,' she said, 'I'm afraid we must get you into the Hospice for the Dying.'

'Horse piss for the dying,' said the old lady in shocked tones. 'Jaysus, these are quare times.'

Eventually, Mrs. Murphy agreed to enter the Hospice for the Dying and myself and my grandmother and Mrs. MacHugh and one or two others went over with her. We left in a taxi about ten o'clock in the morning, and the minute the public houses were open Mrs. Murphy suggested the 'message.'

'Ah, dear Jesus. I don't like to pass that old pub. Many's the pleasant hour spent. Can we not go in for the last drink?'

My grandmother was always amenable to a request of this nature. 'Certainly, Mrs. M.' she said, and she banged on the glass partition between us and the cab driver. 'Jarvey, pull up here at the pub on the corner, Jemmy Gills.'

So we climbed out of the cab and I was delighted at what these old women would be got up to but I had to let on to be terrified.

'Give us four pints and four half ones of whiskey,' said my grandmother, 'and I think the lad will have a dandy glass of stout.'

I had my wine glass of porter and the others had their pints and their whiskey. The chat between my grandmother and Mrs. Murphy came to me and my grandmother told Mrs. Murphy not to mind my drinking stout for if I had it now I would never know the taste of it later when I grew up. Alas, that was where Aughrim was lost.

In and out the next pub we were, and in like a shot with us to a third, until eventually we were over to the south side of the city and across the Liffey, of which river it was said when I was a child: 'You pull the chain and in a jiffey, your shit is floating down the Liffey.' Somebody once said that 'Joyce has made of this river the Ganges of the literary world,' but sometimes the smell of the Ganges of the literary world is not all that literary.

After having visited about seven public houses on the north side of Dublin, we proceeded to do a little drinking on the south side. We emerged from a public house opposite the Hospice for the Dying at eight o'clock in the evening, having left our native north-east at ten o'clock in the morning and I was twisted, as the saying has it, physically as well as in the other way; my head was sunk on my left shoulder.

In the spills of rain, an old gentleman came over to my grandmother. 'That's a beautiful boy,' he said. ''Tis a pity he's deformed.'

'The curse of Jaysus on you. That child is not deformed. He's just got a couple of drinks taken.'

The Reverend Mother came to the door of the place and seeing the condition we were in told us to go away.

'We have a patient for you,' said my grandmother, and 'That's right,' puts in Mrs. Murphy. 'I'm your patient and you'll be doing my soul the height of injury if you do not let me in.' And she breathed the fumes of drink so much, that the holy nun herself was nearly set drunk by it, but not relenting. 'This place is for the dying,' she said.

'Ah,' said Mrs. Murphy, 'I am dying and if I'm not dying now, I'll be dying in the morning.'

We made our easy way home. Now in this tenement where Mrs. Murphy lived, there would have dwelt about thirty people and they had all taken out an insurance policy on her life, and although they liked her, the pain of her death would be eased by the fact that the Prudential and the Royal Liver and the like would be handing over what to them was substantial sums of money when she died. The holding of her body, below on this earth, mattered to them all.

'Poor Mrs. Murphy,' they'd say happily. 'She had a very bad night,' or they'd say unhappily, 'Mrs. Murphy seems to be improving.'

But Mrs. Murphy was doing all right. She was getting a drop of whiskey from one and a bottle of stout from the other and Minnie, the cat, was getting her quaker oats and altogether it was quite a happy deathbed. Until this day when Mrs. Kenny, from the Strawberry beds, was laying her out and she pulling the wedding ring off Mrs. Murphy's finger.

'Kenny,' said Mrs. Murphy, waking up,' put back me bit of gold,' upon which Mrs. Kenny fainted, because she thought she was dealing with a corpse.

Mrs. Murphy had a nephew who, like herself, often alternated between all religions. At one stage of the game he even attempted to become a Jew, but an examination of his physiognomy would have shown that he was not one. The neighbours gathered round the nephew and told him that his aunt did not seem to be dying very happily, but you might as well be out of the world as out of fashion, and they kept it up like mad things, until at last the nephew sent for a wise woman from the country, Mrs. Cloonoe.

Mrs. Cloonoe was distinguished by the fact that she'd pushed her drunken husband into the canal at Mullingar and, in the opinion of the neighbours, this made her a very wise woman indeed. Her husband was a former sergeant-major in the British Army and he used to get his wife out on the floor at half-two in the morning doing foot-drill and bayonet practice with the sweeping brush.

'Right,' he would say. 'Shoulder arms, present arms, FIRE,' and would then do a bayonet charge on her as if she was the German Army and he the British Infantry. She got kind of fed up with this and, as I say, she pushed him into the canal.

Mrs. Cloonoe was now sent for to give her expert advice upon Mrs. Murphy and her passing.

'Ah, well, Jaysus,' she said, 'how could the woman die with a pillow under her head? Pull the pillow out for Jaysus sake.'

And for the first time in my life I saw Mrs. Murphy terrified, as well she might be, as the pillow was pulled out from under her head. In a second she was gone to her maker, under the auspices of which Church I'm not quite sure.

She lay that night in the mortuary chapel and we had a few prayers and Mrs. Kyle, our coalman was there, the mortuary being nice and handy on her way to delivering the coal to the neighbours. She had a son and how either one of them came into the world is beyond me, for she was extremely mannish and her son was extremely girlish. Though I don't think any of us ever had the price of a hundredweight, Mrs. Kyle would heave sacks of coal up four flights of stairs while her son stood below in the street with Neddy, the horse, and cart. Neddy, I remember, would roll himself in the lane, I don't know for that reason, but he seemed to enjoy it.

When the son got married, we were introduced nightly to the saga of what happened between himself and his wife. Apparently they didn't agree and he would give a round by round account of it all and the mother would say in a gruff bass voice: 'God forgive you, son. You were very foolish to marry her,' and the son would reply, 'I didn't know, Mummy. I was innocent.'

Honest to God, we had arrived in Manchester before we knew it.

I suppose nobody goes to Manchester with greater reluctance

than the intellectual native of that city and Stephen got off the train like an early Christian martyr.

The morning was cold, but bright, and the sun shone through the smoky buildings with a fair heart. I was in fair heart too and did not notice the two men until they were upon me, but I could see by the looks of them that they had not come to enquire if I'd had a good trip to London. The young one, with a bloody big bull's head on him, grabbed me by the arm while the older one searched me. From an inside pocket he took the airman's identity card and Service paybook and Jaysus, Mary and Joseph, I was disgusted with myself for giving in so easily to these whore's melts of coppers, but by now they had me gripped by both arms.

'We have reason to believe that you are Brendan Behan,' said the older man who was obviously in charge of the proceedings, 'and we are taking you into custody charged with unlawfully returning to this country and being in possession of false documents.'

If the bastards had offered me the Victoria Cross along with the King of England's blessing I could not have been more surprised, and my thinking in my own mind that the only exercise I would be getting for a long time would be at night— in the kip—and a stretch in front of me for helping a man escape. Maybe this was to come when I got down to the Station.

I was bundled into the wireless patrol car and taken to the lock-up where I was formally charged by the Station sergeant. There was no sign nor mention of Dick Timmons. Later on I was to learn that William Scurrie had brought Dick to Galway on the *S.S. Monalene*, so he was free and I was not.

I was shoved in the cell for the night by an ignorant class of animal who took my shoes and my braces as had been done at Lime Street, in Liverpool, in 1939.

The following morning when I heard the doors above being opened, I knew they were going to court, and I could hear some of the other prisoners shouting to each other and the Black Maria back into the yard. I went to the spy-hole as the turnkey unlocked the cell door. He did not say anything but nodded to me for to follow him. I thought it best to say nothing either, but let the hare sit.

At the court, Chief Detective Inspector Edward Pierrpoint read the charges against me.

'Brendan Behan,' he growled, 'is stated to have been expelled from England under the Prevention of Violence Act (1939) and has entered the country illegally and is in possession of false documents. In view of the provisions of this Act, I shall have to communicate with the Secretary of State.'

I was remanded for a week and the magistrate asked me if I had anything to say. I told him that while I admitted having been served with a deportation order, I failed to see why my case could not be dealt with immediately. He was not unfriendly and smiled at me as he explained that, owing to the seriousness of the case, this was not possible. I could see the sense of this too, as I got rightly out of the court, for my people at home would know where I was and would see that I was not done in.

Back in the cell, the day was beginning to get gloomy with the light fading from the sky and I heard steps on the stairs. The turnkey opened the door and brought me up the passageway. 'Someone wants to see you,' said he.

Maybe they were going just to send me home after all, and God knows I would go and stop away and be thankful. I kept up with him and was shown into the Governor's office. I stood to attention, said my name and number and all to that effect, when he puts up his hand and stops me.

'How well do you know the Pope, Behan?' he said as he handed me a telegram which read: 'I'm flying to defend you. The Pope.'

I gulped a few times and nearly burst my arse laughing but stuffed it back and kept my face straight. 'I know him fairly well,' I said, which was the truth, though not His Holiness himself. I have a friend, Eoin O'Mahoney, a Cork barrister, whom we called the Pope and he must have read of my case in the newspapers.

'I don't believe you,' said the Governor in a stern voice.

'I don't care whether you do or you don't,' says I, 'but you can read for yourself that the Pope is coming over to help me.'

At Manchester Assizes the following week, the Pope O'Mahoney did defend me, and he defended me so excellently that I got away with four months, having been sentenced by Wesley Orr, a collateral descendant of the first man to die for the Irish Republic.

I WAS taken under the court to the cells which are not solid wood and steel like prison cells, but open bars with gates chain-manacled to the bars. And I could see the other prisoners waiting to go up to Manchester Gaol, or Strangeways Gaol; it's all the same, whatever way you look at it. I think that Strangeways is a very good name for a prison, unlike the other ones I mentioned.

With our lot were about twenty men whose ages ranged from seventeen to fifty. It was the most pathetic sight I've ever seen in my life, for they were all wearing their Sunday best and they were obviously bemused by the fact that they were going to prison. They just stood there, very downcast.

I turned to another prisoner, a Yorkshire kid who was an ex-soldier of the Eighth Army. 'Look at those poor bastards,' I said.

'Don't you know about them?'

'No,' I said and I looked at him as earnestly as I could, wondering if I had picked a craw-thumper who had been used to gazing over wide open spaces from the gate to the hang-house. But he only said, quietly, that they were coal-miners who had been caught screwing each other down the pit. And I remembered George Orwell's story of the mines and how sometimes the miners worked in shorts and sometimes they worked with nothing on at all. Mother of Christ, I put it to myself, how they stand it in the pits, I do not know.

Now I have heard of very many depressing human situations, but the idea of having sex of any kind down a coal mine seems to me to be about the most depressing human situation that you could possibly find. And these men were highly respectable; they had worked hard all their lives and now they were exposed between the devil and the deep sea because they would meet the same temptations all over again in the nick. Now I don't know who should be in prison, but sometimes I think the people who dish out the sentences should try their luck in them.

I felt sorry for these men. 'Look,' I said to one of them, 'nothing that you have done, except that you interfere with a little child, is shameful. I'm here because I am a member of the Irish Republican Army and I'm obviously an enemy of the British Empire, but I have been over it before and I'm going to get over it again.'

'Paddy,' he said, 'that may be all right for you, but you don't know my old woman.'

In the afternoon we were brought up to the day-room where we had our possessions marked off and we fell into line ready for the Black Maria. The noise of the traffic as we passed through the city made me sad and as it is impossible to see out of these English prisons on wheels I stared at the floor, not giving a fugh one way or another.

Sitting opposite me in the Black Maria was a red-haired youth who had been charged with obtaining money by means of a trick. He thought he was getting his own back on the Egyptians but it turned out that they were the West Kents, and he got weighed off with six months. The policeman with us was friendly and attentive, cocking his head and nodding according to the conversation though never a one spoke to him. When the Black Maria pulled up, he told us to get out and stand in line with no more talking.

The big main door of the prison had the same snake in chains over it as I had seen at Walton gaol. A warder came out to meet us and we were marched single file inside. The door banged out behind us. The four month stretch had begun.

Mostly all of the fellows who were with me were Englishmen of roughly my own age, although there were one or two older lags. I asked one ould one, who was doing a long stretch, if there was anything to break the monotony of the kip.

'In Strangeways, and I was in it during the war, we used to feel the same way as you and even wished for an air raid, but not any more,' he said. 'We had one and we were locked up in our cells. We stood up on our tables and took the black-outs off the windows and had a grandstand view of the whole city burning away under us. The screws were running round and shouting in the spy-holes at us to get down from the windows, but they soon ran off down the shelters. We had a great view of the whole thing till a bomb landed on the Assize Court next door and the blast killed twenty of the lags. They were left standing on their tables without a mark on them, stone dead. Sure, anyway, we all agreed it broke the monotony, but not any more.'

I had just had my twenty-fourth birthday, which to me now seems to be very young, though I didn't think so at the time. But these fellows were supposed to be the tough guys of the Eighth Army, in the Desert Rats, and they were in for shooting their officers, and by the looks of them I'd say they could have shot a few more.

For myself, I could say I never met more decent chaps in my life. They were extremely good, honourable men, and further than that I would say that they were very good Englishmen. Some of them had fought for two and for three years against the Germans and the Italians in the Desert and had had a pretty rough time. When young bastards of eighteen and nineteen arrived over from Sandhurst in the middle of a campaign and proceeded to use the cane on these veterans, or in one way or another generally fugh them about, the hardy desert fellows turned round and plugged some of them. And knowing a few I.R.A. officers, I must say that I do not blame them. But these young British officers were brave enough so far as I could hear about them, but thick and ignorant where the men were concerned.

At one time the whole of Ireland was in arms against England and the sympathy of the world behind her, but in Strangeways Gaol my whole sympathy was for these poor bastards who were even ill-treated by the warders. I was contented enough, however, and experience of prisons had made me more independent of the shouts of the screws.

Until this day when I could not eat all my scoff at lunch. I was sitting next to a young Yorkshireman whom we called 'John the Baptist' on account of his love for telling stories from the New Testament. He had fought with the Eighth Army at Tobruk and at Benghazi and had had the misfortune of falling across an officer who didn't like him. It was the usual lunch of bully beef, two soggy potatoes and cabbage, but I was not able for it and I handed my plate to Johnny. Our warder,

116

the stocky cruel-faced turkey-toed bastard, known as the Iron Man—though he was not very Iron out at the front by the sound of things—snatched the plate out of my hand and flung the food in the dustbin.

I collected my breath to speak without stammering. 'I don't know if that sort of treatment is provided for in the regulations, but I would have thought you might have more respect for someone who has defended England and the likes of you at a most perilous hour in action against the Germans and against the Italians.'

There. It was done, and as I searched his face steadily keeping the anxiety out of my own, I knew, relieved, that he was shaken. All the men behind him were grinning and delighted with a fearful joy.

'I'll regulate you, Guy Fawkes,' he snarled. 'I don't notice any of you bastarding I.R.A. men doing anything except to blow up new battleships and to kill innocent people who have never done you a day's harm.'

I did not object to this manner of speaking for to a certain extent I deserved it. I objected to it in the sense that I didn't like it, but at the same time, I was an Irishman and a member of the I.R.A. As Reginald Dunne, a British ex-serviceman of the First World War, remarked when he was in prison for the assassination of Field Marshal Sir Henry Wilson, Chief of the Imperial General Staff: 'We didn't think they were going to give us a cup of tea up at Brixton.'

I did not, however, expect this to be England's thanks to her bravest soldiers, the Desert Rats. I thought at the time to ill-treat and insult these men was pretty disgusting and I still think so. How and ever, I do not expect very much thanks myself from Ireland, but this is a different story. This is the thanks that a soldier gets and I'm afraid this is the thanks that a soldier deserves.

I could not complain of my treatment. The screws in Strangeways were getting more used to me and the prisoners who had not fought in any war were easy in their minds that if they got it up for me too much, I'd make a bollocks of them. They were afraid of me and we'll keep it so, I said in my own mind.

Some of the boys who'd been brought in to Strangeways were serving life sentences for rape—perhaps some of them are

117

in yet. It was alleged that they had commited offences against the Germans. While I do not approve of rape nor of any pressure being brought upon young people of any nationality, on the other hand I do not approve of taking boys from their homes, sticking them in a foreign environment and allowing them to do all sorts of atrocities against the Germans in 1945, certainly encouraging them to kill, then all of a sudden in 1946 expecting these same men to behave like little angels. These unfortunate youths did not ask to be sent to the front and I think the British Government should have given them a fair shake. They could have been given a few months inside, or a year even, but that's all under the circumstances. But in the post-war period, the War Office dealt very severely with their own soldiers.

Now I am not concerned with the honour of the British Army either during the war or after the war, but it struck me that most of the boys I met in gaol who were on rape charges in Germany and other occupied areas were not there as a result of anything else except British Government policy. The men were not rapers, because they were not rapers by nature. I knew them and spoke to them and I would say drank with them, except that we didn't have anything to drink. In my opinion they were not rapers nor sex maniacs, but had simply been with girls who, with a very few exceptions, had reported them to the authorities under a species of blackmail. To the eternal discredit of the British War Office, these kids were railroaded. I would say it was pathetic, except that they were brave soldiers and there is nothing pathetic about bravery. However, they were regarded as worse than murderers and it was the best of my play to keep easy and say nothing.

I met one of these post-war heroes one time in the baths. He was on remand, waiting to go to court, and was literally shaking with fright. I stood up in the cubicle to soap my legs and I looked over the half-door and saw him. He smiled at me and seemed glad for a few minutes' chat so I told him he must be fughing mad to stand there shivering, because at first I thought it was on account of the cold.

'I'm on a charge for raping a girl in Germany,' he said, seriously.

'How old, kid?'

'Well, I thought she was eighteen, but it turns out she was only sixteen,' and he began putting his underpants and his vest on as he spoke. I smiled into his serious eyes and, being something of a stir liar, asked him if he had raped her all the same.

'No,' he whispered, shaking his head.

'Straight up?'

'Straight up.'

'Listen,' said I,' don't you go letting them put the wind up you in court. You keep your pecker up and stick to your story and tell the bastards that the girl just fell for you.' Which is obviously what happened, because I know of very few people who believe that there is such a thing as rape, except in the case of a number of men or youths attacking a girl all together.

This unfortunate individual hadn't raped anybody. He was simply being used by the British Government who wanted to make an example of somebody and who felt that the German regime had to be placated. That was about the height of it.

I only ever knew one man in Strangeways whom I did think was guilty of this sort of behaviour. He had interfered with a little girl and none of us spoke to him. We neither walked with him, nor talked with him.

One of the worst and most horrifying acts of the war years in England, was the arrest of Ivor Novello, who as a young man had played a very big part in the First World War and had kept millions of people happy singing his songs:

Keep the home fires burning,
While our hearts are yearning,
Turn the dark clouds inside out,
'Till the boys come home.

He was arrested on a very foolish charge. Foolish, not from his point of view, but from the point of view of the Government. He was charged with buying black-market petrol and if the Government had dished out medals for this, there would hardly be a person in England who would not be getting one.

He was given a month in Brixton gaol, which very effectively killed Ivor Novello. Most of the blokes inside with him didn't fancy his silk pyjamas and his manicured finger nails and instead of saying it's a desperate bloody pity about them, poor Ivor Novello took it very much to heart. I would have made shit of the whole fughing lot. Anyway, he was suddenly one of

119

England's greatest enemies, instead of one of our greatest heroes, the poor decent old bastard.

The screws at Borstal were a different breed altogether, but the ways of the Lord being what they are we did some very unfair things to them, and used to give them the rub because they had done no active fighting except against the Indians at the Fakir of Ipi or some such place like that. The reason for this, of course, was that most of them had joined the army in 1919 after the First World War and their twenty years service was up before the beginning of the 1939 war.

I gained a certain knowledge of wrestling from one of these men at Borstal who was in charge of the garden party. His name was Sullivan and he had red hair, narrow eyes with a slight squint, and a face with the look of a boxer. He was extremely proud to have been a member of the East Lancs regiment and was stationed for many years at Fulwood Barracks, their Headquarters, in Preston. One of the boys on the party had been in the same regiment and had known, if not that particular Provoke Sergeant, at least another one very like, and when they got into conversation the rest of us listened with attention with the hope that it would extend our break beyond the allotted ten minutes.

Sullivan was a Black Sash man at the judo which meant that he knew a very great deal about wrestling too, and in a pronounced Lancashire accent he talked about that, when he was done with the Provoke Sergeant for a while.

When we were working in the fields, we sometimes used to coax him into showing us tricks which he could not resist doing because he was a natural teacher.

'I heard, sir,' I said, 'there was a grip you could use, even against a fellow armed with a knife.'

'Or a gun, Paddy,' he said grimly. 'But it is against the rules for a screw to be showing a prisoner his tricks—makes him as good as himself.' And he smiled with his narrowed eyes as he began showing us all the same.

Ah, Jasyus, he was a good old skin. The only time he ever reproved me was for using bad language on the grounds that his father came from Mayo and his mother was a Sligo woman and they were both good Catholics and that I shouldn't lower myself to using bad language, of which I am extremely fond.

120

In my very early childhood I never used bad language because I didn't hear it in my home, except when my father had a few oils on him, and that was only at weekends. During the earlier part of the week he would read us Dickens and Shaw and Charles Lever, who wrote *Charles O'Malley* and who was Shaw's first model in writing. They were great gatherings and I sitting at his feet round a big fire, taking it all in. The preface in *John Bull's Other Island* I knew almost by heart, but happily I forget everything he read from Marcus Aurelius which put years on me.

Our big fire-place in the kitchen had been there from the time of the gentry, as they are called, who had left Ireland in 1800 after the abolition of the Irish Parliament by the Act of Union. The abolition of the Irish Parliament was a big loss to us because the Colonial Parliament would have evolved, in the course of time, into a National Parliament without war and without the insolent business of killing people. We would not have had a famine and we would have had our own government, in so far as we wanted it, with a Customs Union, not of law but of fact, with the rest of the British Isles of which (I make this confession at the age of forty) we are a component part.

If I learnt about wrestling from Provoke Sergeant Sullivan in Borstal, I learnt in Strangeways, from the men who fought alongside them, that the London regiments didn't get much credit for their bravery during the war. Apparently the Londoner, or the Cockney, was expected to fight and to fight well and had to go first up the line whether he liked it or not. On the other hand, the British Government seemed to think that they had to coax, not alone the Irish, the Welsh and the Scots, but the men from the North of England as well. I can only repeat a famous remark made by one German general to another in the First World War.

'The British Army fight like lions,' he said.

'Yes,' said the other one, 'but they are led by Donkeys.'

Now sometimes I like to argue about politics and to savage the boss class and their peasant supporters but I must give one of these donkeys a fair shake. He founded the British Legion who gave me a bed one time. My brother, who had been in the Royal Air Force during the war, went to them and asked if he could have a bed for himself.

121

'Yes,' they said, 'but we know why you want it. You want it for your brother who is shortly out of prison. He's an I.R.A. man. But we'll give him a bed.'

And I slept there and never a word was said about it.

But the people who bore the brunt of the war on the Allied side were the English, I would say speaking as an outsider, as the Americans were until Pearl Harbour, the Norwegians until they were invaded, and the Dutch until the bombing of Rotterdam.

To my way of thinking, the behaviour of the Channel Islanders was quite shameful. Their great contribution to the war effort was to print the Lord's prayer in German, French and English on the front page of the local newspaper. A collaborator there, according to a friend of mine, had a special order passed in Council that no one should be tried for acts of collaboration with the Germans during this time. The act was passed on 8th May, 1945, so they didn't waste a deal of time getting it through.

As far as I could tell, the only people to fight the Germans in the Channel Islands, were the Irish labourers who were stranded there. And they only fought them because it was their custom to fight the police on a Saturday night, no matter what nationality: British, Irish, French, or German.

A friend of mine was locked up in the Channel Islands at the height of the war. He had gone there and robbed a few things round the place under the impression, and a very foolish one, that small countries have nicer gaols than large ones. He soon learnt the folly of his ways. After the German invasion, the warden of the gaol put a churnful of water in his cell and about one hundred loaves of bread and told him he'd be getting no more exercise this day nor the next.

'You'll have to stop there,' he said, 'because I'm off to help with the tomato picking.'

They say that people take to hard work as easily as to drink but I've never found it so. I'm inclined to have a contemptuous attitude to work of any description, but I did not like the treatment some of the blokes got in Strangeways and a trade would have kept my mind off it. And Satan will find work for idle hands. John Howard, the Quaker, must have had terrible little to do when he invented solitary confinement. I think there was more what we call in Irish—*Uaigneas gan ciuneas*, loneliness without peace, in this gaol than I ever experienced anywhere else.

Until this day, July 22nd, 1947. It was the kind of day that you'd know Christ died for you and to hell with the devil. All loneliness was forgotten and there was great agreeing going on amongst ourselves, we were so grateful and holy for the sunshine.

The little Yorkshire orderly told me. He had only been in the place for two or three days so I didn't know his name even. 'You're going out this evening, Paddy. Remission for good conduct and all that.'

And so it was that I came to be driven along the East Lancs road to Liverpool on a fine summer's evening and once again placed aboard a ship about to leave Great Britain. Deported and not for the first time, nor I am afraid for the last.

'If you wish to make representations to the Secretary of State for Home Affairs against your expulsion, do so or forever hold your peace.'

I held my peace. I thought this was the least I could do.

NEVER being one to remain in concealment, I went through immigration, down the gangway and straight to a pub in Grafton Street. I decided to walk there as the bit of air would do me good for, when I was able, walking was a pastime of which I was extremely fond. Besides, on this day I was half doped from the sun, and when I reached Grafton Street the pavements were like the top of an oven and I was glad for the high stool in the pub for the safety of the soles of my feet.

There are some pubs where it's all widows. Young widows, old widows, thin widows, fat widows, rich widows and poor widows. They sit talking about their late husbands all night until they start crying over them. It would put years on you. But this pub was largely inhabited by intellectuals of a sort and people who had been in the I.R.A. during the war and British and American servicemen who were now at Trinity College, Dublin—the Americans on the G.I. bill.

When I was sitting down having a smoke, a man came over and introduced himself. He was an American from Michigan called Lester Jeus, formerly of the United States Navy, but now he was on the G.I. bill at Trinity College. He spoke not like an American at all, but in the most beautiful English, using Cromwellian swearwords like, 'by the bowels of Christ'.

Not that I have any great affection for the memory of Cromwell who, as is popularly known, is not one of our national heroes. I didn't mind him cutting off the king's noggin, because that just showed that a king's head can come off like anybody elses. But his actions in Drogheda and Wexford were those of a Heydrich and a Himmler combined. In the town of Wexford he massacred 200 women grouped round the Cross of the Redeemer, and delighted his soldiers with the slow process of individual murder, stabbing one after another. When his soldiers were running their pikes through little babies, in between psalms, they would shout, 'Kill the nits and there will be no lice.'

The genuine revolutionaries in Cromwell's army were left behind in remote parts of Ireland so that they could start a revolt against the landlords back in England. Ironically their descendants speak the Irish language in one of its last strongholds, the Aran Islands off the west coast of Ireland, but according to Liam O'Flaherty, the internationally famous writer and a native himself of the Aran Islands, they speak Irish to this day with a Cockney accent. They have names like Perkins and Piggott, gaelicised to O Peircín and O Piggoíd, and visitors are surprised that so few of the inhabitants are dark-haired. I am bound to admit that most of them are blondes, with English roses rather than Irish *cailíns* predominating amongst the girls.

However, nothing alters the fact that these Cromwellian expressions sounded exotically elegant from the North American mouth of Lester Jeus. Although he said he was twenty-seven, he wasn't much taller than I and certainly much lighter. This surprised me as I always imagined anyone in the United States Navy as being of stalwart build. His name seemed to be an embarrassment to him.

'I have often received letters addressed to me as Lester Jesus,' he said. 'In fact, once the Dublin General Post Office refused a telegram for me on the grounds that it was blasphemous.'

We were interrupted by a hungry-faced man with puffed eyes, Edwin Lang, formerly of the Royal Canadian Seaforth Highlanders and the brother-in-law of Lester Jeus.

'You mean,' I said, 'that your sister is married to Jesus,' which I considered a legitimate piece of blasphemy, and we laughed together.

This talent for blasphemy I inherit from my father. A jolly and placid man in the home, he would have to put up with great histrionics from my mother when she'd be in a passion, for her side of the family had been in the theatre for generations and she was not slow to get in on the act. There was this Saturday when he came in pretty drunk and she started in at him, shouted the odds and comparing him to Fleming, a shop assistant who had killed his wife with a blow of a hammer and then tried to blame it on an insurance collector. And he had killed her because he had a young girl in the family way with whom he could not go away while his lawful wife lived. He was a daily Mass goer and communicant and all to that effect, and a member, nay, President, of the Saint Patrick's Anti-Communist League.

'Sacred Heart of Jesus,' my mother screeched, 'you are worse than Fleming. He killed his wife decent, like a humane killer with one blow of the hammer, but you are slowly scourging me to an early grave.'

My father wearily took a newspaper out of his pocket and pretended to read it, holding it up in front of himself as a bit of sound-proofing. My mother lost her patience, or what was left of it, and screeched some more.

'Have you nothing to say for yourself? Can you not answer me?' and she shoved a pot through the paper as she spoke.

My father had to say something now in case worse would befall, so he said by way of no harm: 'Kathleen, if Jaysus Christ was married to you, in two weeks he would be back up on his comfortable fughing Cross.'

Lester had met his wife, Jessica, during the war when she was in the A.T.S. and they were both posted to England. And they had one big thing in common. They were both extremely proficient in the morse code and for some time they sent highly secret government messages to each other across the telegraph wires of Great Britain. One day in an idle moment Lester tapped out a message to his correspondent in the headquarters of a British war citadel, somewhere in England: 'Are you a guy or a girl?'

Jessica tapped back, 'I am a girl.'

'Would you like to meet me for a drink?'

The tapping continued furiously. 'Sure. I feel we have known each other for years.'

Jessica was seventeen at the time and Lester nineteen and they duly met and got married. The first night of their union was spent in the Police Station at Northampton because they had been arrested for being in a condition of as much drunkenness as was possible to make in England during the war years. But the police were very kind and understanding and allowed them to spend the honeymoon night together in the same cell.

Strange to sa, the annuityy Jessica received from the British Government was larger than the grant that her husband got from the American Government, a fact which was apparently a great bone of contention between them.

She joined us now. 'How did your first night of marriage go in the police station?' I asked her.

'It was all right, but my arse sure hurt me because we were sleeping on a wooden bench,' she answered civilly enough, though I could see she was in a bad temper. She tapped something on the counter to Lester and he tapped back. Their facility with the morse code they obviously had not lost on their emergence from the American or from the British forces. I knew they were having a row, because many married couples in Ireland use the Gaelic language only when they are fighting, in the fond hope that nobody will understand what they are saying. Unfortunately this is not always the case, and in this instance there was a rugged looking individual standing at the other end of the counter who seemed to understand perfectly both the morse code and what they were tapping. He blenched visibly. (I would have said blanched, but he didn't blanch, he blenched.) I went moseying over to him, for God send, if you don't get up and ask you'd hear nothing and I didn't want to be out of the fashion.

'Who are these friends of yours?' he asked.

'The divil looks after its own. They are husband and wife.'

'Well, they can certainly use more filthy language in morse than I have ever heard in my life before,' he said, reddening at the gills.

'Come, sir. What could they have said to cause you such distress, annoyance and embarrassment?' For, cute sliveen that I am, I was determined to find out.

'The girl tapped out that her aunt was coming down from Belfast that day and she would like her husband to come home, whereupon the gentleman replied: "Screw your aunty and I'll tell you more if you care to listen." The girl said, "How dare you say, screw my aunty, you American pig," and the man replied, "You Canadian bitch, where would you be only for us?" '

I pretended to look shocked, but I shrugged my shoulders.

'You know, sir, the way it happens,' I said. 'Compliments pass when the quality meet.'

However, the next remark tapped between the two of them must have been so disgusting that my translater dropped his glass and walked straight out of the pub.

I went down to have a piss and to think of the times we were in and the quarrellings both in peace and war, of men with men, men with women and women with women. When I returned to the bar there was another man in our group. He was an Englishman, late of the Royal Navy, called John Fraser. He had flaming red hair which I noticed finished on the smoothness of his neck. He had met Lester Jeus in a pub in London during the war and they had become friendly in rather a strange way. They were both in uniform and, in the course of a conversation comparing their respective navies, Jeus told Fraser that the United States navy dismissed King Lears, officially known as homosexuals, the minute they caught them on.

'Although I am already married,' he said, 'I would not have any scruples about trying this dodge on myself, only I am saving it up for D-Day in case they send me towards the Continent. I have no intention of leaving my present job as a telegraphist in the London office of the American Navy, that's for sure.'

John Fraser nodded approvingly with a best of British luck grin on his face and then fell to thinking himself. He was on destroyers at the time, which were highly dangerous, not to say uncomfortable if you were eating your dinner and the ship took a sharp lurch one way or another. He ordered another two pints of bitter, a drink I particularly detest, but a drink for all that.

'I wonder whether our lot would wear that lark?' he mused.

'It's worth trying,' answered Jeus. 'It's bad enough to be in this bloody war, without having to spend it on destroyers:

'Try it, I will,' says John Fraser. 'I've to be back on board by eleven o'clock tonight, so I'll be off now.'

Jeus called out to him to let him know how he made out.

'Right mate. See you here tomorrow night around eight o'clock,' answered Fraser.

The meeting with the Captain took place early the following morning.

'I have a confession to make to you, sir,' says John Fraser.

'Really, old boy,' said the Captain tugging at his beard, 'How interesting.' And when after a pause, 'Push on old man. What is it?'

'Well, sir, I find myself sexually attracted to my oppo.' (Oppo. meaning the bloke who sleeps in the bunk opposite you and has the chair opposite you in the mess.)

'Indeed,' said the Captain sternly. 'And who might he be?'

'He is 350166 Smith, Able-bodied Seaman, sir.'

'There are so many Smiths, Fraser. Would you describe him to me and tell me what his function is on my ship?'

So Fraser gave a loving account of 350166 Smith, Able-bodied Seaman, whose guts he hated, more especially because the bastard snored like a pig all night and he could hardly ever get a wink of sleep.

'Ah, yes, I know whom you mean,' said the skipper when the description was over. 'Pretty nice looking lad. I couldn't blame you for fancying him, but you know how it is. The course of true love never runs smooth. Try and concentrate on your work a bit more.'

He stood up and with a gesture of the hand dismissing Fraser, he said, 'Good luck, my boy.'

'Mean old fughpig,' Fraser called him as he told the story to me and we all nearly burst from laughing, but stuffed our laughter back for he was serious with it.

'You're a funny sod and no mistake,' I said to Fraser.

Said Edwin Lang, 'He's an Englishman *and* a foreigner.'

I nodded my head, but before Edwin Lang could say anything else I said, 'Well, everyone is a foreigner out of their own place.' Him being a Canadian, that shut *his* bloody mouth on the matter.

John Fraser had just returned from the Isle of Man were he and his sister had been placing their dead father, so they wouldn't have to pay death duties. The old man was the proprietor of a very large woollen mill in Yorkshire and, when they found that he was failing in his health, they brought him across to the Isle of Man in an aeroplane.

'When we got there,' said John,' the old bastard was as stiff as a board. He had failed us on the way out, in spite of the fact that we gave him champagne and we gave him blackers—which is a mixture of champagne and Guinness, commonly known as black velvet.

'Gee, what waste,' Jeus said, taking a drag of his cigarette. I smiled at Jessica and Jessica smiled back, but Edwin Lang only nodded as he was still needled with me over my last remark to him.

'Ah,' said Fraser, 'all was not lost. When we discovered that the old fellow was quite stiff, we pretended he was drunk and assisted him off the aeroplane and into a taxi. The taxi driver was a decent chap and he helped us stick my father into the back seat. "Now father, bear up. You'll be all right in a minute. Come along now," I said to him and the man was as dead as a doornail the whole time. We had rented a house on the Island and we carried him, all that was left of him, up to his room and we had a Manx doctor certify that he had died fifteen minutes after his arrival in the Isle of Man.'

I asked,' How did you know it was a Manx doctor?'

'Because,' he replied shrewdly 'he said he had no tales.' And with that anglo-saxon chivalry of which he was ever the master, he explained that his father had died in a good cause. He had saved them about thirty thousand pounds.

With that piece of information, Gabriel McCarthy, an ex-I.R.A. friend of mine who had by now joined the merry throng, suggested that we might see some of the thirty thousand pounds that he had saved. 'Set them up, John,' he said.

'Okay,' said Fraser though his hand trembled at the thought of it as he reached out on the counter for a tumbler to grip.

'Come on then, before your thoughts go from the straying,' said Gabriel.

The order was given and taken and a young poet sitting at the other end of the counter called out that he would have a drain of the other as well. When the drinks were set up, there was no glass of whiskey for the poet.

'The trouble with that fellow,' said the poet looking at the barman, 'is that he hates me because I am Irish.'

We had begun the morning on the totally false declaration that we were only going to drink Guinness, but after a while we all started to drink whiskey.

John Gough came into the bar. He was an Englishman who had been in the Fleet Air Arm, but he had only been in it after the war and even to the Irish Republican Army this did not constitute effective service and he was not entitled to a Government grant. As a result he was not so much respected in our company but it wasn't the poor bastard's fault because he was too young to have been in the war. Whatever military service he did, he did it after the war, which didn't amount to the same thing. He was not in the 'farewell to arms' lark like the rest of us, because he had no arms to say farewell to. He was too late for World War II and too early for Korea.

Myself and MacCarthy had both got money from the Clan na Gael, the Irish Republican organisation in America, on our emergence from durance vile, and the rest of the boys in the pub that day were living off the British Army or the American Army or other sorts and sizes of Armies. We despised Gough because we considered any self-respecting man, fit for our company, should be getting a pension for something, or should be getting some kind of allowance or an educational grant. He certainly should be on some fiddle. Also he was living on his own money and supported not only himself and a wife, but also a large moustache which looked quite ridiculous. The only good thing to be said about him was that he spoke with a very healthy Yorkshire accent which he never tried to disguise. As a matter of fact, I think he somewhat accentuated it since he came to live in Ireland.

Gough tolerated me largely because I had a brother in the Royal Air Force who received a pension for war service and who had been invalided out, and he tolerated Gabriel Mac-Carthy for the simple reason that he was a friend of mine.

But Gabriel, at the best of times, particularly when he had a drink on him, was violently anti-English. He detested Gough and he was not a man to hide his detestation.

'Hello there, Gough,' he said.

John Gough answered. 'Hello, MacCarthy,' affecting the attitude of a bluff officer of the old school tie. His pretty little blonde wife Gloria, was with him and Gough politely pulled up a stool for her to sit beside him.

'You'll sit over here beside me,' Gabriel snarled at her.

Gloria took it in good part and only pretended to go for him. 'Don't speak like that,' she said. 'I'll sit between the pair of you.'

'In that case,' said I, with that courteous wit of which I was ever the master, 'you will be like Jesus Christ between the two thieves.'

I thought Gabriel would do his nut, but I was wrong for he was very much improved in his humours.

'Give us a rebel song there, for Jaysus' sake,' he said to me.

I looked up at the large notice board reading, 'No singing,' and began sobbing with emotion, *September Song*.

> For it's a long, long time,
> From June to September . . .

'Not that fughing song,' interrupted Gabriel, so I struck up, *Home on the Range*.

'Go it, Brendan,' said Gloria. 'I like that song.'

'Doing a great business,' said the publican. 'Nice place isn't it? Next year I am going to start a bear garden in the back.'

Gough said stuffily: 'It strikes me you have a bear garden already in the front.'

'They are American bloody songs and I don't want to hear any of them,' said Gabriel. I had forgotten that he hated the Americans at the present time because he thought they were too pro-British. 'I suppose you will be singing *God Save the King* next.' he said spitefully.

'Ah,' I said, 'I don't know. I've a certain admiration for the old skin. He took up speaking as a doctrinaire Republican. He took up a job that he didn't want and he carried it through very courageously.'

'Good on you, Brendan lad,' said Gough and Edwin Lang smiled out his approval.

Gabriel's wattles flamed in anger. 'If you won't sing a fughing rebel song, then I will.' He struck up:

> In Dublin town they murdered them,
> Like dogs they shot them down,
> God's curse be on you, England now,
> God strike you, London town.
> And curse be every Irishman
> Alive or yet to live
> Who'll ere forget the deaths they died,
> Who'll ever dare forgive.

132

The song finished and by way of no harm, he shouted, 'Up the Republic. We defy you,' straight in the face of John Gough, 'and to Hell with the British Empire,' and his face was as pink as a baby's from passion and drink.

With the help of the Holy Mother of God, he'll carry on his Plan of Campaign by himself, all honour to him of course, if only he leaves me out of it, I said to myself. I was enjoying the day, but by the looks of the publican I wouldn't be enjoying it very much longer. I was just wondering what to do when Gough spoke.

'I don't like that song, you know, nor the remarks that followed.'

'I don't give a fish's tit whether you do or you don't,' said Gabriel, 'and there's an end on it.'

Edwin Lang said, 'Give the man a fair shake. I didn't like it a lot either.'

'By the bowels of Christ,' said Jeus, resorting to his Cromwellian expressions, 'I cannot see what you are all getting so excited about. It's a song just like any other song.'

I was thinking about Jeus and what a hard man he was to please, because although he was dead against the I.R.A. he was also against the British upper class and the Royal Family, when I heard John Gough ask Gabriel why he had found such delight in getting it up for the English.

To tell the honest truth I could never understand the relationship between these two, and somehow I wondered if Gough was not pushing his luck by asking this question, for although Gabriel was a short squat fellow he was well able for the fists and to me looked exactly what he was: a little Irish Tyke, rather resembling myself in appearance. If you have ever seen a matchbox turned horizontally and walking on two human legs, you will know what I mean. But Gough, like a great number of English and American people, was fooled by Gabriel's size and had the idea that the fighting Irish are a tall race. This stems from the fact that most of the emigrants from Ireland are from the West and they are huge looking bastards but they couldn't fight their way out of a paper bag. At my best days I could take on two of them because they will always give warning beforehand that they are about to fight. 'Did you do this, be Jaysus?' or 'Did you do that be Jaysus?'

133

and, if I was merciful enough, while they were shouting the odds, I would give them a right cross-counter. Sometimes, I am afraid to admit, I gave them what was called in my old school, Borstal, the 'Bowery Belt'.

Anyway Gabriel MacCarthy and John Gough seemed to play on the Anglo-Irish conflict again now, and as I was out for a bit of a hooley I was wearying of the whole business.

There was another thing as well. For my own sweet self, at this stage of the game, I really could not see why two small Islands off the coast of Europe, which are neither acceptable to Europeans as being part of the Continent not acceptable to the Americans as being part of America, required four capitals. One is enough, and we should live off the better one, which is in England. However, according to a great number of people, not according to me, England is not now in her better days.

I do not see why we require the Common Market or the patronage of America or Russia, or, for the matter of that, of China.

The older I get, the more I see the sense of my grandmother's statement: 'Do you know the difference between having an Irish Republic and being a section of the British Empire?'

'No,' says I, 'what is it?'

'You'll get an eviction order written in Irish with a harp, rather than one written in English with the lion and the unicorn.'

My grandmother had four sons fighting for the cause of Ireland and in the barricades of Easter Week, 1916.

In the lengthening afternoon, I put these thoughts away and, asking the publican to set up another round, we drank until MacCarthy and Gough lost their bad humour in the merriment that followed.

I THINK it was Jeus who actually mentioned giving a party for me, though all the others were for the idea as well.

I had been given a great welcome home and by this time none of us were very much interested in politics and had more or less forgotten the war aims of the various organisations we had been in.

Besides, up to this, the Dublin intelligentzia were very friendly disposed towards me because I had published very little and for a garrulous man, one of the very few things I don't talk about is my own writing. I started writing for Irish Republican and Irish Left Wing papers and was published first in a magazine called *Fianna*, the organ of Fianna Eireann, the Republican Scout organisation founded by Countess Markievicz, of which I was a member from the age of seven until fourteen, when I was transferred to the I.R.A. as a courier or messenger boy.

I was very much incensed by the Spanish Civil War, in which many of my friends took part on the Republican side. The Irish who fought for Franco appeared to achieve the remarkable military feat of coming home with more men than they went out with. The Irish on the Republican side formed part of the International Brigade and they fought well and valiantly to the extent that they lost eighty men killed, a great number wounded and many taken prisoner. And us who were fourteen years of age were left with the women and children, and a humiliating place it was for tough chiselers like us. We were left collecting tinned milk and packets of cocoa and bags of flour for the food ship and we were only consoled by street fights and stone-throwing.

> Sure with money lent by Vickers
> We can buy Blueshirts and knickers;
> Let the Barcelona Bolshies take a warning,

135

Though his feet are full of bunions
Still he knows his Spanish Onions
And we're off to Salamanca in the morning.

The British decided to adopt for themselves the name of the Oliver Cromwell Battalion, but the Irish, who would do most things for Spain, decided that this was one thing they would not do—fight under the name of Oliver Cromwell, and they formed a column of their own. I could have understood it better if they had refused to fight alongside the British at all. Their atrocities to the Irish were committed in far more recent times than those of Oliver Cromwell. All of us in Fianna Eireann had lost some relation or other during the Troubles, and my mother was only two years married to Jack Furlong, a '16 man. My own father was involved in the burning of the Customs House although, as he says himself, the only useful thing he did during the whole War of Independence in Ireland was to burn his own birth certificate. Nobody over the age of sixty-five is supposed to work in either England or Ireland, and my father, who is certainly over sixty-five, has worked in both places.

The Irish in the International Brigade always liked fighting alongside the Basques, because they had Catholic priests who would take the confessions of the wounded. But in that period there were also people who shot members of the Christian front and I was accused of suffering from amnesia because I did not know about these things. (Perhaps I suffer from amnesia still.)

In 1936 I began writing articles for the *Irish Democrat* about Spain and they are the only articles I have ever written that I was not paid for and enjoyed writing. Any writing I have done since I have done purely for money.

The first article I was ever paid for appeared in the June, 1942 issue of *The Bell*, which was edited at the time by Séan O'Faolain. It was called 'For the Assizes', but published under the title, 'I Became a Borstal Boy', and I got a couple of guineas for it.

Séan O'Faolain, with the late Minister for Defence in the Irish Republican Cabinet, Mrs. Cathal Brugha, also supplied me with a blue sports coat and a pair of flannels but, by this time, I was in Mountjoy Gaol at the beginning of a fourteen year stretch.

When I came out four years later, I wrote silently, starkly, as my mother did not approve of my literary efforts.

'God preserve me from geniuses,' she would say.

I sent a short story to Cyril Connolly, who was editor of *Horizon*, and I consider his reply very civil. 'I'm afraid we cannot use this, not even in *Horizon*.' But he also sent me a cheque.

So on this July day, 1947, there was no cause for anyone to be jealous of me, and a party in my honour was suggested.

When we came out into the street, it seemed years since the morning, with the sun scorching the pavements and the sky rosy and pink over the head of Howth as I came off the boat. It was a fine mild evening though I could see already the mists rising off the city and knew tomorrow would be fine as well.

The party was held in the Catacombs, a flat in the basement of a large Georgian house in a Georgian square in Dublin. It was rented by a tall, willowy Englishman called Cecil, a very kindly person in his own way and a great favourite of my father and mother. The lady who owned the Catacombs was a painter and she let the flat to Cecil rent free, apparently because he posed for her pictures. Years later I was to see some of them.

The literary editor of the *Irish Press*, M. J. MacManus, an old comrade of mine who had been in the I.R.A., asked me to write a column for his newspaper, which I did for a couple of years. I got barred off it sometimes because I had too much to say against the clergy and the politicians, for it is owned by the President of Ireland, Eamon de Valera. I understand that although he could not read the column himself because his sight was going, he used to have it read to him.

However, M. J. MacManus was a very kind man and a good friend to me. When he died, as Eamon de Valera's biographer (the book was first published in 1944 and reprinted many times since) and literary editor of the government organ, his funeral was very widely attended.

I was met at the church door by Benedict Kiely, the assistant literary editor of the *Irish Press* at the time and a novelist and a good one.

'While you are in the church, Brendan,' he said, 'they will be watching you because you are supposed to be anti-clerical.

For Christ's sake try and behave yourself and don't give them any excuse for criticising your behaviour.'

I nodded in agreement and thanked him for the warning, but when I looked round the church, I discovered that the Stations of the Cross had been painted by the lady who owned the Catacombs and that her model for Jesus Christ was Cecil. There he was in various 'camp' attitudes, as they say in England. Cecil arrested by the Roman soldiers; Cecil cruelly scourged at the pillar; Cecil meeting the pious women; Cecil with his afflicted Mother, and last but not least, Cecil nailed to the Cross.

And Cecil lay on the Cross rather like some handsome young Italian sunbathing. He reclined on the Cross so to speak. I burst out laughing and Kiely jabbed me in the ribs. Quickly I bent my head though my shoulders shook and I had to pretend to be sobbing.

Cecil had a lodger in the Catacombs known as the Baron. He was a Dutchman who had spent the war in Ireland though his family, who were very wealthy brewers, lived in Holland. I do not think they were very anxious for to have the Baron join them.

At one stage of the game, Cecil noticed that an electric kettle was missing from the Catacombs and he suspected that the Baron had stolen it, so he told him that if the kettle wasn't returned, there would be very serious consequences. In actual fact the Baron had not only stolen the kettle but he had pawned it, so he had to wait until he got his allowance from the family in Holland before he could reclaim it.

'Cecil,' he said, 'after days and nights of searching, I have found your kettle,' and his face broke into a wide grin.

'You found the kettle,' answered Cecil sternly 'because you stole it in the first place and then pawned it. I sentence you to two years washing up, otherwise I will get you deported,' which was an empty threat as Cecil was pretty lucky not to be deported himself. But the poor old Baron, rather than be sent back to his native land, agreed to his sentence.

There was some sort of a party practically every night at the Catacombs. A crowd of people would assemble in the flat, each one bringing a bottle of gin, or whiskey, or a dozen of stout. There would be men having women, men having men and women having women; a fair field and no favour. It was all highly entertaining.

On this night of my party a good time was had by all. I was busy getting the credit of my travels with a girl who lived on the first floor of the Georgian building that housed the Catacombs. She had been the wife of a very famous English artist and was in Czechoslovakia when the war started, where she was nearly occupied by both the Germans and the Red Army.

John Fraser was attacking Lester Jeus over the negro problem and Edwin Lang was attacking Gabriel MacCarthy over the power of Catholicism in Ireland, and he in turn, was attacking John Gough for the crimes of the English in Ireland, India and the rest. By way of no harm, Cecil began to attack the Baron over the behaviour of the Dutch in Indonesia. Everyone else was listening with wide-eyed astonishment and the unknown warrior at the Arc de Triomphe on the Champs Elysées had nothing on the unsung heroes of the Catacombs this night.

By way of being a natural coward and not wishing to get it up for anyone, rich or rare, except the girl who wasn't having any, I joined in with three other blokes and a girl who were ignoring the drunken rows over politics. I could hear Gabriel swearing at Gough from a height and telling Fraser that the lowest ruffians in Ireland were the Protestants.

'I've never heard of a Protestant ruffian,' I said by way of introducing myself, 'for all the Protestants I ever knew were rich people in Dublin.' The girl smiled. Her name was Ruth and she was Jewish and her husband, sitting opposite, was Seamus McCafferty, a sculptor. The other bloke was Mickey Brennan and looked the sort of fellow who would go anywhere he could get his head in. It was great gas and I sat talking with them until two o'clock in the morning when the drink finished and then we retired to Mack's studio, which was a little distance out of the city, and where Mack said there was plenty more to drink. I left my aforesaid friends still arguing the toss, but in better humour now and occasionally striking out the stave of a song.

Mack's studio was in the loft of what had obviously been an eighteenth century coach house, but in the coach house he kept sacks of plaster, casts and materials that he used for his statues. We went upstairs to the loft where there was another man, Ben Isaac, a Jewish painter.

Man-sized glasses of whiskey were given us to send off the night in good order and we talked far into the early morning on the rim of the light from the dawn. When Mack and his wife and Ben Isaac left, I began discussing with Mickey, and him being a Northerner from Belfast, the lamentable fact that everyone, only the poor Irish, is allowed to have a difference between North and South.

'Damn it,' I said, 'we can't open our mouths but the stranger has it made into the basis for a thesis on racial relations.'

In France, the miner from Pas-de-Calais and the Norman farmer even refer to their countrymen of the South as 'les negres', and all combine to heap the foulest abuse on Paris and its people. In Italy, the Milanese and the Calabrian speak what are nearly two different languages and in England itself the Geordie from Newcastle-on-Tyne speaks a dialect incomprehensible to the Cockney, who incidentally despises him as a 'swede-basher'.

But nobody has set up a Boundary Commission to separate Cannes from Caen, nor has it been suggested that there should be frontier posts from the Severn to the Wash, with a border in Birmingham cutting the Bull Ring in half, with the Mitre one side and the Rose and Crown on the other.

We heard voices downstairs in the coach house, Ruth's low at first and then rising later, Ben's grating voice mixed in between times. Then we heard her crying. Mickey looked at me and I looked back at him. If he was going to say anything, he changed his mind and went on listening the more.

'It's all right dear,' Isaac said, 'they hid the cup of Benjamin in your sack.'

Said Mickey Brennan and up like a shot with him, over to the door, 'Jaysus, that's some special Jewish drink, the cup of Benjamin, and they have hidden it downstairs in one of those sacks of plaster.'

Yes, said I in my own mind, and you'll have your head in there too, that's for sure. And he did. As soon as Ruth and Ben came back up to the loft, he slipped down and proceeded to up-end all the sacks full of plaster looking for this cup of Benjamin. Apparently he did not know that it was merely a

Jewish metaphorical term for saying that somebody was getting somebody else into trouble, and I wasn't in mind for telling him.

The following night Mack and Ruth asked if I would like to go to the French ballet with them. Now I have got very strong views about the ballet. I do not consider it an art form. I think it is nice to see the kids hopping round and so forth but the significance of it is lost on me. Also, this night, the only seats we could get were up in the Gallery and the wits were frightened out of me in the first place as I am very much afraid of heights.

In one ballet, there were a lot of French youths dressed up as sailors, with little pom-poms on their hats. And their pants were so tight that I began to be concerned as to their physical well-being. When they began to dance, for a tender youth of my age this was too much.

'Up sodomy,' I shouted and, in honour of those poor fellows out there strangling themselves, I had to retire to the bar to give myself a rosiner.

Next morning, I didn't feel so good but in the summer-time nothing lasts long, and I was back at the Catacombs before the night was out. Now the reputation of the flat around the city of Dublin was not a very high one and some oul' ones even paid us the compliment of suspecting that we took drugs there. But such was not the case. Once or twice an American student might have pinched some drug from a hospital, but whatever it was, it usually got drowned in the whiskey or the gin. The poor old drug addict really didn't have much of a chance.

Sometimes the Catacombs could be quite dangerous, though for a different reason. Cecil was not always sure whom he would be bringing in and some of the young criminals—I don't know as I would call them criminals any more than the rest of us, but they were criminals in civil crime—used to get tough after they had a few drinks on them. But they were very much in the wrong shop, for we were able for them.

Eventually Cecil gave up the flat and went to England where he ran a bar in Welwyn Garden City and he used to bring my mother and father down to see him and gave them lots of free drink. He was a good old skin but we have now lost touch with him.

There were two sorts of official brothels in Dublin that I used to attend and neither for their official purpose. They were simply places that stayed open until three or four o'clock in the morning and where you could get the glass of malt beside. One was called Smokey Jack's and the other known as Mary the Whore's. It was in Mary the Whore's that I re-acquainted myself with Sheila. Always slim and light on her feet as a feather, she was up from the corner of the room and next to me.

'Did you ever see one of these before?' she said, and I thinking she was pulling up her clothes to show me was going to say yes, when she pulls out from her pants a hundred pound note. Actually I had never seen one before, but the more I looked at it, the more certain and easy I was in my own mind that it was a hundred pound note, for not only was it written on it, but there was the Custom House printed on the back.

Irish paper currency has on the back of each note, pictures of the sculptures around the Dublin Custom House, which I understand represent the different rivers of Ireland. In each case the river on the reverse side of the note is represented by the venerable head of an ancient.

On the ten shilling note, the ancient representing the River Blackwater is looking non-commital. On the pound note, the head is the River Lee in Cork and he's smiling, just ever so little, while on the five pound note and the River Lagan in Belfast he is giving quite a smile. Come the ten pound note which is the River Shannon, the old one is laughing. The twenty pound note is the River Liffey, and he is laughing himself sick, while on the fifty pound note the head is the River Corrib in Galway and he is splitting his sides laughing. The hundred pound note has the Custom House itself, alone, on the back.

'Yes, sure,' I said confidently, 'that's a hundred pound note.'

'Is it real?' she said seriously.

'Of course it's real. Why shouldn't it be?'

'Somebody has stamped on it, "Not Negotiable",' and sure enough there it was.

'Oh,' I said, 'probably some shiner playing around with a child's printing set.'

So she tells me I am a very intelligent man and all to that

effect and asks me if I would ever change it for her? By a master stroke and real presence of mind, she agrees to my getting as much as I can for her in notes and a tenner for myself for the trouble. We arranged to meet the following night and like the hammers of hell I was out of the place and over to see a friend of mine who I knew had a banking account. So anxious I was not to be lost out on the transaction, that I stayed with him all that night and nearly driven out of my mind and above in the puzzle factory with the waiting.

In short order, we were first in the bank that morning for, as I told the man, it wasn't lucky to stand in a queue for money. The hundred pound note was handed over the counter along with some other currency to be deposited and a cheque duly drawn for one hundred pounds. They were to be given in ones and fivers.

Outside on the pavement and the sun high in the heavens, 'I'll give you seventy pounds,' he said.

'You will in your arse,' for my nerves hadn't gone from the straying without some reward. 'Give me ninety pounds,' I said, 'and that's the cheapest ten pounds you'll ever know.'

When I met Sheila, I gave her the seventy pounds and I needn't have worried about the tenner. She gave me that too. I would like to put on record that this is the only time in which I have ever shown any acumen with regard to finance. However, I first started making money out of brothels at a very early age and for this reason.

I came from a poor home. Not so poor however as some American or English homes in the sense that my father would read to us for the four nights of the week when he hadn't enough money for beer, and my mother would sing to us. But poor enough that the first eight years of my life were spent in a back parlour.

In the front parlour, divided from us by folding doors, was a brothel. It wasn't much of a brothel, God knows, but the inhabitants enjoyed themselves or seemed to. I think they did more drinking there than anything else; it was more a shebeen than a kip, kip being the Dublin word for a brothel and shebeen the Irish for a place where people are able to drink after hours.

One of the girls, Winnie Flanagan from Sligo, used to come

143

to the hall door in the morning, just before we went to school and we got to realise that this was her custom. She would stand with her client, who was usually a little Dublin bourgeois very anxious to get away from our district, which is not one of the best known socially in the city (but is best known in the world of literature as Joyce's 'Night Town') and she would ask him to send me across the road for a package of cigarettes.

The client would then fumble in his pocket and maybe come up with a half crown which he would give to me. When I returned with the snout and offered the guy the change, she would say: 'Ah, give the kid the change. He ran the errand.'

The only smart thing I did in this case was to make sure I was around for the taking.

THE next day, my mother gently suggested that I might go and look for a job, and to avoid hearing further, I got out of the house by a mutter about going down to the Union Hall.

And by way of no harm, I went down by Davy Byrnes' where the height of good humour prevailed. Lester Jeus was there, telling all and sundry that he was off to France with the mot and small son, and Edwin Lang was going with them.

I reflected, as I covered the distance home to collect my passport, that a trip to Paris would improve my health considerably, a fact which I did not intend to disclose to the ould one.

Three hours later, as I tottered onto the B. and I. at the North Wall, Gabriel was on the gang plank to tell me that the others were already improving the day up at the bar. And we improved the day from Holyhead to London and back to Newhaven for the cross-Channel boat to such good effect that as I handed the Immigration Officer my passport—albeit under the name of Francis Behan—I was able to point out to him that, as I was going and not coming, his proper title should be Emigration Officer. The Deportation Order against me troubled me not at all. I went through the Customs with my friends and took the opportunity of watching the white cliffs of England receding in the background as we tossed our way across the Channel.

At Dieppe I dodged out under the boat train at the Gâre Maritime—it's out in the street—and snaked over to a wineshop for some cheese and *vin rouge* and was back on the train again as quick as an ass's gallop. The shop was owned by a Limerickman who called it the BBC Wine Store. A few hours later, the Dieppe-Paris express, with a couple of dozen stops at intervening points, arrived at the railway station of Saint Lazare.

We were told that there was a shortage of buses, the Germans

145

having taken a great number of them with them on the retreat of 1944. Judging by the length of time it took us to bus our way to St.-Germain des-Prés, they couldn't have given any of them back yet. Though looking up at the destination board on the lamp-post, I felt I could forgive a lot to a vehicle that made regular journeys to places like St.-Germain des-Prés, the Louvre and the Pont du Carrousel.

We were all kipped in a small hotel at St-Germain des-Prés, on the Left Bank or on the south side of the Seine. This area is to the post-war intellectual, genius or phoney, have it whatever way you like, what Montmartre was to the artist of Picasso's youth before the first war and, as a refuge of sinners, has succeeded Montparnasse, stamping-ground of Hemingway and Scott Fitzgerald in the 'twenties.

It gained notoriety as the headquarters of Jean-Paul Sartre, just after the Liberation. He had a flat on the corner of the Rue Bonaparte, and the adjoining licensed premises, the *Deux Magots* and the *Café de Flore*, became the twin cathedrals of existentialism of which philosophy he is the high priest.

As regards 'existentialism', Cecil ffrench Salkeld, my first wife's father, defines it as teaching 'that man is sentinel to the null.'

And as good an excuse for robbing all round you as any other, as Monsieur Jean Genet has proved, with great profit to himself. This man was a burglar for many years and also a poet. He was arrested many times for breaking and entering and each time refused to recognise the Court. Like Marlowe, who countered all objection to his home production of the coin of the realm with the remark that he was as much entitled to mint money as the Queen of England, Monsieur Genet told the Court that he robbed as an existentialist and had a conscientious objection to keeping his hands easy.

In a less civilised country, he would have been engaged in the production of mailbags, four stitches to the inch. But Sartre and a number of other writers demanded that they leave the boy alone. And he is now an honoured French writer, a credit to his country and the proprietor of an estate in the country. He does not need to do any more work in the burglaring line and lives on the proceeds of his books.

I had extracts of his autobiography read to me, some of

which rose the hair on my head. And, as my mother once remarked, that which would shock Brendan Behan would turn thousands grey.

Oscar Wilde died in a hotel down the street from us, in the Rue d'Alsace, and tradition has it that it was a priest of St-Germain des-Prés who attended him on his death bed. Later I was to write a poem to him.

Then there was the Bonapartist who would march along the Boulevard St-Germain each day in his long coat and cocked hat, sword ever at the ready to avenge the slightest insult to his Emperor. We subsquently discovered that he was a collaborator and he was put in gaol.

The atmosphere in the Latin Quarter at this time was quite extraordinary. Nobody gave a fiddler's fugh for your connections, who you fought for, or why you fought. All they wanted was a drink, a smoke and *that*, and were totally uninterested in any armies or arms.

I was in the company one evening of Samuel Beckett and his cousin, a Jewish girl from Dublin. Samuel Beckett had been in the Resistance and he introduced his cousin to a great many of his friends, both French and otherwise, who had also been in the Resistance. We started off in a bar at Montparnasse and wound up almost a day later somewhere around Pont Royal, and despite the many introductions I had this little Jewish girl to myself all the way, and for the following reason. Every time Sam introduced her to one of his compatriots I would click my heels and she would hear the clicking and assume the innocent fellow was an ex-member of the S.S. and refuse to speak to him; despite the fact that the poor bastard had probably spent about four years in Ravensbruck or Belsen or some such godforsaken hole.

Nearby our hotel, in the Rue Dauphine, was the Studio Bar where Jeus had his small son's C.A.R.E. parcel delivered. Now C.A.R.E. is an organisation whereby Americans supply other Americans in Europe with food and Jeus' parcel consisted of olive oil and an assortment of baby foods, mistakenly sent by his father for his little grandson. Jeus, however, would sell the parcel and usually got two thousand francs for it.

Also in the Rue Dauphine was old Raymond Duncan who ran an Akademia of Greek culture, and often I watched him

147

in the midst of his disciples, elderly ladies and gentlemen dressed in blankets and sandals—a sort of kilted costume that bore as much resemblance to the clothes of the ancient Greeks as the uniform of the Fintan Lalor Pipe Band to that of Brian Boru—march in solemn procession to greet the dawn at the bottom of our street.

A little further up at Odeon Metro Station was the Pergola restaurant frequently inhabited by an old Chinaman or something, who specialised in one branch of English literature, and that a bilingual catalogue from Messrs, Whiteleys of London. He would read it by the hour so that we might know how 'three-piece Chesterfield suite, twenty pounds ten,' or 'Oak double bed, eleven pounds ten: mattress, best flock, extra,' sounded in Chinese.

Jeus christened him God, whom he rather resembled. And we dared not move an inch till the last huckaback towel was disposed of, for he was a man of wide culture and, in addition to his literary talents, was a ju-jitsu expert.

We hadn't been in Paris very long and it being summer and you'd die from the lack of a breath of the sea when Jeus and myself sat in the Studio Bar trying to cure two hangovers with very little money. The patron man, by the name of Pierre Kharlamoff, was a decent man but he could do nothing for us. The real governor of the place was in behind the counter checking the accounts. And the most our kind patron could do was to offer us two hundred francs to go up the street to the Pergola and get a little *pastis*.

But the cure was worse than the disease. Because I was expecting to meet members of the Irish National Pilgrimage of Repentance to Lourdes, and Jeus was expecting his small son's C.A.R.E. parcel to be delivered and this was the time for the both. The pilgrims were the cause of our hangovers this morning, for we were after having a tremendous bash the night before. As one of the repentant pilgrims put it, as soon as they reached Lourdes the repentance would really start, but in the meantime they had to have something to be repentant about.

Jeus, after a half hour of waiting, looked glum about his son's C.A.R.E. parcel and I prayed more fervently and desperately that the steps of the repentant pilgrims might be directed towards the Studio Bar, before the depression got the better of us and we accepted the patron's loan and bought a bottle of *Calvados* with it.

A tall man came in, in the midst of our misery, and started walking up and down the floor alongside us. Twice or three times he looked over and smiled anxiously in our direction.

'God's teeth,' muttered Jeus with some irritation, 'could that fellow not go away?'

I suppose he had as good a right to be there as we had, although it was beginning to wear me down too. 'Hey Mac,' I said to him when he looked over at us again, 'pore tront frank donnery moowah une image.' Which was my simple translation of the Lancashire remark to starers; ''Ere, luv, for a tanner you can 'ave a photograph.'

He made a strangled sound in his throat and looked sad like King Kong. 'Urm .. sorry, bat urd do nit spurk Fhrunch.'

Well that's a bond anyway said I in my own mind, but Jeus called the patron and demanded the removal of this man who was destroying his nerves already destroyed from the hospitality of the penitent pilgrims.

'Ah, dees poor man, M'sieu Jeus, he does not speak French.'

'Well, they've got the Berlitz up the road there, why doesn't he go and join that?'

'Maybe he will, now. He's just won the Loterie Nationale and he has no one to celebrate with.' Pierre sighed. 'Le poevra.'

'He won the Loterie Nationale? And you allow the poor fellow to walk around there in loneliness with neither kith nor kin to share his joy? Shame on you, Pierre,' said Jeus with indignation as noble as that of Brutus's. 'Sit down at once, my good fellow. You are amongst friends now,' he shouted to the big fellow, who came over and sat between us with eagerness and a big smile on his face.

'Urm Schweed,' said the big fellow.

'No matter a damn,' said I, 'if you are itself, whose business is it but your own and so long as you interfere with nobody.'

'We will not let you down,' said Jeus, 'do not worry.'

'Be not afraid,' I echoed.

'Three bottles of champagne here,' said Jeus. 'Pierre!' he roared like a sergeant-major of a low type.

Pierre, delighted at doing such good business at ten in the

morning came down beaming, and our big friend produced a ten thousand franc note and off we went. By twelve o'clock Jeus and I were cured, the big man was in great humour and we decided to go and eat at the Brasserie Lipp.

Coming down the Boulevard St-Germain I met some of the penitent pilgrims, who shouted at me, 'Ah dere you are, Brindin boy.'

'Away from me ye hypocrites,' said I with dignity, and marched up the street. And then the thought struck me. These pilgrims were not on to such a bad deal and I knew from the experience of the night before that nobody screws like a pilgrim on his way to Lourdes. I suppose he thinks he might never come back. Final passions are strong in death.

I mentioned this to Jeus and on the heels of the reels we became members of the Pilgrimage of Repentance to Lourdes, carrying a large wooden Cross, on which you could have easily crucified two men of normal size, from the *Café de Deux Magots* on St-Germain des-Prés to Chartres. On a fine summer's morning Jeus and I set out with hundreds of other artists and phoneys of all description. Jeus carried the Cross for five yards and then handed it to a Dutchman.

'I'm not worthy,' he said. 'You should carry this Cross and put the arm on the guy for two thousand francs.'

We got off the electric train on the route at Rambouillet, which I understand is the summer residence of the President of France. The young clerk at the booking office directed us to the Café where lunch was laid on for the pilgrims.

Our modest statements that we were the advance guard of the pilgrims, brought forth *le patron* himself, no less, and his entire *entourage* and the best of food and the best of wine as well. We decided to do an auto-stop, or a hitch-hike as the saying has it, for the rest of the trip, with an adjournment here and there, eating and drinking what the pilgrims were supposed to be having.

British tourists sometimes stop, Americans seldom, women and clergymen never, and our best bet each time was a truck. The driver would get out and have a look at us, and on hearing that we were two of a band of happy pilgrims, would eagerly give us a lift. Finally we got to Chartres Cathedral itself which is famous, amongst other things, for its stained glass windows, but as they are so high up I couldn't tell a deal about them. Towering and mighty, since the age of Faith, Chartres Cathedral was decorated by a group of sculptors, unpaid, and giving themselves, mind and muscle, for God's sake.

Jeus and myself wandered about the churchyard and didn't see the pilgrims arrive carrying their huge Cross and we had to hide quickly behind the tomb of an Archbishop so that we couldn't be seen. But Aughrim was not lost, for as they entered the door I hurriedly grabbed the Cross from the proud pilgrim-bearer and brought it up to the altar. And for my religious efforts, the National Pilgrimage of Repentance stood myself and Jeus that night many litres of *vin rouge* of a good year.

We got a lift back to Paris the next morning from the correspondent of a London newspaper who was in Chartres to report on the proceedings of the previous day. He told us he was staying at the Hotel Trianon and invited us along for a drink. I think he only stayed at the place because he had a large expense account and used to give it a plug in his column.

He introduced us to an Englishman—whom I subsequently discovered was a crook—who had a fund of fantastic stories, one of which I remember quite clearly.

Now I don't understand finance very well, but apparently to get gold into France was considered quite a good idea. There was this man who arrived in Paris wearing a gold boot. Unfortunately, as he got off the aeroplane one of the Immigration Officers happened to notice that he had a slight limp, and suggested to him that he might like to sit down while waiting to go through Customs. The gentleman became so nervous that he eventually fainted. They undid his tie and his shoelaces and discovered, with alarm, the gold boot.

When we got back to the hotel that night, Jessica, Jeus' wife, began tapping messages furiously in morse on the table, and thinking it is better to be insulted than ignored, I went to bed.

We stayed in Paris four months, and on our last day, we sent Jeus out to buy the breakfast, which consisted of a litre of *vin rouge*, a long French crusty loaf and a box of Camembert cheese which was sold at the corner of the street for twenty-five francs because it was rotten. The French, contrary to popular belief, do not like to eat rotten cheese.

An hour later Jeus returned, very ornate and very sweet

smelling, but without the wine, without the bread and without the cheese, but with George, a Hungarian fellow.

'Where the fugh is our breakfast?' I asked sourly.

'I felt I needed a bath,' says Jeus, 'and there wasn't enough left over for the breakfast.'

'You didn't need a bath that bad, you bastard,' said Gabriel, but Jessica only shrugged her shoulders.

'Don't any of you guys ever take a bath?' Jeus snarled, baring his teeth like a dog at the show.

'No,' I answered. 'Only dirty people have to wash. It's like the Sacrament of Penance. When I am asked in Ireland if I have been to Confession recently, I always answer, "no, that's only for sinners." '

Once or twice, in the heat of the Paris summer, at the cost of two shillings I had gone into the Piscine, which is a sort of floating swimming pool on the Seine. But for one hour only. They control the length of time by a system of coloured tickets, and when they shout out that it's time up for the yellow tickets or the blue tickets it's no good gaming on that you don't know what 'jaune' or 'bleu' means. And you can't stop there till the place shuts and be charged the difference afterwards—like travelling first class on a third class Metro ticket. The inspector, if he catches you, will waste no time bemoaning the dishonesty of any part of the human race, yours or his. He'll hold out his hand for a ten-shilling fine.

Gabriel and I thought this American emphasis on washing a bit much. And then George comes up with the suggestion that he stands us all beakfast at the Studio Bar, but first he has a proposition to make to me. 'Would you like to work in a brothel?' he asked.

At the time I had all my teeth and weighed eleven stone, two pounds.

'Sure,' I said, 'if it's soft money.'

'During the week you will have to satisfy old women, but at the week-end you'll be satisfied by old men.'

'Thank you very much,' I answered politely for I didn't want to hurt his feelings. Every cripple has his own way of walking. 'But this is not a proposition that appeals to me.'

'What about me?' chips in Edwin Lang.

'Oh no,' says George, 'you are much too ugly.' And I thought

Edwin would do himself damage for he pretended to be very vain about his personal appearance. He turned his head to the wall and became an upset bloke.

'Is it a condition of our getting breakfast that I work in this co-educational brothel of yours?' I asked, for my principles did not stretch as far as the hunger in my stomach.

'Certainly not,' said George.

But Edwin was very hurt and said to go and have breakfast for he was going back to Ireland on his own. I thought maybe he'd snap out of it, but he didn't follow us out. So I said in my own mind, what can't be cured must be endured. We went on out without him.

George explained over breakfast that one of his extra-mural activities was writing pornography, and if ever I was in the need it would be no trouble to put the writing of one or two articles in my way. I thanked him very much for I knew I would come back to France which I had grown to love very dearly and felt was part of my inheritance.

After all, you might say that the Latin Quarter was bounded by the Rue de Bac, on the north-west by the river, and the Irish college on the south-east at the Rue des Irlandais, up behind the Pantheon, where Wolfe Tone plotted to free a people and destroy an empire on one hundred guineas and a hard neck, and where the students waved their black shovel hats and cheered John Mitchel, and the old Republican Ulsterman, son of a Unitarian minister, wiped his eyes from the warmth of a Papist welcome.

'Always Ireland with your people,' said Jeus. 'You think of everything in regard to yourselves.'

Even the French Revolution—and who is more entitled? It was an Irishman led the people in the attack on the Bastille. He was a Wexfordman and a cobbler, by the name of Kavanagh.

I was home for Christmas and went with my mother to see the eldest of us and we drank potheen and right and all as it was, I fell to wondering what, in the name of our sacred and dearest old creditors, was I going to do for readies? In between hopping to France and trotting, lepping and dancing. I had got through all readies.

The following morning I was feeling like a corpse that didn't get Christian burial, but after I had backed two winners at the dog track on expert advice, back I came to relish a bit of turkey. In my childhood I spent lovely Christmases and we had a sight less than turkey but youth at our side to make as merry a Christmas as ever you saw. But when all is said and done, with advancing years a bit of turkey is very light, highly nutritious and altogether delectable and acceptable of a Christmas time. After turkeying and coming out on the street again and meeting people, all of whom were moaning and groaning and wondering how they'd get through January after asking one another how they'd got over the Christmas, I felt great.

I wrote my first play at this time for the Barnes and McCormack Commemoration Concert which was to be held in the Queen's Theatre in the following month. It was called by the nonsensical title of *Gretna Green*, and I based it on the execution of the two innocent I.R.A. men, Barnes and McCormack, for their so-called part in the bomb explosion in Coventry in 1939 which killed five people.

A bit jarred one night, I had agreed to take part in it myself but the rehearsals put years on me and I told Séan Mooney, the stage manager, who was later to hold this position with honour and distinction in the Abbey, that I was a writer not an actor. I watched it from the side of the stage and Jesus, Mary and Joseph, it would be better to forget it.

On February 9th I was twenty-five and after taking as many weeks as there are since the New Year to recover from the festive celebrations, my mother gently suggested to me, once more, that I might go down to the Union Hall and look for a job.

154

> Now Autumn leaves are falling,
> And the light is growing dim,
> The painter wipes his pot clean down—
> And —ks his brushes in . . .

O R, as the old saying has it, 'Cover me up till the First of March,' and look at it anyway you like, the time had come to be uncovered.

I went down to the Painter's Union but had time over on the way for a word with Cathal in the Irish House to steady my nerves and to put me in the humour for regular employment. The secretary, or the delegate, gave me a card and sent me down to a firm of painting contractors on St. Stephen's Green. When I arrived the foreman looked at me. 'Oh, Jaysus,' he said, 'it's yourself.'

Now I am bound to admit that though not devoid of ambition in the graining, lettering and marbling line, my real talents lay not in painting. My father and grandfathers were painters, and at an exhibition of Patrick Swift's, Victor Waddington remarked that of all present my father was the only painter with a Union card. My granny was forewoman gilder in Brindley's of Eustace Street and on my mother's side the Kearneys were and are similarly engaged. For all that, maybe because of that, I am allergic to painting. Not to paint mark you. But to putting the stuff on.

I even like looking at a job well done and have been known, in the middle of Debussy's *Pelléas et Mélisande*, to force the attentions of John Ryan and Frederick May, who had the good fortune to be sitting either side of me (otherwise they might have missed it), to a rather neat bit of repair filling on the

Gaiety ceiling in Dublin. And in company with another literary refugee from the trade, Joseph Tomelty, I commented adversely on the papering of a night club in Villiers Street in London. Joe and I agreed that it was 'lapped' where it should have been 'butted', which drew from the cynical lip of Con O'Leary—the Lord have mercy on him—the comment that in a new town the first thing a tinker looks at is his horse.

Strangely, there are few house-painter-painters. I mean, few *peintres en batiment* become *artistes peintres*. There have been firemen-artists, grandma Moses peasant-artists by the acre, priest-artists, policemen-artists, child-artists, and there are people who would claim that the famous English artist, Sir Winston Churchill, is an author. For the matter of that, there are not wanting those who make out that his colleague, Sir Alfred Munnings, is a horse. But seldom do you ever hear of a house-painter-artist.

I remember once there was a fisherman-artist, and his work was hung in very august surroundings and a big ha-ha in the papers about him being an uninstructed simple man and all to that effect, and at the opening of the exhibition old ones from the cultural areas were all gabbling round this chap who had cleaned off the herring leavings for the day. He stood rather more stylishly dressed than the ordinary artist-artists, modestly giving his opinions on life and art.

Then the door burst open and a very well-known Irish artist stood there, his massive frame adorned in the habiliments of a trawlerman. Enormous seaboots, a blue woollen jersey, sou'-wester and rubbers he wore, and trailing from his shoulder was about twenty yards of tram net. The first to recover from this apparition was the then chief among artists, an old man of ancient lineage who directed a stern and indignant inquiry towards the figure in the doorway.

'Sir, what is the meaning of appearing amongst your friends and brothers in this preposterous costume?'

From the doorway came the drawled reply: 'Oh, I thought you knew. I,' and with a nonchalant shrug of his net-draped shoulder in the direction of the serge-suited fisherman-artist, 'am an artist-fisherman.'

Howsome-ever, as the man said, first carefully removing the butt from his lower lip, this foreman of the painting contractors on St. Stephen's Green had to employ me as I produced my card for he wouldn't have been able to get any more men if he hadn't done so. He gave me my kit, which was a set of brushes, and he told me to go down to the Gaiety Theatre. Now many's the time I had been there, as a member of the audience at least, since I was four or five, and the *piece de resistance* was always a solo bit by a tiny tot who came in front of the line when the rest of the orchestra knocked off for a minute and danced on her own. With all due respect to tiny tots and their fathers and mothers and teachers and the whole world of tiny tottery, I had as little time for that as I had for painting the joint.

But when I got to the place, good Christ, what had I to do? The ceiling had to be painted. To get to it there was a single six-inch plank leading out from the gallery (where I had been even afraid to sit two nights previously with my friends, Mack and Ruth) to a number of planks where one single board was lowered to take you up a further three foot of empty space to the roof. Underneath was an eighty-foot drop to *terra firma* below. I nearly died seven deaths but being a natural coward I was more afraid to go home to my mother and tell her that I'd left the job than I was of getting on to the plank, so I climbed up there in a cold sweat.

However, in the course of a week I got more used to it, although I kept looking down on either side of me to the eighty-foot drop below. Anyone who says that you get used to heights is talking complete and absolute nonsense. I was terrified the whole time, but the way some of the painters were hopping round the board you'd think they were walking on the pavement.

In the course of the first morning, when I got off the plank to look for fresh colour—which I frequently did—I met an elderly gentleman with a moustache called Jack Guilfoyle. He was wearing the old time celluloid collar which was favoured by some painters because they were able to wipe the paint off it with a turpentine rag and then wash it with soap and water. Jack Guilfoyle was a Protestant. He was a member of the Church of Ireland and one of the very few Protestants in the painting trade or in the building industry in Dublin who had never been a foreman and by reason of the fact that he was a drunk.

Somebody told me that during the Depression, Merrion Hall in Dublin was the headquarters of an extreme brand of Protestants who didn't have any clergy apparently, but held services which were conducted by building contractors and builders' foremen. Because it was a good place for getting a job, Guilfoyle, who was not a notoriously God-fearing man, went to a service at Merrion Hall. A contractor called Jones was taking the service and he began to recite the Lord's Prayer and when he got to the bit, 'Give us this day our daily bread,' all the unemployed workers assembled there shouted out 'Amen! Amen! Amen!' but Guilfoyle forgot himself even further and he shouted: 'Amen! Ah-fughing-men!'

A fellow feeling makes us wondrous kind, so when Guilfoyle suggested that we went down to the corner in the lunch hour and give ourselves a couple of drinks, despite the fact that I told him I hadn't any money, I was only too happy to fall in with him.

'That's all right,' he said, 'but just carry this box for me,' and he handed me what looked like a child's coffin, only twice as heavy.

'Jaysus, Jack,' I said, 'what ever is this?'

'Oh, it's only my tool box,' came the reply.

Now the height of tools that Guilfoyle would ever be owning would be perhaps a scraper and a putty knife from Woolworths of the sort that women use in the home, but I wasn't in mind to be asking further, so I just let it go at that.

In the pub, he asked the barman if he might leave the tools with him. 'I'm up on a job at the Gaiety here,' he explained, 'and I'm only using brushes, and such tools as I want, I have taken out of the box. I would like to leave the rest here in case some of the other skins (meaning the painters) would steal them. They are a very valuable set of tools.'

In my own mind I thought, Jesus, they must be a motor mechanic's outfit.

The barman took the box and put it behind the counter and we ordered two glasses of whiskey and two pints of stout. Guilfoyle hurriedly swallowed the whiskey and I followed suit, taking a large slug out of my pint at the same time. We then ordered another round, and the barman, who was an innocent country boy, asked us for the money.

'That's all right,' says Guilfoyle, 'I'll see you on Friday, pay night.'

'Oh, we don't do that here,' said the boy. 'I'm afraid you'll have to pay now.'

'Look,' said Guilfoyle, 'haven't you got my very valuable box of tools as security? I have to come in on Friday night to collect them.'

So eventually the barman agreed but rather doubtfully and we went back to work the better off for a few jars.

I remember at the time the Gaiety was putting on a show called *The Winslow Boy* and rehearsals were taking place in the afternoon. Guilfoyle, on account of his age I suppose, was not shoved up in the roof but was painting the hallway leading to the stage. He had his ladder right across the entrance. The Winslow Boy, or the boy who was acting the part, was a blondie-headed youth of about fourteen and he suggested to Guilfoyle that he move his ladder a bit so that he could get past.

'If you don't get out of my way,' retorted Jack Guilfoyle, 'you'll be getting a kick up the arse and a mouthful of three-penny bits that you won't be forgetting this day nor the next.'

The Winslow Boy had to squeeze by the ladder as best he could.

Although we went to the pub on the corner almost every lunch hour, in the evening we availed ourselves of different drinking places. One evening we went to a pub that was owned by an old man from Galway who had, however, spent most of his life in Manchester, where he also owned a public house. Now it turned out that he was a great Gaelic singer and himself and myself went into the back room and threw back our heads and sang Gaelic songs to the darkened ceiling over the upturned toil-worn faces of the men and women listening to us. There is no gloomier place, incidentally, than a Dublin pub because, as a rule, no singing is allowed and most of the talk is in whispers. It is a funny thing but you very seldom get a Dublin man owning a pub. The proprietors nearly always comes from off the tops of the mountains and are to be recognised long before they open their mouths by the strange way they have of walking.

It is said that the sedan chairmen of eighteenth century

London were Irishmen. It is believed that their peculiar gait, from long practice in bog-trotting, made them lithe and delicate carriers of frail and elegant *grandes dames* to and from the ball and the rout. (Don't ask me what the rout was. For long I have suspected that it described an entertainment similar to a meeting of tinkers at Ballinasloe horse fair. That sometimes finishes up in a rout, but the London aristocracy wouldn't be decent enough for that sort of sport.)

Sure enough in a matter of moments this old man's son, who had been reared in Manchester, comes over and asks us, 'might we not give over this carry-on and speak English like everyone else and stop singing and making a show of ourselves.' I answered him in the mellifluous tongue of Shakespeare, Milton and Johnson before I left with Guilfoyle.

The next night we chose a different public house and on the way we found a temperance badge in the gutter, which Guilfoyle promptly stuck in his coat. Now this badge represents an organisation in Ireland of about half a million members who favour total abstinence.

There was a young apprentice barman of about sixteen behind the counter who was not more than a month or so off the bog, I suppose, and he looked at the badge and then in horror at Jack Guilfoyle when he ordered two pints. He left the bar and went across the room to a man standing in the corner talking to some people, and back again meeting himself coming back, having been told by the proprietor that he didn't give a damn what badge he was wearing provided he had the money to pay for the drinks. The young boy slapped down the Guinness in front of us as if as much to say, I hope it chokes you.

Many years afterwards, I met this young boy again and by now he was a fully-fledged barman. I deliberately got him talking on the organisation for total abstinence.

'I don't believe in them,' he said. 'I spent two weeks in Dublin as an apprentice barman and an old fellow came in with a younger man—funnily enough Brendan, the younger fellow he was with was not unlike you. He might have been a brother of yours—and he was wearing the badge of a total abstainer but that didn't stop him from drinking two pints of Guinness.'

On the Friday, after we had been paid, I suggested to Jack

160

Guilfoyle that we went to the pub on the corner on our way home and give the guy what we owed him for the drinks.

'We'll go halves,' I said. 'How much do you think it will be?'

'Oh,' said Guilfoyle, 'about one pound I should think.'

So I gave him the money and waited to go with him to help him carry the tool box which he had left in the pub.

'Go away, for Jaysus' sake,' said Guilfoyle. 'I discovered that box here in the theatre and I filled it up with bricks and empty beer bottles. The barman is welcome to it. He can fughing-well have it.'

And I lost a pound.

After I had finished working the Gaiety, I worked on the reconstruction of the church at the bottom of York Street, which was being turned into a hostel for the Salvation Army, and then I was asked by a Union delegate if I would like to work for the Irish Lights. Now the Irish Lights is the organisation that controls the lighthouses of Ireland, both North and South, and the headquarters are in Dublin. It is perfectly obvious that despite politics, partitions and borders, there is not a deal of sense in having a lighthouse on a border, black one side and white the other, and it is more convenient for all concerned to have them under the one authority. The usual custom is that the glasses and the lights themselves are made in Birmingham—that noted seaside resort—and the maintenance of the structure is done by Belfast men, while the painting is done by Dublin men.

The English and the Welsh lighthouses are controlled by Trinity House, which means that myself and Winston Churchill were once upon a time in the same organisation, he as an Elder Brother of Trinity House and I as a painter for the Irish Lights, his position being more decorative than functional however.

I agreed to do the job and was given a card. Also with me was a friend of mine who was a notorious drunk. He had been in the British Army during the First World War and had little to distinguish him from any other drunken Dublin housepainter, except for the fact that had he gone to church at all he would have gone to a different one from the majority of us. He was a Church of Ireland man despite his name being O'Leary.

His son had escaped from the slums in which he was living

by becoming a clergyman in the Church of England, and when his father arrived over in England for his Ordination he was so blind drunk that he nearly made a bollocks of the entire proceedings.

O'Leary was the only man I ever knew to be barred from an Ordination, but the authorities put him out and kept him out.

On this morning, however, the pair of us arrived at the Irish Lights office in Dublin, sober and correct. We were to go to Donaghadee in the County Down in Northern Ireland and paint the lighthouse. (Since this day, I have painted striped lighthouses, banded lighthouses and spotted lighthouses.) We were given our equipment which consisted of paint brushes, wire brushes, a blow lamp, knives and scrapers which were put into two wooden boxes and these were to be sealed with the official stamp of the Commissioner for Irish Lights, so that they wouldn't be searched at the border. If the Northern customs officers insisted on doing so, we had the alternative of coming back, as the boxes were as much the property of the government of Southern Ireland as they were the property of the government of Northern Ireland. Or Western Ireland for the matter of that, or Eastern Ireland where I happen to come from.

By the same token, I wonder how Ireland lost one of the cardinal points of the compass. We have songs, sneers, jeers and cheers for the *Men of the West*, the *Gallant South*, the *North Began* and the *North Held On, God Bless the Northern Land* and all to that effect, but damn the ha'porth about the East. There's not a mention of our geographical direction, nor a line for the Men of the East. When someone calls me a 'Southerner', I feel like Old Black Joe.

'What part of the South do you come from, Rastus?'

'Ah sho' don' know, massah. It was dark when Ah left!'

A lot of people are somewhat puzzled when I say that I come from neither Northern Ireland nor Southern Ireland. I am a wise man from the East, I tell them, and by the looks of my two little slitty eyes like Fu Manchu, it's easily seen that's where I do come from.

However, myself and O'Leary were given an advance of £5 and the two boxes and as the man put the seals on them, he turned to us:

162

'We always trust our men,' he said, 'that they are not going to take advantage of these seals to smuggle anything into Northern Ireland?'

'Certainly not,' says I and O'Leary who had a great habit of saying 'beyond a shadow of a doubt,' echoed: 'Beyond a shadow of a doubt, no.'

As soon as we got outside with our equipment, says O'Leary:

'The first thing to do, before we waste our substance, is to buy four bottles of whiskey this side of the border,' for at that time there was a considerable difference in the price of liquor between Northern and Southern Ireland.

We went into the nearest pub, which wasn't an ass's bawl from the Irish Lights office, and ordered a couple of pints of Guinness. O'Leary then called for the whiskey and proceeded to break the seals off the boxes and shove in the whiskey. On my enquiry in a sarcastic tone of voice as to what he was going to do about the seals, he put his hand in his pocket and produced about a hundred of them, which apparently he had nicked from the office when the bloke wasn't looking. Very carefully, with a razor blade, we removed the old seals and replaced them with the new. I could have said new wine in old boxes, I was that gone in a weakness.

We drank so much that eventually we had to go to the Union Hall and borrow the money for the fare and a couple of quid besides and we got on a train at Amiens Street Station where we arrived at the border, I am bound to admit, still pretty drunk.

After opening our battered looking attache cases containing our personal effects, if a couple of old dirty shirts can ever be so described, the custom officer's eyes focused on the boxes.

'Open these,' he said.

'I can't do that,' I answered. 'These boxes are sealed by the Commissioner for Irish Lights. Have a look for yourself.'

The officer began to read slowly, 'the C-o-m-m-i-s-s-i-o-n-e-r . . .'

'That's the lighthouses,' I interrupted him for I wasn't in mind to be arguing with this pox-faced bastard of a whore's melt. 'And furthermore,' I said, 'you'll be falling out with Winston Churchill amongst other people if you make us open these boxes. You know that the Irish Lights control the lighthouses of Ireland don't you?'

So this guy had never heard of them, but after a consultation with a colleague of his we were allowed to proceed.

We arrived in Belfast about noon and after a bite to eat and a sup to drink, we moseyed round to the Labour Exchange in Corporation Street for to get Social Security Cards and ration books for food. And Jaysus, in the Labour Exchange didn't we find this half-wit of an eejit to end all eejits?

'Ah,' he said, 'you're birds of passage from Eire,' but he pronounced it Ayr.

'Ayr,' says I, 'is in Scotland, but I would not be ashamed to come from there because one of the greatest poets that ever lived, Robert Burns, was a native of Ayrshire, but you're such an illiterate bastard, you probably wouldn't know that.'

His face reddened up. 'How dare you speak like that to me.'

'Like what?' says innocence.

'Using that foul language in here.'

'I didn't use any foul language,' I said. 'It's obvious, despite the fact that you are English (no disrespect to the breed, for you get objectionable folks from all classes, creeds and nationalities, I've seen them at home) you don't know your own language, for the word I used is a piece of Norman French and is a legal term relating mostly to royalty. However,' I continued, 'I did not come here for a discussion on either literature or geography. I came here to get Social Security Cards and ration books for the pair of us to enable us to fulfil our rightful jobs in the North of Ireland.'

I walked away from this junior Hitler and went across to a member of the Royal Irish Constabulary who was standing nearby.

'What's the trouble?' he said.

'Myself and my colleague here,' I explained, 'have come up from Dublin today to do a lawful job of work for the Irish Lights, which is a Thirty-Two County organisation. As a matter of fact, it is a department, indirectly, of Trinity House in London.' I didn't like to mention the fact that I had often been in Belfast before on an unlawful job of work—hat in hand goes through the land—'And, furthermore,' I said, 'if this man refuses to give us our cards, I will find out his name and I will go back and make out a report of the whole incident to

164

the Irish Lights and I will personally see that he returns very smartly to whatever slum in East Jesus, Fulham, S.W.96, he comes from.'

'Take it easy,' said the constable, 'here is the manager,' and a tall dark-haired man with an easy smile came towards us. I noticed that he was wearing a masonic ring, but he was a Belfast man so I explained the position once more to him.

With a 'yes, sir, no, sir, three bags full, sir,' from this half-pay of a limey idiot, our cards were filled out shipshape and Bristol fashion. Funnily enough, Behan as a surname he didn't seem to particularly object to, because, I suppose, he didn't think it was Irish enough, but my Protestant British ex-service friend, O'Leary, had his cards flung at him, 'beyond the shadow of a doubt.'

'Listen,' I said to him. 'What is the good of fighting and arguing? Will you answer me one question and a civil one? Have you enjoyed your eight years in Belfast?'

'How did you know I'm here for eight years?'

'Well,' says I, 'this is 1948. The war got rough in England in 1940, so I presume that is when you decided to dodge over here,' and I drove this dervish to such a dance of fury by this last remark that we decided not to push our luck and left. So if he got medals for insulting people at the Belfast Labour Exchange, he certainly was not so good at insulting the Germans and the Italians.

'Goodbye, now, Dodge-the-War.'

WE GOT on the bus for Laganbank Road where we were to catch another one to Donaghadee. On the way down from Laganbank Road to Donaghadee, a schoolboy sitting beside me in the bus, pointed out Stormont, the Government buildings of Northern Ireland, and I must grudgingly admit, one of the most beautifully set Parliament buildings I have ever seen. It stands on the top of a hill out in the country and in the front of it is a large statue of the late Lord Carson which I am happy to say—in my bollocks—was shown to the old man before he died.

Lord Carson was at school with Oscar Wilde, whom he also prosecuted at Wilde's famous trial. And as Oscar himself remarked, he prosecuted him 'with the added bitterness of an old friend.' But the right name of this clam-headed old butcher was Carsoni; he was the son of a Dublin Italian and not from Northern Ireland at all, any more than Galloper Smith, the first Lord Birkenhead, who also interested himself in our affairs.

But I did not let on to this schoolboy that I had seen Stormont before and I have one great memory of it, which concerns a much later time, however.

There is an organisation of Poets, Publishers, Playwrights, Editors, Essayists and novelists called P.E.N. It is an organisation of writers, at least in everywhere else in the world it, is, except in Dublin. I am afraid in my native city, but for a few rare cases, it is mostly an organisation of phonies: However, in 1953, the P.E.N. held an International Congress in Dublin and I was quite well-known as a writer by that time.

It was quite an occasion and the President of Ireland—South, West and East—gave a garden party at his house. Not to be out-done, the Government of the Six Counties of Ireland laid on a special train to take the delegates up to the North where they

166

were to be entertained, not only to lunch at the Belfast City Hall but also to dinner at Stormont.

And I saw all these Dublin phoneys of our democratic Republic hastening up to the Phoenix Park for the President's garden party, with the men in their Ascot suits and the women in their picture hats. Some of them even condescended to give me a salute as they passed me on Stephen's Green.

When the Belfast P.E.N. arrived in their lounge suits and normal hats, Roy MacFadden, the poet, said to me: 'Funny thing. You're supposed to be the democrats in the South and we're supposed to be the monarchists up in the North and yet your lot are all wearing morning suits and picture hats, while we are wearing our every-day clothes. Several hundred of them have gone to the Park. Are they all writers?'

'Oh, yes,' I said. 'In the Free State, or the Twenty-six Counties, or whatever you like to call it, they don't just fall in as writers and poets in reality. They all become writers and poets in their own mind and the Kerry writers fall in—novelists in front—then the Kerry playwrights, then the Kerry essayists and by the time you have covered every county, that's quite a few people.'

'I suppose you are going up to the Phoenix Park, Brendan?' says Roy.

'No, indeed I am not.'

'Why, Brendan? Are you not invited?'

'No. I am invited to stop away. In the first place I do not own a morning suit, although my aunt owns a few thousand of them because she operates an agency for hiring these things out and my cousin, Seamus de Burca, who runs the business, wouldn't have left me short. He could have fitted me out all right.'

'Well,' said Roy MacFadden, 'I think it's a disgrace but I'll tell you what we will do. You come up to the North with John Hewitt (another very old friend of mine who I understand is now Curator of a museum in Coventry) and myself tomorrow, and come to the luncheon given by the Belfast Corporation and to the dinner at Stormont.'

'That's very nice of you, Roy,' I said, 'and I don't like to look a gift horse in the teeth, but let me ask you something. When you are at these functions given by the Government of

Northern Ireland, I presume you toast the Queen of England?'

'Yes,' he said.

'Now I've nothing against the Queen of England,' I replied. 'She's a wife and a mother and, as far as I can tell, an inoffensive person. But I will not toast her as the Queen of England nor the Duke of Edinburgh on Irish soil. I'm willing to toast them as private individuals—good luck to them—but the Queen of England is not the Queen of Ireland. At the same time I would not like to insult her or to embarrass my friends so I will take the will for the deed and I won't forget it of you for asking me.'

My schoolboy guide next remarked that Purdysburn Mental Hospital was further down on the opposite side of the road to Stormont. I think it is most appropriate that any Parliament building, whether in Dublin, Belfast, London, Vladivostock, Moscow, Peking, West Berlin, East Berlin, South Berlin, North Berlin, New York, Washington or any place else, should have a mental hospital *en face*.

'The bus is now passing between misery and madness,' I said to O'Leary who was sitting across the aisle from myself and my new-found friend.

'Beyond the shadow of a doubt,' echoed O'Leary.

I laughed in my rich southern brogue, low but musical, and an acid-faced lady in the seat in front called the schoolboy to order. When the seat beside her was vacant, she called your man over to it and, glaring at me, breathed fiercely in his ear and he answered, 'yes, auntie,' and 'no, auntie,' and sat staring straight in front of him for the rest of the journey.

It appeared that she didn't like 'southerners'. I had not encountered this kind of carry-on before and it made me feel important and tragic, like the dust-jacket of a Peadar O'Donnell novel in the big block letters of the 'thirties. When I heard her speak to the boy at the end of the journey, I was surprised to notice that she had an American-type accent.

However, it was a lovely summer's evening and I put the incident out of my mind while O'Leary and I went along and got a room at the Lighthouse Cafe where we handed our ration books to Bert, the proprietor. And he expressed himself as well pleased, because it appears that we were given extra rations; we got sailor's rations, though I don't know why we did because we were not sailing anywhere. Thanks be to God, the lighthouse we were to paint was a shore station at the end of the pier.

In the bar that night, I remarked on the acid old one in the bus to the fishermen I was with.

'Och, aye,' said one, 'that'll be Miss Mackenzie. She's from Toronto and she's in some Ulster Society to save us from yous. She can't bear the sight of a southern man and it's very dacent of her, seein' as she was never in the country before in her life.' And to cheer me up: 'Of course, yous have a crowd in America, too, that goes around blackguarding us.'

The Fosters and the Nelsons were the names of the fishermen. A quiet, decent crowd with names of magic to the Belfast children—generations of them—who know that the sea is blue and misty soft where it is nearing the smudge of Scotland and the Lough a drowsy blue all the way to Bangor; that it's always summer at Donaghadee.

The next day was a beautiful one and O'Leary and I went to meet a Harbour Master who was called by the good old Northern name of William. After bringing us down to the lighthouse he came back up to our room at the Cafe to have a couple of shots of whiskey.

'Although this is Dublin whiskey,' I told him, 'it is Protestant whiskey; it's Jameson's.'

'I don't give a fish's tit whether it is Mohammedan whiskey,' he said, so we opened two more of the bottles we'd carried across the border and after a bite to eat, we opened two more, so not a deal of work was done that day.

In the evening I left my friend O'Leary with William for I was still young enough to be interested in female society and was not sufficiently alcoholic at the time for it to make any difference. I changed my clothes, put on a tie and had a shave in readiness.

Round the North of Ireland they are very fond of holding what they call 'Beach Meetings', so I went to one where I noticed a girl who was wearing a C.E. badge—the initials for Christian Endeavour. Yes, said I in my own mind, I am going to do some Christian Endeavouring with you.

I looked up at the preacher and turned to the girl. 'You know,' I said, 'that man has many cogent and logical arguments.' In actual fact all the silly bastard was doing was shouting the odds about the Pope. But in matters of prick, there can be no principle.

'You're R.C.,' she said.

'Arsey,' I replied.

'I beg your pardon?'

'Yes, sure. I am a Roman Catholic but this man is seriously affecting my views on religion.' And he was shouting out: 'The Vatican spreads its tentacles all round the world!' and in a form of lunacy known only in Northern Ireland, he continued: 'There is an alliance between the Pope in the Vatican in Rome and Stalin in the Kremlin in Moscow!'

'Don't leave out Maurice Chevalier in the Place de Vendôme,' I shouted.

'Quite right, sir,' he answered, not knowing what I had said.

After the meeting, the girl decided that I was a brand to be plucked from the burning and she agreed to go for a walk with me. If I said I seduced her, I would be telling an absolute lie but I would have liked to. After all I would be only striking a blow against heresy. Unfortunately I had nothing against this little heretic although I would certainly have liked to have had!

'I can always tell a Fenian,' she said. (Fenian is the Northern expression for a Roman Catholic, dating from the Irish Republican organisation of a hundred years ago, but they have long memories up there).

'How?' I asked.

'By their wee button noses.'

Now religious prejudices are not usually logical, but if you could see my nose you would see how utterly and absolutely illogical this statement was. By the same token she was nearly fit to be in the Ku-Klux-Klan or the Catholic League of Decency—fair field and no favour.

However, I undertook to meet her the next day after work for to go for a swim. I'd really no hope of even getting a good look at her heretical little person, but I wanted to see what kind of swimming togs she wore. I presumed it would be a double-skirted kilt.

In the morning O'Leary and I started work on the lighthouse and I had to re-write the lettering on the board: 'Permission to view this lighthouse must be obtained from the Secretary, Commissioners for Irish Lights, Westmorland Street, Dublin.'

Although I had done a small amount of lettering, I must be one of the worst signwriters in the world. And I don't think any signwriters in Ireland are very good but their housepainters are the best in the world.

Only a portion of the old sign showed through the fresh paint, but enough to let Miss Mackenzie, the miserable ould strap on the bus, know that an Ulster lighthouse had some connection with the rebels. She was amongst a crowd of holiday-makers out for an after-breakfast stroll, and she breathed fury as I rewrote the sign on a surface previously coated with raw linseed oil: 'Permission to view this lighthouse must be obtained from Eamon de Valera, Leinster House, Dublin.'

I thought Miss Mackenzie would explode. She fulminated in the crowd but the people that go to Donaghadee in the summer have a deal to bother them, fishing young Sammy out of the harbour and trying to save wee Bella from death by ice-creamitis. They gazed with mild interest after her as she dashed up to the Harbour Office. By the time she got back, of course, I had the board rubbed dry and the official legend rewritten. She put her hand to her head and searched, distracted, for the offending words, nearly having a heart attack into the bargain. It was all the one to me. If anybody gets a heart attack over political matters of this sort above the age of twenty-five, they deserve to have one, in my opinion.

William looked at her and then at me and muttered something about the heat and ould ones going round in their bare heads. With innocent diligence I went on with my work.

There was an old age pensioner and his wife down from Belfast on a holiday on what little savings they had, which I don't think can have been very much. After they had read the notice, they explained to me that by the time they had written to Dublin to get permission to view the lighthouse their holiday would be over.

'It's a pity,' the old man said, 'because I have never seen over one and I would really like to.'

Heartened by the experience of the early morning, I decided to push my luck. 'Come right in,' says I. 'It's all yours. Be my guest.'

And I showed them both round and told them a bundle of lies about how everything worked because I had never been in a lighthouse before in my life. At the end of the tour I gave them both a slug of whiskey and they were well pleased because your man said it was a long time since they'd seen the drop.

'Irish Republican Whiskey,' I said.

Your man looks round nervously. 'I'm an Orangeman,' he says, 'but who's to know?'

On the eleventh of July, I was tactfully requested to refrain from servile toil the following day, the anniversary of William III's Protestant victory over James II's mixed Irish and French Catholic army at the Battle of the Boyne in 1690.

I put up with this check on my industry as best I could but only after I had persuaded William, the Harbour Master, that eleven and a half hours pay—which is what O'Leary and myself were getting each day—was in order for inhabitants of the Free State who did not recognise the Twelfth of July as a Bank Holiday.

In fact, so well did my morale stand up to the enforced idleness that I was in singing order amongst a pubful of Orangemen that night. When called upon for a song, I was lit out of school, and as cute as a Christian, discretion being the better part of valour, I chose *The Dear Little Town in the Old County Down*. Though the company were decent Protestant fishermen, you never know what half-fool is lying in the background waiting to make a name for himself by crowning the stranger with a porter bottle—you get them everywhere. However, though it's me says it that shouldn't, the song went down like a dinner.

We went down like a dinner for another reason as well, though O'Leary could nearly be wearing a plaque round his neck he was so anxious to be telling everyone he was a Protestant: we flogged the fishermen gallons of paint for the price of a pint and a chat up at Anderson's snug.

Later in the evening, I was in the hotel bar. Myself and the French chef stood chatting with Anna, the barmaid. Myself and the French chef were not that gone on each other for the simple reason that Anna was nineteen and I was twenty-five and the chef nearly went mad when I pointed out he was born the same year as I. He said I was born at the beginning of twenty-three and he at the end of it. Three more days and he'd have been born in twenty-four. Now I could hardly be responsible for the chef being born on the twenty-ninth of December. The arrangements were none of mine.

The coxwain of the lifeboat came in and told us to take it easy and not to be making a show of ourselves in front of Anna. He was a great little man who won the George Cross for his efforts to rescue people from the *Princess Victoria* which sunk in the few miles of the Irish sea between England and Ireland: a great example of British and Irish seamanship. We are constantly sneering at the Greeks and the Italians, but this ship was lost on a trip of twelve miles with never a man, woman nor child saved, although all the crew were rescued.

Although I think the coxswain rather liked me, I think he had it up a bit for O'Leary who spoke in a flat Dublin accent the same as my own but was constantly telling everyone he was a member of the Church of Ireland. I think the coxwain was a little suspicious of him and didn't appreciate him very much. He understood me however because I did not conceal the fact that I was a Catholic fanatic and a daily Communicant and I went to Confession every week—in my sweet imagination.

'Are you going to stop here in Donaghadee all day long tomorrow, Brendan?' he asked.

'Yes, sure. I'll go for a swim or something.'

'But there won't be anyone here. We march out to Millisle for to celebrate the Twelfth. Why don't you join us?'

'It's all right for O'Leary,' I said, 'but I might feel a little embarrassed and who's to know but that some of the boys might get a little jarred and look around for someone to lynch?'

'That's ridiculous,' said the coxswain. 'Everybody knows you're all right and the boys often do a deal with you for a drop of paint and they will all be there. You can travel out with us in the bus and see the whole affair from the back window. Unless of course you have any objections on religious grounds?'

'Not at all,' I assured him. 'I would watch anything if there was any beer on the job.'

'There'll be plenty of that. It is not a dry hooley. There are temperance Freemason Lodges of the Orange Order, but ours is not one of them.'

The following morning we went out on the bus halfway to Millisle where the boys got out and marched the rest of the way with their Lodge, under the banner of William crossing

173

the Boyne on his white horse. It is said that William was never born and his horse was never foaled: they were both obtained by Caesarean operation. How the fugh anyone would know is a mystery but that is the kind of shit one hears about these historical figures.

I decided that I might as well be into bed without a barracks— I decided I might as well hear the proceedings—so when the bus got to Millisle I got out. Now I always enjoy any kind of religious or political screwiness, and when it is directed against myself I find it extremely entertaining. The next thing I knew I was pushed right up to the front, next door to the speaker, a very prominent Northern Ireland Unionist Orange Member of Parliament. I suppose the boys thought that if they put Brendan up in the front where he can hear it all, there would be hopes of converting the heathen.

'Would you hold my hat, son?' said the prominent Northern Ireland Unionist Orange Member of Parliament as he rose to take his place up on the platform.

I just nodded because I did not want him to hear my accent.

'Brethren and sisters,' he began and up like a shot with him, he launched into a bitter attack on the Dublin government and how sorry he was to say that the Control of Employment Act in Northern Ireland had not kept out a vast number of Fenians. 'There are Dublin scum in our midst,' he said. I clapped along with everybody else. 'They shall be driven out.'

'Hear, hear,' I echoed with the masses.

Finally, frothing at the mouth in a professional fashion, he revealed the joint conspiracy of the Kremlin and the Vatican.

'I gave it to them, there, didn't I?' he said as he returned to his seat.

'You certainly did, sir,' says I.

And I thought he would pass out in a weakness. 'Jesus, where are you from?'

'I'm from Dublin, sir.'

'Ah, of course, you're one of the Dublin Brethren?'

'I'm a brother of all men,'I said.

'You mean you're an Orangeman?'

'No,' says I, 'I'm an ex-I.R.A. man.'

'And a Catholic?' He hissed the words as though he was not able for them.

174

'A great number of people in Dublin are in serious doubt as to what I am, sir, but from your point of view I am a Catholic and my father and mother before me. Nobody belonging to me was ever anything else, but I won't say they were very good Catholics. The only thing I will say, however, is that none of them were ever fughing Protestants. And furthermore I'll tell you one thing and that's not two: you are sure to be elected at the next election. I cannot see the people in the North acquiring any more sense than the people in the South, and there are enough suckers here to put you in.' He put up his hand to interrupt me but I was not done yet. 'I notice you didn't say anything about unemployment in the North,' and I looked straight into his face for I was full of Dutch courage, or Gaelic courage, from the flask of whiskey in my pocket.

The Minister looked a bit surprised but not angry and I didn't care now. 'The part I really enjoy in all the speeches of Orangeman and extreme Protestant Ministers is the pronouncement of a joint conspiracy between the Vatican and the Kremlin. I will tell you this much,' I continued. 'That is, if you went out into the world—and there is a world outside of Northern and Southern Ireland—and you stood up on the platform and told your audience this in Paris, London, Rome or New York or in any of the main capitals, you would have them rolling in the aisles. I think this is a wonderful angle. The native Protestant Irishman is the only person on the face of the earth who is intelligent enough to see the fughing menace of Stalin and Pope Pius XII.'

That lovely summer's day I'll remember too for the singing of an old man from Millisle. *The Bright Silvery Light of the Moon* and *The Yellow Rose of Texas* he sang, and disappointed me because he didn't sing something more Orange. We had a great day of singing and drinking and eating and though I did feel a bit shamed by my slanging of the unionist Member of Parliament and by the bright sunshine when we came out blinking into it at closing-time, it wasn't long before we got indoors again. There were some that did not go to bed at all that night. A few devoted revellers had made a night of it. They stood wearily on the corner and an ould one asked me what time it was. I told him.

'Thanks be, it's over for another wee while,' he said. 'I'm beat out.'

I wasn't so favourable to it myself when I'd to get out of bed in the morning but I was soon swimming around the harbour like a two-year-old with Anna and my little Protestant heretic swimming it out beside me. And if I says it myself that shouldn't, at that time I was a pretty good swimmer. Alas, nowadays I don't seem to be pretty good for doing anything else except swimming in malt liquor.

'Tomorrow,' I said to William who had come to the harbour to have a look at me, 'there's another feast, le Quatorze Juillet.'

'Is it a Fenian do?' asked old William.

'It's the greatest Republican feast of the year,' said I. 'The Fourteenth of July and you had better come down to the hotel with O'Leary and myself in the evening.'

'It'll kill me,' he pleaded.

'Well, we celebrated yours,' said I.

' 'Deed yous did,' said old William resignedly, 'and fair is fair.'

It was a great day and my rounding it off in the hotel by singing any songs about France that backed my own side. Everyone joined in, for as I said, apart from the hatchet-faced ould strap on the bus, I never encountered opposition from the North. Didn't my own family find refuge in Belfast after 1916? It was like this.

My mother had two husbands, not at the one time, of course. She married the first a little time before Easter week, 1916 and spent her honeymoon carrying messages for her husband, brother, brothers-in-law and generally running round with my aunts and her sisters in misfortune, shifting one another's dumps and minding one another's babies for a long time afterwards.

The peaceful Quaker man that founded the business would be very surprised that, with the Post Office, where Uncle Joe was, and Marrowbone Lane, where Uncle Mick was, his biscuit factory was, to my childhood, a blazing defiance of mausers, uncles and my step-brother's father against

> . . . . odds of ten to one,
> And through our lines they could not pass,
> For all their heavy guns.

176

They'd cannon and they'd cavalry,
Machine-guns in galore,
Still, it wasn't our fault that e'er a one,
Got back to England's shore . . . .

Give over, before I hit a polisman!

Belfast figures as the refuge in cosy remoteness and peace,
after the battle had ended and the hunt left behind, because
it was there my mother had her first home and her husband
had his first job after the Rising. It was there that she began her
married life and after the guns and the bombs and the executions
began a stock of more homely domestic anecdotes, like the
time she tried him with a curried stew and he ran to the tap
after tasting it, wondering why she was trying to poison him.

They weren't the only refugees either. A former Captain of
the Guard at Leinster House is remembered with indignation
for coming in amongst the twenty or thirty people assembled
in close formation for the Sunday night *scoráiocht,* and remarking through the haze of Irish tobacco smoke that the place
was like an oven.

And after Rory, my step-brother, was christened Roger
Casement in the church, my uncle Peadar, the same that wrote
the Irish National Anthem and a sort of walking battery of
Fenianism, held him in his arms on Cave Hill, and with the
baby's father acting as sponsor swore him into the Irish Republican Brotherhood.

The little house in the Mount became a clearing house for
the Dublin crowd to and from Liverpool and Glasgow. And
to this day my mother remembers the kindness of the neighbours. Their great interest was the baby Fenian, though being
polite and respectable they never referred to his politics, nor
to the comings and goings and up-country accents of the young
men visiting the house at all hours of the day and night. There
might be a satisfied remark about the larruping the Germans
were getting on the Somme, but when the Peelers came nosing
round the quarter it was the widow of a Worshipful Master came
up with the wind of the word.

'There were polis round here this morning, ma'm, enquiring
about some people might be hiding from the military in Dublin.
Rebels, if you please, round here. Sure, as we all said, it's an

insult to a loyal street to think the like. Rebels, Sinn Feiners, hiding round here. And how's our wee man the day? Did you do what I said about the . . .'

My first visit to the North, or for the matter of that to any part of Ireland outside Dublin, took me to Newry, with a train-load of Soccer players, accordionists, corkscrew operatives, the entire production under the masterly direction of my Uncle Ritchie. He was a non-military uncle, and indeed had been accused of only remembering the significance of Easter Monday, 1916, by reference to a gold watch, his possession of which dated from that day.

Another souvenir of the six days was a pair of fur-lined boots, which were worn out by my time, though they still hung in their old age under the picture of Robert Emmet and 'Greeting for Christmas and a Prosperous 1912' card from 'Dan Lehan, the Patriotic Sand Dancer and Irish National Coon. Performed the Soft Shoe before the Crowned Heads of Europe, also Annual Concerts, Mountjoy, and the Deaf and Dumb Institution.'

When Uncle Ritchie had a sup up, he'd fondle the old fur boots and looking from Robert Emmet to the Irish National Coon he would remark 'By God, there was men in Ireland them times.'

When the other Jacobs and G.P.O. uncles were hard at it remembering the sudden death of a comrade, Uncle Ritchie shook his head with the rest. 'When you think of what they did to poor Brian. Poor pig. Cut the two legs of the man. Them Danes.'

Gritting his teeth and controlling his temper, he would look round the room and a good job for the Danes that there weren't any of them knocking around our way. He wasn't really my uncle at all, but a far-out relative of another bunch of our family from around north-east Dublin. Mostly he didn't bother much about the cause of old Ireland or any of that carry on. When he was bent in thought, it wasn't the declining Gaeltacht was knotting his brow, nor the lost green field, but we respected it just the same. He sat in a corner and looked the same way as our uncles remembering the time they met John Devoy, or killed one another during the Civil War. But we knew that this deep cogitation meant that Uncle Ritchie was thinking up a stroke.

His final stroke brought me to Newry. He hired an excursion train for a deposit of thirty shillings and our team went up to play a team representing the Ancient Order of Hibernians.

In consideration of his putting up a set of solid silver medals for the contest, Uncle Ritchie's nominee was allowed to take half the gate, and he collected the ticket money from the people on the understanding that he would bring it to the G.N.R. on Monday morning and receive a small percentage for his trouble.

The whole street saved up for a while and the train was packed with old ones, young ones, singers and dancers on the way up.

Uncle Ritchie got the team in a corner and swore that by this and that they had to win those medals and seemed very serious about it. Someone asked who were the Ancient Order of Hibernians and was told they were a crowd that carried pikes, and someone else said they'd lodge an objection that you wouldn't see the like of this day nor next.

The Ancient Order of Hibernians had no pikes, but before half-time they could have done with them. They were all over our crowd in everything except dirt. The double tap, the hack, the trip, the one-two and every manner of lowness, but to no avail. The Ancient Order of Hibernians won two-nil.

Uncle Ritchie had to hand over the set of medals and though he wasn't a mean man, you could see he felt it. He muttered to get us down to the station quickly and lock the carriage doors. He wouldn't be long after us.

Neither he wasn't, as the man said. But came running down towards us with half the town after him, and they shouting and cursing about the medals. Someone said they weren't bad medals considering they were made out of the tops of milk bottles.

The crowd were in full cry after Uncle Ritchie, but gaining little. We shouted encouragement to him, 'Come on, Uncle Ritchie, come on, ye boy, ye,' till at last he fell against the gate of the Residency and we hauled him in the carriage in the nick of time from the berserk natives. Carrie Swaine, a Plymouth Sister from Ballybough in the south, called out in triumph, 'Go 'long, yous Orange beasts,' which for some reason drove the Ancient Order of Hibernians Amateur Football Club to a very dervish dance of fury.

Past Clontarf Station, Carrie smelt the Sloblands, and from excess of emotion shouting, 'Law-villy Dublin', put her head through the window without taking the trouble to lower it and nearly decapitated herself.

Uncle Ritchie gave a big night in the club and was seen off by the whole street to the Liverpool boat. He expressed no bitterness against the town of Newry or its inhabitants except to remark that the medals were waterproof. I don't know what he told the railway company.

Howsomeever, as the man said, all good things must come to an end and having stretched the Irish Lights assignment to include worthy celebrations of Orangemen and doctrinaire republicans, O'Leary and I returned to Dublin.

WHEN we arrived in Dublin, O'Leary found he still had enough of the readies for to visit his clergyman son in England, and I had enough, and more beside, for to get me to Paris. We made the trip together as far as London, where we parted wishing each other good luck, beyond the shadow of a doubt, and all to that effect.

Once in Paris I got on a number ninety-five bus in the Avenue de l'Opera for St-Germain des-Prés and in like a shot with me to the Studio Bar. I was not disappointed. George, my Hungarian friend, was still there, sitting with two other fellows that I did not know. Donal, the smaller man with a mass of fair hair rising straight up from his head, was working for an American-owned magazine called *Points* while Desmond was the Paris correspondent of the Irish Times, which is not only the smallest of the Irish newspapers but the best. And he seemed to be on quite a good deal, for the French thought the Irish Times must be as influential as the London Times apparently and Desmond was invited to nearly all the diplomatic receptions.

After I had agreed to write pornography in English for French magazines and poems in Irish and stories in English for the American magazine, *Points*, we settled down to more serious business. With the drop of *pastis* in my hand and the noise of clanging pots and pans in my ear, I fell to wondering whether I was no longer able for it, when Desmond said he heard them too. It was the band of the Ecole des Beaux Arts or School of Fine Arts in Paris.

In the popular imagination, the Beaux Arts School is a sort of *Tir na nOg* (land of my youth) of young geniuses, painting and sculpting with fresh, savage efficiency during the working day, cursing the professors, damning all academies, till the light fades, the stars rise over the garret and Mimi, the little midinette, knocks timidly on the door and comes in with the

181

bottle of wine, the piece of veal, the garlic, the bread and cheese purchased, mayhap, with the fruits of her long day's stitching for the rude and haughty ladies of the Rue de Faubourg St. Honoré.

And apparently, I said in my own mind, they have a band.

During the summer nights, Desmond said, they have a march-out, at least every Saturday night, up and round the narrow streets of the Latin Quarter, playing in close harmony, on buckets, tin cans, biscuit tins, old motor horns, acutioneers' hand bells, basins, bowls, with a male and female voice choir, in sections variously represented: the howl, the screech, the moan, the groan, the roar, the bawl, the yell, the scream, the snarl, the bay, the bark, in time to the steady and rhythmic thud of the big brass dust bin, and the more sombre tones of the tin bath.

Along the street, the foreigners smiled and nodded indulgently at each other. Dear old Paris. Dear old Latin Quarter. Has never changed since Gene Kelly's feet were hot, since the last time we were over. We wondered at the sour looks on the faces of the French, and the disgruntled voice of the big vegetable porter who cursed the noise and said people had to be up at five in the morning to go to work. Don't worry about work I said in my own mind. Those lads outside aren't worried about work. Free spirits. I ordered another cognac and *le patron* handed it to us in man-sized glasses.

Outside they were advancing on St-Germain.

I turned to Desmond and, amidst the satisfied sighs of the foreigners in the place, shook my head indulgently and remarked apropos the vegetable porter and other native grumblers: 'Woe to the begrudgers. Aren't they gas men, the art students? *Is maith an rud an óige.*'

'They manage an imitation of it,' said a voice beside me.

I turned and saw that a girl had come in and was standing beside us.

'What does who manage an imitation of?' I asked.

'You said in Irish that youth is a great thing. You were obviously referring to those dreary architects making a nuisance of themselves up the street.'

'What architects? Anyway how did you know what I said in Irish?'

'I suppose I went to school as much as you did.'

'That'd be small trouble to you. But what architects are you talking about?'

'Those fellows going around the place, doing the hard chaw, keeping everybody awake. You, like all the tourists . . .'

I choked with indignation and Desmond, Donal and George gazed at her with disgust. The foul word that had just left her lips stamped her. in all our eyes, as a cad or a caddess. It's not a word used in polite society along the boulevards, unless you are speaking of somebody else, of course.

She went on relentlessly. 'You people think it's all very romantic, but those little architectural students, as soon as they qualify, buy a nice suit, grow a moustache, and refer to this period as the time they were sowing their wild oats. I wouldn't mind that, but I've got to get up and go over to Neuilly and be at the church of Saint Pierre in the morning to do some work.' And she held up what looked like a kit of tools belonging to a bricklayer.

Kathleen Murphy said good-night to us and went off up the Rue Dauphine, a trim slip of a girl, as they say at home, but swinging her hammers and chisels with an air.

The Church of Saint Pierre is the parish church of Neuilly in south-west Paris. It is about the size of the Dublin Protestant Cathedral and is nearly a hundred years old, no older than the University Church on Dublin's Green, and as beautiful, in a different style. The parish priest of Saint Pierre had about enough money to keep the church in repair, to pay a couple of charwomen, and a verger. He had nothing over for ornamenta tion of the lovely stone that practically shouted for a chisel.

God's help, they say in Irish, is never further than the door; in this case the door of the Ecole des Beaux Arts. Someone in the school heard of all this lovely stone going unadorned, and the next thing a squad of students are out, fighting to divide the church up amongst themselves. Kathleen Murphy comes away with three pillars, and with hammer upraised poises her slim self to strike a blow, *do chum ghlóire Dé agus onóra na hEireann.*

These pillars represent, in their tortuous Celtic way, the struggle of Christian France against the Huns, the Creation and the Deluge. Standing there one morning in the quiet of the

183

Avenue de Roule, in the Church of Saint Pierre, the noise of the traffic round the Etoile and on the Champs Elysées dim in the distance, I noted lovingly the twisted features of each cantankerous countenance, thought of Raphoe, Cashel and Clonmacnoise, and heard the waves of the Atlantic break on the Aran shore, and the praising voice of the holy Irish, long since dead, soft in the gathering bustle of the day. And I blessed the chance introduction to Kathleen Murphy in the Studio Bar.

Soon I was earning an existence—if it ever can be so called—by writing pornography and by supplementing with one or two of my poems and stories which were published in the American-owned *Points*. Anyway, I had sufficient enough to enable me to frequent many of the bars in the Latin Quarter and for them to recognise me too. Also, I naturally gravitated, as all *clochards* do, to the markets.

On this morning, I was in a market bistro called *Le Nouveau Siècle*. These enormous glass-roofed enclosures, built by Baron Haussmann when he redesigned the city in the last century, are known as *Les Halles* in French. And I was drinking a demi of beer, having not eaten for about forty-eight hours, and I was over it for about two hours. Even if I had the fare I didn't wish to return to Ireland, because I happen to regard Ireland in the same way as Séan O'Casey. It is a great country to get a letter from.

For the want of another beer and the price of a chat, I engaged the barman in conversation, And sure enough, God's help is never further than the door, for didn't this girl come up and introduce herself?

'I'm Jenny Etoile,' she said, which means 'Eugenie's star,' but really meant that she had formerly been operating up round the Etoile, which is all the streets leading off the Arc de Triomphe at the top of the Champs Elysées. 'I heard you speaking to the barman and I think you're English.'

'I'm not,' I said. 'I'm Irish.'

'Well, you were speaking English. Can you speak American?'

'Sure,' said I. 'They're much the same language.'

'Would you like to work for us?' Would ducks like to swim I said in my own mind, but to her: 'Who's us?'

'Myself and Monsieur Tony, the chef.'

The following day, at *Le Nouveau Siècle*, I met Tony, the

184

trés bien maquereau (the pimp) and after wining and dining me ·
I was duly appointed the *sous-maquereau*. And I was taken to the
Trois Quartiers and introduced to seven or eight girls—manna
from heaven—and fitted out with several suits of clothes,
shirts, shoes and ties. I hadn't felt so well in ages and all I had
to do was to go to Harry's New York Bar and pick up a little
trade for the community. It was owned by a Breton, a celt
like myself, but the four barmen were Irish-American, because
most of the clientele were American. I would contract my
business from the corner of the bar by the telephone.

Jesus, Mary and Joseph, I have never seen anybody slower
than the Yank. If he was let loose in a convent he couldn't get
a woman. I would be sitting up at the bar and these middle-
aged Americans (alas, that I could be adjudged middle-aged
myself now) would come across and ask the barman what had
happened to all the girls they'd heard about in gay Paree?

'That's O.K. friend,' I would say, 'I'll fix you up,' and I
would go to the telephone and contact either Jenny Etoile or
Monsieur Tony and the girl, like a shot with her, would be outside Harry's New York Bar in a taxi before we'd had the first
drink.

'That the giving hand may never falter,' I would say, as the
Americans peeled off a few dollar notes for my trouble, and I
entertain the astonished company with songs about my native
land. Rich in liquor, my voice carried round the room.

'Paris is full of them,' someone remarked.

'He's Irish,' another said, 'and there was never any shortage
of them.'

Practically every night an extremely fat man would come
into the Bar with his mother, but not for the want of hearing a
stave, as I discovered. I always thought of them as inseparable,
for to tell the honest truth I had never seen them apart. Until
this day when the fat man asks me if I would get him a girl; his
mother had left his side for the few minutes it takes to attend
to the call of nature.

'Sure,' I said, 'but it will cost you a bit extra; weight for age
and all that. Beside, the girl that's going to have you has a
kind of proposition on top of her.'

It was all the one to him, he said, but what was he to tell his
mother?

185

'Tell her you're going to midnight Mass and it is a Mass only available to men; it's a men's sodality.'

So, in a matter of minutes, but before the old one had come back, the prostitute gets out of the taxi and comes into the bar looking for her client.

'There's a midnight Mass in Notre Dame,' I shouted for everyone to hear me, giving the prostitute the wink as I did so. As he left, the fat man slipped me ten dollars. Sipping the *pastis*—a bird never flew on the one wing—I was able to explain to his mother the fundamental principles of men's sodalities and the custom of some Orders in France of dressing their nuns in plain clothes.

During the course of my activities in Harry's New York Bar, there was an American who sat by me by the hour and he sat in silence. For Jaysus sake, it would put years on you, and I got to the point of asking him if he wanted a girl.

'You know,' he said seriously, 'there are some people who don't like girls.'

'I haven't met many, but is it a boy you're after?'

He looked aghast. 'Look buddy,' I said, 'this is Europe, not East Jesus, Kansas.'

Eventually he agreed that he would like a boy and I was after fixing it up with Monsieur Tony, being more in the men's department, when the question of colour arose. There was a coloured boy who met all the required specifications, for my American friend would not be fobbed off with common bowsies or the likes of them.

'Did you want a white boy or a black boy?' I asked.

'How dare you insult me,' he remarked. 'I will have nothing to do with a black,' and I remarked, in passing, that if he had any future need of his gizzard and didn't want to be at the loss of it, it would be as well if he kept his own company.

A man sitting at the table rose and shook hands with me. It was another Irishman who had been in Paris since 1930 for the simple and sufficient reason that he had remained in Ireland, he would have had to pass a few years in Glencree Reform School. During the war he dealt in scrap iron which made him a target for the F.F.I., because it was a strictly collaborationist activity in that it assisted the German war effort. In actual fact, he was only collaborating with himself and on several occasions sheltered fellows on the run from the Gestapo and the French militia.

Afterwards when he heard the F.F.I. were looking for him, he went into hiding because he thought he would be shot for his scrap iron activities. However, instead of six ounces of lead, he got the Croix de la Liberation for sheltering men from the 'dirty Boche.'

For many months I worked in Harry's New York Bar, until this day the Breton manager tells me he has observed my activities and this is not a bordel or a maison tolerée and all to that effect and I must go. So go I had to and go I went.

However, before leaving each of the barmen insisted upon buying me a drink.

In 1959, my play *The Hostage* represented Great Britain at the Theatre des Nations and as I was quite a big shot at the Festival, I was given a car by the French Government and also a guide. The guide was an old friend of mine, but not from today nor yesterday, but of eleven years previously, and anxious to get in a bit of tee-hee before he'd ask me how I was ever since, I shot forward to tell him how happy I was to be shown round Paris, being a stranger in these parts and unversed in the language, and conversing with fluent sleeveenery we piled into the car.

My guide was well equal to the ploy, and the hazardous business over and my just getting down to my second wind, when Jesus, Mary and Joseph, didn't I notice the tricolour flag on one side of the car and the Union Jack on the other?

'In the name of the Blessed Virgin Mary, would you mind telling me the meaning of the Union Jack? Why have we got this disgusting rag on the car?'

'Your play is representing Great Britain.'

In terror at what he might be saying when we first met in front of the dignitaries, my blood had gone cold at the sight of the guide and I had forgotten the reason for my visit. Now it was beginning to flow red, white and blue.

'I'd forgotten that,' I said. 'Stick up another Union Jack and I might get a bit more trade.'

Flaunting my glory before the world, we drove round the

Latin Quarter and into the Pergola restuarant where the still large and affable proprietor welcomed me warmly, bidding me farewell even more warmly when I left several hours later, having entertained his customers with Pernod and many verses of the 'Internationale', sung in English.

Alas, it was the *pastis* and the Marseillaise in the Theatre Club that destroyed us.

The next day, my guide remained in his room, the heavy curtains drawn to keep out the bright light of the Spring day. I was to go to the reception at a famous American bar with a guide from the French Ministry of Culture, he told me.

'Oh, good Jaysus,' I moaned. 'Harry's New York Bar. I never have an hour's luck.'

As we started out on our stately drive, flags fluttering in the April Paris air, I kept telling myself that this was ten years later and more, and probably the staff had all changed. We stopped for a while at a place off the Avenue de l'Opéra, with Desmond in mind, for I knew he was still often in the place, but the few shots of absinthe would taste none the worse in his absence. My man from the Ministry of Culture was getting restless. Like an early Christian martyr with legs of lead, I walked into Harry's New York Bar.

The same Breton manager who had expelled me for my pimping activities came forward to 'welcome Mr. Behan,' and the same staff echoed, 'Hiya, Brendan.'

And my guide, astonished, 'You know Mr. Behan?'

'Sure we know him,' said the Breton manager. 'He used to work over there, in the corner by the telephone.'

The Ministry of Culture enquired when my treatise on Harry's past would be published, but the answer was lost in the clinking of glasses.

IT SEEMED a century standing there shouting: 'For the love of Jaysus, will you ever open the door,' before my father came down the stairs and opened it.

'You're not coming in here in the middle of the night upsetting your mother,' he said. I pushed past him. 'You jackeen from the North City slums,' which is an expression I am extremely fond of and often use about myself. My father said nothing but went on up the stairs and I followed him up.

Nor did I tell him how I had occupied my time in Paris and the reason for the suddeness of my home-coming. I was grateful for his silence as I banged out the door of my bedroom.

I was up early in the morning and went downstairs to the kitchen to say good-morning to the oul' one. She was in the kitchen, standing over the stove.

'Ah, there you are, Brendan,' she said in her easy, gentle way. 'The Da said you were home. You're just in time for your breakfast.'

'I don't want any, thanks,' and I was surly with it too.

'You don't want any? Sure, it's ready and the tea is wet and all.'

'I'm in a hurry out,' said I, in a sulky tone so she would know there was something up.

'It's not out to work so soon you're going?'

I went out of the kitchen for the smell of food was making me sick, and I could not eat anything till I'd got a few drinks into me. That was really why I did not stay for breakfast, though I was hoping to get a bit of consideration for my wounded pride at my cold reception at the same time.

I hurried down to the Markets for a drink.

'Ara, Dia dhuit,' says Michael to me. A nice old skin, though I'd sooner heathens than publicans. 'God Bless you.'

'God and Mary and Patrick, Bríd and Columcille to yourself, Michael, and to every decent person in your house.'

189

Cathal Goulding, Gabriel MacCarthy and the crowd lined up at the bar and, sitting in a row along the wall, all intoned the responses. 'Amen, amen,' answered the porter sharks, whiskey kings, wine lords and cider barons. And Michael, the publican added, 'Amen, O Lord God,' for he was a genuine religious man and one of the few religious men that was not a worse bastard than ordinary people.

Considerably improved in my health, several hours later Gabriel and I came out blinking into the sun, but it wasn't long before we got indoors again in Davy Byrne's. Here we met the Fixer. Now the Fixer stood about six foot tall and was a native of the North East of England and was known for the fact that he'd been a British agent during the war in Italy, though some said he was an Italian agent during the war in England. I personally think that he was an agent for himself, but Scotland Yard gave him the benefit of the doubt and freedom from all his sins, past, present and future. He was also a very good man with boats and I heard him ask Gabriel, whom he had met before, whether he would care to take a trip with him.

'We're going first to Newry in the North of Ireland, then to Rouen in France, and then back to Glasgow,' he said. And to Gabriel's remark that this was one hell of a strange way to go to Glasgow, he replied: 'I've got business to do—on the wrong side.'

My ears pricked up (though I have never seen anybody's ears prick up) for I was more in mind of becoming a smuggler than I was a house-painter.

'And what the hell could you do on a ship?' asks the Fixer.

'I could steer,' I said truthfully for I had learned the art off my family. In the winter, when there wasn't much work at house-painting, some of them used to get employment as 'hawsers.' They would take a little dinghy out of a sailing ship, take a heaving line off the ship and take the line into the shore. The line was put round the capstan and the seamen turned the capstan which brought the ship in. As a chiseler I had watched them do it many times, almost as if I was steering the ship myself.

It was agreed I should join them and after the formalities of getting a British seaman's certificate and the Fixer calling

up to my father, who was twenty feet up on the roof of a corporation house, that he was taking me away to sea and my
father shouting down to take me anywhere he liked and to
fughing drown me at sea if possible, I boarded the *Sir William*
on the Liffey.

It was eighty-six tons register with no plant for electric
lighting and had been originally owned by a man called William
Johnson from the west coast of England, who had one arm
and was always full of rum. Apparently he felt that as the King
hadn't given him a knighthood he wouldn't be troubling the
the King but he would give himself one. So he called the ship
Sir William and himself Sir William Johnson. There is something
to be said for these old English salts, for with his rations,
which consisted largely of bottles of rum, he sailed the ship
single-handed all round Land's End in Cornwall and up to
London where it was purchased by the Fixer.

We sailed with a mixed crew. Some had been on a boat before
and more hadn't. The real sailors were the Skipper, the mate,
and the Welsh fireman, Taffy. Because the Fixer believed
in the Munster School of economics, he believed in buying in
the cheapest labour market and selling in the highest, in this
case to himself, for Taffy had been on the pool of seamen which
meant that he was entitled to a salary every week, whether or
not he had a ship. But to remain on the pool he had to be
medically examined and it was discovered that he was suffering
from tuberculosis so he was sacked. As a result, the Fixer
was able to hire him for about two thirds of his normal wages
and work him about one third longer the hours he would
normally be working on board ship.

The Skipper was a very pleasant and talented man—an
engineer, a very good navigator and a good seaman anyway it
took him. He was also a radio expert and had worked in that
capacity for the BBC during the war. Unfortunately he had a
weakness for backing horses and every time we got into port
he would lose everything he had. The rest of the company were
merchant adventurers and Gabriel and myself were merchant
adventurers' labourers, so to speak. The real sailors slept
forrad, and we had accommodation aft, where villainy could
be plotted in peace.

Smithy and Jonesy came aboard wearing very natty London

suitings and Windsor knots of some dimensions. Smithy's tie was scarlet silk with aluminium leaves and Jonesy's was blue silk with gold leaves. Yes, said I in my own mind, if the Duke of Windsor invented this way of fixing a tie he had to have some way of passing the time. Both of them were shareholders in the enterprise and had come on board to see how the good work was going. I don't think either of them had ever been on a boat of any description before and, till they heard from the Fixer, thought they'd been done away with like the trams.

The sailors we left forrad, brewing their tea, darning their socks winding the dogwatch and, with infinite skill, putting little ships into bottles. The Fixer, Gabriel, Smithy, Jonesy and I retired aft to drink rum, like sailors. There would be no shortage of bottles.

We sailed up the coast to Newry on November 11th and arrangements had to be made with the Urban District Council for the shipment of a cargo of apples and a British Customs manifest to say that we'd come from a United Kingdom port and therefore would not be subject to the usual customs examination.

'When we get our cargo of apples,' said the Fixer, 'we will dump them three miles outside the coast except for a few boxes which we will need as a cover-up for the real cargo we'll be collecting from Rouen to take over to Glasgow.'

We all nodded our heads in agreement as we marched up the main street of Newry on Armistice Day, and the Fixer goes into this shop and comes out like a shot with him carrying large poppies.

'Look,' I said, 'I want to explain,' but the Fixer turns round and puts up a warning finger, saying, 'Nark it, Brendan, will you. I don't want any explanations.'

'No, we don't,' said Gabriel. 'Nor for the matter of that, any principles about wearing poppies and us going to sea to do a stroke.'

So I said nothing until we got to the hotel where we were meeting the Chairman of the Newry Urban District Council, all decorated with large poppies in the lapels of our coats.

'Listen,' I said, 'I am trying to explain to you that although this is Northern Ireland, it is the southern part of Northern Ireland and up here they don't go in for poppies.'

The Fixer, always a fair man in matters of porter, thrashed this out over whiskeys and gins and tonics at the pub opposite and it was generally agreed that we should throw our poppies into the gutter before going into the hotel. 'Only a nicker wasted,' said the Fixer.

We met the Chairman of the Urban District Council and the Fixer shook him by the hand. 'I'm very upset about what the dirty bastarding Protestants have done to you 'ere in the name of England.'

The Chairman's plumbeous face turned blue and his stomach heaved the protest. 'How dare you,' he croaked. 'The Vice-Chairman of our Council is a highly respected member of the Presbyterian community.'

His indignation collapsed for the want of breath and over a couple of drinks, gave the Fixer the chance to explain that it was a joke. We got the apples and a few days later we were out to sea on our way to France.

For the first two days, Smithy and Jonesy were as sick as dogs and when they finally emerged from lying in their death agonies, looking rather pale and shaken, they went up on deck. It was a fine morning with a nice fresh wind blowing behind us. The Skipper had left the mate up at the wheel and had come down the companionway carrying a wooden box. Smithy and Jonesey, who were feeling a bit peckish by this time as neither had eaten anything for forty-eight hours, enquired as to whether the box contained sandwiches for them.

'I'm sorry, lads,' said the Skipper. 'I've no sandwiches in this box; I've got my father.'

And it was assumed that the Skipper, who was no mean partaker of the rum and orange (I think he took a couple of subsidiary rosiners to make up for the orange) had been over-indulging himself.

'Be reasonable Skipper,' said Smithy, 'how could you put your father into a little wooden box like that?'

So the Skipper explained that his father had been cremated and that he left a wish that his ashes be cast off the coast of France, which we were now nearing, because the Skipper's mother had been a Frenchwoman. He proceeded to open the box to cast forth his father's ashes upon the waves and Jonesy stood sadly by, mainly because he never took his hat off. He wore it on the Kildare side, even in bed, for he had not a rib between him and heaven. Gabriel sang under his breath a rebel song while I hypocritically made the sign of the Cross and gabbled some of the Lord's Prayer.

But the Skipper was so overcome with emotion that he flung his father's ashes into the wind, rather than with the wind, so that they blew back at us and more down the ventilator where the Fixer was brewing his hot rum.

'What dirty bastard is throwing out clinker into the wind again?,' he shouted up.

As quick as an ass's gallop we were down to explain that it was not clinker, but the Skipper's father, and revered and respected with it too.

At the Wake a few minutes later the entire crew were drinking to the Skipper's father, and not alone were we drinking *to him* but we were drinking the father, because some of the ashes had got into the rum. However, no harm to that; they were perfectly hygienic ashes.

In the half-light of the following morning, we went ashore at Rouen and collected a cargo of more sensible goods: brandy, a small amount of wine and nylons, all of which were in short supply in England at the time.

After we had loaded up our little ship, the Fixer got a fit of nostalgia for Paris where he had spent some time as a British agent during the war. He offered to take Gabriel and myself with him and I was eager to accept.

We piled into a taxi, no less than a big Delage which, once on the main route, ate up the distance. We arrived at a place opposite the Dupont in the Boulevard St-Michel and the Fixer indicated to me a spot where a collaborator had been shot stone dead by a Resistance man, who was now a member of the Police Force.

We went to an hotel on the Left Bank in the Rue du Bac and, standing at the bar, dressed in the uniform of the *flic*, was the very man himself. The Fixer introduced me and invited him to join us for lunch.

And as the Paris police are mentioned, let me say this much about them. Some people from the island across the way, and Irish visitors from those strata of society that would eat cooked Kenyan if they thought the quality over the way were doing likewise, adversely criticise them as armed State police, as compared to the dear old village constable in Dry-retching-under-the-water. My grandmother's favourite toast was: 'Here's to the harp of old Ireland, and may it never want for a string as long as there's a gut in the peeler,' and I am not that mad about police of any sort myself, but my experience of the Paris police, on the whole, has been a pleasant one.

In a spirit quite in keeping with the democratic tradition of their country, they will reprimand the wealthy *rentier* in his Delage and the workman carrying his child on the backwheel, and as freely assist them. French or foreign, rich or poor, they are at everyone's disposal and, if your papers are right, they don't care how little else you have in your pocket; you can go home and the sleep will do you good.

Sitting in the corner of the restaurant, drinking a fruit juice or looking at it, was a girl I recognised instantly. She came towards the Fixer with outstretched arms.

'This is Jenny Etoile,' he said, and if she recognised me, as recognise me she must, the muscles of her face barely flickered and she discreetly left.

The Fixer ordered us an excellent meal of *soupe de l'oignon,* a dish of which I am extremely fond, and steak, but the slaughterer of the collaborator declined the steak on the grounds that he was a good Catholic and never ate meat on Friday. The rest of us sinners did the meal more than justice.

After the bill had been paid, We went up as far as the Mabillon, where we had a *café fine,* and then across the Place St-Sulpice, up the Rue Servandoni, over to the Jardin du Luxembourg and into the Boulevard St-Michel again for another one.

I had never seen the Fixer in such form. He was as carefree as a boy on a school treat, as indeed so was I for the matter of that, and our lungs felt the better for the use they were put to as we sang our way back to Rouen, en route for Glasgow.

On leaving the boat in the Clyde, the Fixer told myself and Gabriel that he would see us at the Celluloid Bar on the Quay in an hour's time. This cinematograph title turned out to be the *Céilidh Bar,* which the Irish spell *Céilidhe* (the gaelic word for dance). But despite the uncompromising Scottish spelling on the facia, we found the place all right.

Over pints of porter, the Fixer suggested that I paint the mast of the *Sir William*, and I readily agreed.

The following morning I climbed up the mast and the ship started rocking. Being very yellow, I didn't know how to hang onto the ladder and paint the mast from the top down, so I started from the bottom up. Given an hour, give or take one way or the other, I would have had it finished, neat and trim and Bristol fashion, but doesn't the Fixer come up from his cabin for the breath of air, just as I am steadying myself on the deck with barely a foot painted?

'Good Jesus,' he says. 'I know you're a kind of a half-hour sailor, but at least I thought you were a painter. Do you usually start from the bottom?'

'No,' I answered a bit sheepishly, 'but I was trying to ease myself up and get myself used to the height.'

'The height? On a little ship like this? I've often pissed higher.'

From this and subsequent trips, I remember every single landmark going up the River Clyde. Before approaching the mouth of the river, on the starboard side is the Island of Aran and the light of Lamb Lash, and there is Greenock and Gouroch and Paddy's Milestone—Ailsacraig rock—right in the middle of the Firth of Clyde. Alongside there is King George V dock and the coaling station, and opposite, the Singer Sewing Machine Factory, built of red brick and looking very up-to-date with a neon clock to the front of it. Then there is Jamaica Street Bridge, with the Clyde Quay on the one side and the Broomilaugh on the other.

But all good things come to an end, and many many months later in the *Céilidh Bar,* the Fixer and I parted company, remarking that Partition was strategically and financially useful.

ON MY return to Dublin, my mother indicated to me that one could be either a housepainter or a sailor in her household (a dear friend of my father, Jack Basnett, a sailor, had been drowned in the East River in America many years ago) but not a writer, embryo or otherwise.

So I went to the household of a good Republican lady which was mainly supported by the efforts of Irish speaking navvies from the West of Ireland, whom she fed mostly on bones; the bones coming from the butcher's backyard behind the house, which had been left there for the rats to clean off the meat. Hilda would collect the bones, fresh out of the rats' mouths, for she was very much up for them for the stock-pot. They were so cheap and nourishing, she said.

But it was as much as these poor unfortunate navvies could do to lean on their shovels to support them and they were anxious to complain about their diet to me, but I pretended not to understand them, although I understood them just as if they were speaking English. For the truth of the matter was that myself and Cornelius Mackie, an ex-I.R.A. man from the West of Ireland, were eating happily, like fighting-cocks, and we were given eggs beaten up in milk, sometimes with a drop of brandy, for to recover us from our supposed ill-treatment in British and Irish gaols.

Finally, one fellow gathered up enough English to question Hilda.

'Madam, 'oo soup me but no meat me?'

And Hilda had to drink a Baby Powder whiskey, for she wasn't the better of herself, and said she would get a handful of old rubbish from the butcher in the way of lights in future, and the bare bones in the stock-pot bubbled angrily at the thought of it.

On bold and venturesome days, the rats would come into

the house. It was bad enough going into the kitchen, but sitting there on Hilda's dressing-table in the bedroom it would put the heart crossways in you. I stood looking at it, in fear and trembling, but Hilda, in her easy way, would shoo the animal off. 'Go down pussy, go down,' she'd say.

With few exceptions, she scorned to use mattresses, sheets and blankets, but rather bought sofas at second-hand auction rooms. The lodger would be told to use his knife and slit open the sofa and slide into it, which is fair enough until this lodger brings a girl in with him. She didn't exactly know where to go or how to screw herself—for screwing was the operative word—into this mattress situation.

Then there was Dick, the young actor, who insisted on sheets and blankets. One night, the Culchiemachs, as we call the Irish speaking people, wished to play a game of pitch and toss, and the only way they could stop the pennies from rolling round the floor was to put down a blanket and to toss the two coins onto it.

Up like a shot with them and into Dick's room, who put his hands lovingly on his groin, for belonging to one of the two theatres in Dublin known as Sodom and Begorrah, he thought he was going to be raped.

'Oh, dear,' he wailed. 'Now you mustn't come at me like that; not in sixes and sevens.'

'Come on,' said one Irish fellow. 'Take your hands off your brains. Give over nursing it. We only want your blanket for to play the game of pitch and toss on it,' and he pulled all the bed clothes off as he spoke, leaving the poor bastard with ne'er a rib between him and heaven.

Cornelius Mackie did not go a great deal on this no bed-clothes lark, so he thoughtfully provided his own, as did myself for the matter of that. But he was in a great state of undoing in case his brother Séan should find out the manner in which he was so unaccustomed to living. But, to the best of my recollection, when the brother duly arrived up, he got into bed beside Mackie and stopped there for six months. And, as was his wont, he developed a great trade in the city of Dublin of flinging himself under the cars of foreign Ambassadors, who would usually settle out of court. Except for a few bruises and a broken ankle, caused by the intervention of a well-meaning dog, Séan didn't do too badly out of this transaction.

Also living in this house was a highly respectable woman who worked much for the church, and on occasions when we met on the stairs, she would take time off to warn me of the company in the kip.

'Everyone in the place is not as good living as you are, you know.'

And at the time I was making my living by helping to dope greyhounds. I became very well informed as to the form of dogs at any race track in England or in Ireland. Whereas house-painting is a trade and gambling a gift, it was the gift that was improving my health in these times, though I don't like racing myself, because the track racing is too dull and the coursing is too cruel. I did go coursing betimes for the screams of the hares gave me the excuse to stop in the tent drinking whiskey for to drown the noise.

I was also writing bits of poems and articles—I never saw myself as anything else but a writer—and a second play, *The Landlady*. The stories and atricles were published mainly in the *Irish Times* and the *Irish Press* but John Ryan also published some in his magazine, *Envoy*. The play I wrote in long-hand and my cousin, Seamus de Burca, typed it for me, but it was never published.

Now I cannot imagine anybody in the ripe years that I have reached writing for fun. I agree with Dr. Samuel Johnson, a very great Englishman, that the man who doesn't write for money is a blockhead. And while I am on the subject of Dr. Johnson, the great man's house is still in London, as ever was, and has survived the war, riot and civil commotion. I passed it and going by, greeted the bulky shade of the old cantanker, with a few words of Irish. He might have learned a bit up there, in the one and three-quarter centuries since his death for he always had a great smack for the language, even though he didn't know much of it.

But the old man's feeling for Ireland was no mere fascination with the time of long ago. In his old age his generous indignation could break out in massive anger for her wrongs:

'The Irish are in a most unnatural state; for we see there the minority prevailing over the majority. There is no instance, even in the ten persecutions, of such severity as that which the Protestants of Ireland have exercised against the Catholics.

Did we tell them we have conquered them, it would be above board; to punish them by confiscation and other penalties, as rebels, was monstrous injustice. King William was not their lawful sovereign; he had not been acknowledged by the *Parliament* of Ireland when they appeared in arms against him.'

Doctor Johnson had good time for us, as the County Clareman say.

Another great Englishman who favoured Catholic emancipation was Sydney Smith—a Canon of St. Paul's, no less. And he said, which is an unfortunate truth for the world, that 'The moment the very name of Ireland is mentioned, the English seem to bid adieu to common feeling, common prudence and common sense, and to act with the barbarity of tyrants and the fatuity of idiots.'

He was a Canon very much out of the ordinary, of whom George the Fourth said: 'A more profligate parson I never met.' Many a one, in that day and age, would have agreed that George the Fourth should have been a good judge of a profligate, but his friend, Dan O'Connell, described Sydney Smith as 'the ancient and amusing defender of our Faith'; Thomas Moore was his friend and his wife referred to him as 'my noble-hearted husband.' Still, the opinion of a wife is no certificate of worthiness, less than a parent's, for the wife does more than love the wayward child; she takes over the matured and finished sinner. Which is why they are not compelled by law to testify against their husbands. But Queen Victoria, who practically owned respectability, apparently went into fits of laughter at the sayings of Smith, which were repeated to her by Lord Houghton. And Dickens, a more important witness, said, ' . . . Old Lady Holland, whom I see again crying about dear Sydney Smith, behind that green screen as we last saw her together . . .'

Old Holland House, which was situated in that part of London that lies between Kensington and Hammersmith, is now a burnt-out wreck. Not that it matters very much. The old Liberal spirit was dead as a doornail long before Lloyd George made Liberalism into a thing taken on a tank to weaker people. But I am sorry for Holland House, surrounded—as its ruins are now—by the dwellings of what Gilbert Harding once described as 'chinless nonentities,' when I think of how the Holland family entertained the most relentless minds in

Europe. What wit in what heads must have been carried up that drive from a road whose present claim to fame is that it contains the headquarters of a firm of caterers, giving employment on a daily basis to thousands of pearl-divers—dish washers.

Sydney Smith was also more blessed than most Englishmen with what they imagine to be an English thing: common sense. And at a time when Napoleon could easily have turned to Ireland rather than to Egypt, he wrote about Catholic emancipation: 'To deny the Irish this justice now, in the present state of Europe, and in the summer months, just as the reason for destroying kingdoms is coming on, is little short of insanity.'

He made jokes about the Scots, though he had happy times in Edinburgh and remembered them to the end of his life. 'Palmerston,' said Sydney, 'when speaking is like a man washing his hands; the Scotch members don't know what he is doing.' (But there is little enough harm in that, any more than in my own father's story of the raffle in which the first prize was a week in Belfast and the second prize a fortnight.)

On the subject of war, he was, as the man said, fumigating with sense. He wrote to Lady Jane Grey: 'For God's sake do not drag me into another War! I am worn down with protecting and crusading and defending Europe and mankind. I am sorry for the Spaniards; I am sorry for the Greeks; I deplore the fate of the Jews; the people of the Sandwich Islands groan under the most detestable tyranny; Bagdad is oppressed; I do not like the present state of the Delta; Tibet is not comfortable! But . . . am I to fight for all these people? No war, Dear Lady Grey! No eloquence; but apathy, selfishness, common sense, arithmetic!'

He died on a Saturday evening in February, 1845, and as Hesketh Pearson writes, 'shook Lord John Russell, silenced Macaulay, caused Lady Holland to forget her ailments, stopped the pen of Dickens, reddened the eyes of Thomas Moore, and upset Lutterell's dining arrangements.'

Sydney Smith for Irishmen is the Smith of Smiths.

And for those who favour Ireland, for myself it was ever Dublin. Show me any one street in the world which can claim a Richard Brinsley Sheridan and a Séan O'Casey, both of them Protestants, incidentally.

For the matter of that, I was born at the one end of Merrion Square and Oscar Wilde was born at the other, near St. Andrew's Church where myself and my wife, Beatrice, were baptised. The Church was one of the last Catholic churches designed by Patrick Byrne, who was the architect employed by the Dublin Catholic Committee to build their churches in the days before Catholic emancipation. They were not allowed to have spires, and the Committees were, as a rule, composed of merchants who were silly born bastards anyway and cowardly, to boot, so they tried to made the churches look as much like Methodist or Baptist chapels as possible. I do not say Presbyterian because the Presbyterians gave us some of our finest fighters and the first man to die for the Irish Republic was a Presbyterian from the County Down, by the name of William Orr. For many years the slogan went, 'Remember Orr.'

Given any sort of fine weather at all, it's hard to beat Dublin. In London, you'd die in a desert of little streets, and in Paris the Luxembourg would be a few tired trees set in a patch of dry dust, while in New York the humidity would be fierce. But go through Dublin's 'Green' in the sun, and the richness of the cool grass and the riot of flowers at lunch-hour, would put work out of your head for the rest of the day. Not to mention the girl students and the typists, shaped, as the poet says, like tulips. Not that you'd want to be minding them poet fellows, a dangerous clique be the best of times.

However I could not manage anything to knock you on the head with such an unexpected belt as Valentin Iremonger's *Spring Jag:*

Spring stops me suddenly like ground
    Glass under a door, squeaking and gibbering.
I put my hand to my cheek and the tips
    Of my fingers feel blood pulsing and quivering.

A bud on a branch brushes the back
    Of my hand and I look, without moving, down.
Summer is there, screwed and fused, compressed,
    Neat as a bomb, its casing a dull brown.

From the window of a farther tree I hear
  A chirp and a twitter: I blink.
A tow-headed vamp of a finch on a branch
  Cocks a roving eye, tips me the wink.

And instantly, the whole great hot-lipped ensemble
  Of buds and birds, of clay and glass doors,
Reels in with its ragtime chorus, staggering
  The theme of the time, a jam-session's rattle and roar,

With drums of summer jittering in the background
  Dully and, deeper down and more human, the sobbing
Oboes of autumn falling across the track of the tune,
  Winter's furtive bassoon like a sea-lion snorting and bobbing.

There is something here I do not get,
  Some menace that I do not comprehend
Yet so intoxicating is the song
  I cannot follow its thought right to the end.

So up the garden path I go with Spring
  Promising sacks and robes to rig my years
And a young girl to gladden my heart in a tartan
  Scarf and freedom from my facile fears.

And in Dublin, you never get dehydrated as you do in places
further from the sea. On the hottest day there is a breeze from
the Bay there, and the mountains to look at and people lift
their eyes to the hills and work on through the heat and burden
of the day in better heart.

O'Connell Street in Dublin is said to be the widest street in
Europe. It is certainly wider than any street in London, for the
very good reason that the people who designed the streets
of Dublin were dealing with other men's property. Fortunately
for us, they could afford to be generous when the land was not
their own.

Which brings me to mind of a story about ex-President
Cosgrave, who was attacked by a Republican lady of my
acquaintance while he was addressing a meeting in O'Connell

Street. 'You murdered my brother and you have my sister in gaol. Why don't you put me in your gaol too?'

And Cosgrave, who was seldom short of an answer, leaned down from the platform to answer, 'Madam, I am not a collector of curios.'

I first noticed Nelson Pillar in O'Connell Street one day, not long ago, when I met a man, a pal of my cradle days. And worse is to come. I have been on top of the Pillar.

I came out of Henry Street, and who should I see but my old school mate, staring up at the top of the Pillar before.

'Me tearing man, Jowls. I didn't know you were out.'

'Aw, hallo, the hard. Yes, this three weeks. Wasn't bad. I was in the laundry during the winter.'

He was still examining your man on the Pillar as closely as he could from a distance of a hundred feet.

'Very interesting that. Up there.'

'Nothing got to do with us.'

'Why hasn't he got something to do with us?'

I had never suspected such loyalty in the bosom of the Jowls who sat with me, a boy, under the watchful eye of the French Sisters of Charity in the North William Gaeltacht.

'Did you ever go up and look at him?'

I started off the usual long spiel about being a Dublin man, but Jowls cut me short. 'Come on up and I'll show you. It'll give us an appetite for a couple.'

We started in, and to cut a long story short, I died seven deaths on the way up, all from shortness of breath. Jowls was in better condition, being just back to this sinful world from his place of retirement.

We got up to the top and I crawled out after him to the platform, or whatever it is called, and knelt before Nelson. I hadn't the strength to stand. Jowls looked up at the Hero of Trafalgar, sighed deeply and reached up to pat the sword—the victorious shield of England, home and beauty.

I looked up at Jowls and said humbly: 'Napoleon wasn't a bad one either.'

He came out of his reverie: 'Wha'? Do you see that?' He tapped the point of the sword. I nodded up to him.

'D'you know what I'm going to tell you? There's about a fiver's worth of scrap in that. It's not much, but not much trouble either of a dark evening to bring it down wrapped up in brown paper: they'd never miss it till the morning.'

Once down, safe in the snug, I reconsidered the proposition and decided that it would have to be a savage of a different variety to me to face going up the Pillar twice in a lifetime. But I still think the least we can do is to knock Nelson off his perch.

While I was still at Hilda's, a friend of mine from the County Clare told me a very interesting way of getting a kip for the weekend, which was to go to a Retreat run by the Jesuit Fathers at Milltown Park in Dublin. On the face of it, it was for free, but the Clergy usually expected that you would put something in the box of a more substantial sum that you would normally be paying at an hotel.

My friend was speaking from personal experience; no less. He had gone to this Retreat, and believing he was more in need of the charitable donations, not alone did he lessen the weight of the box but he left wearing a priest's overcoat in which he found, tucked in the leather-lined pockets, the price of several pints.

There was great agreeing going on in Donal's public house off Grafton Street, the night I borrowed it, and be Jaysus I would stand for no competition in the singing line for it was a smart outfit, when a slap on the back which sent my spine crossways through me, and the breath with it, softened my cough.

'Father, that was massive,' said the stranger. 'What are you having?'

Cathal and Gabriel swallowed a few times and looked at me as if they'd drop dead before giving way to the laughter and I covered up my embarrassment and, to a certain extent, my shame in the over-indulgence of bravado.

'I'll have a glass of malt.'

'You're a very jovial man for a priest. Will you give me a blessing with the glass of whiskey?'

Fugh off, you old bolloxy-faced craw-thumper, I said in my own mind but to him: 'Sure, sure I will, if you get me another one.'

At one time, before I'd got a few glasses of whiskey into me, I'd moan and groan about my past and sinful life, and quite sincerely pour myself a couple to give me the strength to get down to Mass. By the time I had recovered sufficiently to get as far as the church door, I was strong in my unbelief again and very coarse, apart from being blasphemous. It was the whiskey I was needing now.

'You're a really good priest,' continued the stranger, stoutly. 'If there were more priests like you, there would be less sinners.'

Jesus, Mary and Joseph, would he ever go away and leave me alone to enjoy the price of a chat? These are quare times. In Grafton Street, which is literally the fashionable centre of the city, the literary intelligentsia had discovered that I had been writing pornography for French magazines, in English of course, and now I was to be plagued by an animal of a different character.

'The blessings of Jesus on you,' I said to the stranger and several hours later, as we walked the Dublin streets, I confided to Cathal and Gabriel that I would be leaving for France in the morning.

Someday maybe, I'll go back to Paris,
And welcome in the dawn at Chatelet
With onion soup and rum to keep us nourished,
Till the sun comes up on St-Germain des-Prés.

I WANTED to return to France for the fact of the matter
is there is everthing to fit an Irishman in France. He can
find a good Irish excuse for getting into any political
argument there.

Paris, as the man said, *est toujours Paris*. Always her own
sweet self. The talk about local politicians and other notabili-
ties in a Paris bistro is like a breath of home to the Dubliner,
far from the scurrilities of pub conversation in his native city,
and just as intimately savage.

And the Frenchman has good time for us. I remember once,
at a party held on a little island, under the auspices of some
students from Trinity College, Dublin, I dived in from the
Pont Notre Dame. The *pompiers*, or river fire brigade, shone
searchlights from their boats. I hardly had my clothes on when
the *flics* were down, wanting to know what I thought I was
making of the place altogether, and where I was from and had I
my papers? I showed them my papers, and they saw the cover
of my passport and bothered no more. One nodded to the other
not to mind me, that I was an Irishman, and tapped the side
of his cap to indicate that I was one of the Gormans of Grange
and a foreman in the puzzle factory.

He saluted and wished me a civil good-night and they went
off, much gratified, to the strains of the Marseillaise, sung by
the choir of Trinity scholars, in the version attributed to its
distinguished alumnus, known as the 'Pope':

'Oh, the Board takes grave except.. chi .. o .. on,
Yours sincerely, Matty Fry. . . .'

I think the Paris river fishermen were under the impression
that ours was a rather premature celebraton of the Quatorze
Juillet, when there is dancing all over France. In little stone
Roman villages, high in the Alpes Maritimes, like Montmichel,
between Grasse and Cannes, which has its quota of Irish children, of families settled there, to dance in the sun for liberty.

In the villages long tables are laid out, with M. le Curé and
M. le Maire to see that a proper respect is paid to the cloth and
the tricolour sash. Man-sized glasses of *pastis* are left out to
give the proceedings a send-off in good Republican order, and
after lunch the sports begin with a seriousness about the young
men taking part in them that easily finish up in a digging match,
if it isn't the day that is in it.

In Port Royale in South Paris, in Belleville, on the other
bank where the hard chaws come from, the old ladies of the
Quarter come out to keep an eye to the capers in the street.
There is dancing in Montmartre and in Montparnasse and in
the Boulevard St-Germain, where they are always very handy
at throwing up a barricade, at which, the legend has it, a young
student from the Irish College fought in 'forty-eight.

As a doctrinaire republican, I seldom lost an opportunity
myself, in the enthusiastic days of my youth, of making pro-
paganda for the rights of man and the principles of 'eighty-nine.

I had no king, nor wanted any, and if I went looking for a
chief, I'd know where to look for him—above in Arbour Hill,
where my old man, not long out of Gormanston himself,
brought me and held me up on his shoulder to give three
cheers with the rest of the crowd on a Sunday morning.

I hope my taste in French politics may be indulged so far as
to permit me to repeat the story of Desmond Ryan, whom I
saw a deal during this trip to Paris. It is about Marshal
MacMahon who was being interviewed by the press shortly
after his installation as President of the Republic in 1873 and was
asked a question about his health.

'I do not feel well at all,' replied the old man. 'Anyone that
ever suffered from cerebral meningitis would be as well off if

they died from it. For it either kills one or leaves one a hopeless idiot. And I should know—I've had it three times.'

One of the avenues off the Etoile, at the top of the Champs Elysée, is named after him. Next but one to Avenue Mac-Mahon is the Avenue Hoche, named for the Bantry Bay general.

When Wolfe Tone founded the Society of United Irishmen in 1791, it was to the French revolutionaries that he turned for assistance to free Ireland from the tyrannies of the English. And after persuading the French to send over an Expeditionary Force under the able generalship of Hoche, didn't the English, with ever luck on their side, have the weather too and a gale of such proportion that, not alone did the flagship of General Hoche lose contact with the fleet, but the fleet itself was prevented from landing. Wolf Tone returned to France with them, a disappointed man. He records in his diary:

'The door opened and a very handsome well-made young fellow in a brown coat and nankeen pantaloons entered and said: "Vous étes le citoyen Smith?" I thought he was a Chef de Bureau and replied, "Oui, citoyen, je m'appelle Smith." He said, "Vous, vous appelez aussi, je crois, Wolfe Tone?" I replied, "Oui, citoyen, c'est mon veritable nom." "Eh, bien," he replied, "je suis le general, Hoche".'

Bad luck to the wind at Bantry, said I to myself many a time, walking down his avenue. Saint Joseph's Church is there and outside you'll see the crowd gathered on a Sunday or holiday, just like any Irish church anywhere The Ambassador and embassy crowd, Aer Lingus officials, some very correct governesses, a few nurses from the American Hospital at Neuilly, an odd artist or musician on a scholarship to the Beaux Arts or the Conservatoire, some business people and a collection of citizens whose most prized possession, next to their Irish passport, is a hard neck.

They are the gayest of the crowd and though the governesses move closer to the Ambassador as they move off, they bow their hard necks in grateful homage to the embassy staff as they move on towards the Arc de Triomphe, and the diplomats smile to each other in resignation, and the stout figure of Father O'Grady, C.P., appears at the door, to wave a benevolent hand on all and sundry, and it would be a poor sort of an

Irishman could leave Paris without a salute in his direction.

Another of the Avenues of the Etoile is named for Victor Hugo, who made a personal appeal to Queen Victoria to spare the life of Pat O'Donnell, who was hanged for shooting James Carey, the informer.

It happened in the Phoenix Park all in the month of May,
Lord Cavendish and Burke came out for to see the polo play,
James Carey gave the signal and his handkerchief he waved,
Then he gave full information against our Fenian blades.

Hugo was born very far from the elegant street named after him, in the Rue des Feuillantines, off the Rue Jacob, and not far from the Irish College, over whose walls, it is said, a student climbed in 'forty-eight to join the barricade at St-Germain. His name was MacHale.

It is for no one event in her history, no one selfish interpretation of this piece of her history or that, that we remember the fourteenth of July, Bastille Day, but for our affection for her place in our own history in bad times, and now in better.

I would pester Desmond to tell me more of her history, and of the Countess in Brittany, with whom he stayed, *en famille,* when he was thirteen and learning French. The old lady came to him one day, not long after he arrived and said she was very worried about his five o'clock tea. It seemed that she was under the impression that no English-speaking person can survive twenty-four hours without a pot of tea, which must be administered at five o'clock.

Though a supply of the raw material could be procured from Paris, or maybe even from as near as Rennes, there was nobody amongst the servants that could prepare the infusion, and to tell the truth, she didn't know much about the stuff herself. Did he think, would he be kind enough, to accept as substitute a bottle of port, a drink of which she knew some English milords were quite fond, together with a plate of sweet biscuits? The wine had not been touched from the days of her late husband, but in his time several of his friends had spoken quite tolerantly of it.

So every day at five o'clock this plucky youth of thirteen summers was sat in state in the library and served with his pint of Cockburn crusted and his biscuits. As he said himself, at first it was the sweet biscuits that appealed to him, but by degrees he was able to put up with the wine too. When I met him, he was more able for the wine than he was for the biscuits, like many another.

On one occasion, in the Hotel Louisien, he was with myself and Albert Camus and a row developed, with the result that Desmond was left with a black eye. And as luck would have it. he had to go to a diplomatic reception that day, for as Paris correspondent of the *Irish Times* he was invited to all sorts of receptions. Desmond asked me if I ever thought he could go looking like that and would I for God's sake mosey over to the druggist and get something for it.

Myself and the man in the chemist had a conversation that passed off very civil, with him telling me that he went a great smack on leeches, though with them all crammed up in the jar I wasn't out of my mind about them.

I came the far side of Desmond and put the leeches, one by one, to suck out the blood that was under his eye, but as each leech worked it dropped to the floor dead, or within the bawl of an ass of it. In a passionate temper the druggist told me they were valuable leeches and he looked lovingly over to the counter where not long since he had tendered them. He bent his head and all I could see was the rest of him shaking, gone in a kind of religion.

'How do you think they died?' he whispered, and then, nastily, 'Are you an alcoholic?' and me admitting that I was.

'Goddamnit,' he said. 'Why didn't you tell me? I've got alcoholic leeches.'

Albert Camus was a great writer. In England, Ireland and America, a great many people sound the 's' in his name, but I happen to know that he did not, for the simple, sufficient reason that he told me so.

Like myself, he was a soccer fan and agreed with myself that the best soccer to be seen is in England, which is the home of football. He suggested to me that I go over to England with himself and the proprietor of the Hotel Louisien, for Arsenal and Tottenham Hotspurs were duelling it out that Saturday. Out of perhaps mistaken loyalty to the British Crown, I did not like to mention that I would have been delighted to go, except there was an expulsion order against me.

As a chiseler, I had watched many exciting matches in Ireland and I remember well the replay of Dublin versus Galway, amidst a shower of rain as thick as the boots we wore those times. I was sitting beside a priest on the sideline and when the people were going off he absent-mindedly gave me an Afton cigarette and remarked that some people were made of sugar. I thought that I must have a kind of dispensation against catching cold and stopped there in the showers of rain till the finish.

In such a downpour I arrived home. I could have changed my clothes and got into bed only half Ireland seemed to have got themselves into our street, looking for shelter, and if they weren't afraid to hide them from the Black and Tans on Bloody Sunday, fourteen years earlier, all but two months, neither would the people of Russell Street put the crowd back into the elements that day of deluge. In our house we had a hooley, and the measure of our accommodation was not such that we could have a hooley and get into bed at the same time. My father played the fiddle, amiable as always, anything from the 'Blackbird' to 'The Lady in Red', and we danced and sang the night away, till in very short order I got pneumonia and found myself in Temple Street Children's Hospital.

Camus was subsequently killed in a car accident with a representative of our joint French publisher, Gallimard, which shows, perhaps, that it is not safe to travel with publishers. They are a breed of men and the only recommendation I can give them is that they make a couple of shillings for us all.

In America they teach journalism, but in France it just overtakes you, and although I was doing a deal of writing, for a man whose needs in the eating line are few, it was, surprisingly, not long before I was without the price of a pint. Reluctantly, I went down to the Conféderation General de Travail, which is in one of the side streets off the Boulevard de Magenta, near the Place de la Republique, and I told the delegate that I had passed the London City and Guilds examination in Painter's Work, which includes lettering, that my father was a top house-painter in Dublin and my ancestors had been for generations in the trade.

He wrote it all down in a little book and passed me on to the section of the union for house-painters, and I was given the job of painting a house out in St-Gratien, west of Enghien, a great resort of Jewish families from Paris. The secretary explained that, as a foreigner, I couldn't belong to the first class section of house-painters for about six months, and he handing my wages for the week as he did so.

'The blessing of Jaysus on you,' said I. 'First class or second class, may the giving hand never falter.'

The next morning, I met some of the other painters on the job at the Gare du Luxembourg where, over glasses of rum, the native drink of the French proletarian, the chat was mainly directed on the weather and there was a sign of rain on the sky this morning and maybe we will have it before the day is out and all to that effect, and on we travelled to the Gare du Nord, where some had coffee but the more rum and the chat more friendly with every sip. Eventually, and a more happy crowd I've yet to meet, we got out at St-Gratien where, to put me in the humour for work, I drank four of five more rums.

M. Monti, the owner of the house, was a decent old skin, for there would be many a one who had led a more sheltered life would hope never to see the likes of us arriving on his doorstep. But M. Monti, after telling us that he had never met anyone worse than himself in the course of his travels, gave us all a glass of wine and a cigarette, which I thought then, and still more now as the qualified bearer of the title of ancient bowseyhood, was very civil of him.

The French, I discovered, are extremely good at filling, at making up a surface, but they use round brushes and I knew as much about painting with this type of tool as my arse did about snipe-shooting. And I had the humiliating experience— and my family and all belonging me in the trade—of a boy of some sixteen summers being put over me on the filling, and giving out the pay on how it should be done.

What can't be cured must be endured, but it wasn't long before I had persuaded M. Monti to let me enamel several of his doors, an art of which the French know nothing because it is not very much used in the country. And if I say it as one who shouldn't, I became quite popular with him as I was fairly good at it.

There was a woman on the *Queen Elizabeth* one time who

told me that the reason English industry was falling behind in foreign orders, was because the working man indulged in too many tea-breaks, though I noticed her aversion to this particular form of indolence did not take into account the gallons of tea she drank herself. At no time during the five-day trip did the steward pass her but she was either drinking a cup or asking for it.

But Jesus, Mary and Joseph, if English industry was falling behind, the French were out of it all together, for didn't *le garçon de vin* come round with a glass of wine in return for a few francs as often as was wanted for to soften the hardships of the day? And you would have to be an animal of a different character to me not to pass off the time drinking with a bit of a chat.

At twelve o'clock we stopped for lunch, and M. Monti would take us to a restaurant for a five-course meal. I offered to pay my share but he told me to wait and settle up at the end of the month, and sitting there we appreciated the comfort. A change is as good as a rest.

The month was beginning to feel its age when M. Monti tells me his son is returning from the army in North Africa, and for the price of my meal tickets would I ever let him work with me and learn how to do enamelling? To tell the honest truth, although the part of North Dublin I come from is as tough as any and I'd worked with numerous people, including Glasgow-Irishmen, in the house-painting trade, I would not have been so eager with my agreeing had I seen him first, for he looked the type to sit up all night with a shotgun on the odd chance of his having to use it. For all his nineteen years he had a hard face, more like an Irish terrorist's than mine, and wore, not alone the French army uniform, but the sword as well.

But his family were obviously very proud of him and a party was given to celebrate his return. M. Monti welcomed me literally with open arms, and François, the son, came over with a glass of *vin rouge* much stronger than anything I had tasted before from Metropolitan France. He told me it was called *Mascara* and that he had brought several bottles back with him from North Africa. Afterwards I discovered it was sold mainly in working-class areas and was very cheap, even for France.

214

But François gave me qualified approval with the glass of *vin rouge* and after a while we sat over drinking it, codding the girls and codding one another over the girls, and then started a sing-song.

Although we all joined in the folksongs, solo performances were well received, and I was encouraged to round off the evening with the singing of a few staves, in French, of Rouget de Lisle's *La Marseillaise*. (Voice from Crumlin: 'You're at it it again, Brending Behan.')

> Allons, enfants de la patrie
> Le jour de gloire est arrivé!
> Contre nous de la tyrannie
> L'etendard sanglant est levé.

So we all got friendly and soft-sugach drunk and everyone friendly with everyone else, which is the happiest thing we have in this world, although not always easy or certain to come by, till I sang the last coherent melody:

> Come, come, beautiful Eileen, come for a drive with me;
> Over the mountains, down by the fountains,
> Up by the highways and down by the byways,
> We'll drive to Castlebar;
> On the road there's no danger,
> To me you're no stranger,
> So, up like a bird on me ould jaunting car.

Bravo! Bravo! They all shouted and applauded vociferously and, well-oiled, most of the guests departed. There was the noise of cars starting and shouts of who wants a lift and you move over there and take Simone on your knees and no carrying on under the rugs please, keep your hands easy I can't get her started, and you're awful get out and push, and then silence and there was only a few of us left.

I found myself, as often I found myself before, in an armchair, and like the other half of a family group, in an adjoining armchair were M. Monti and his son, François. With an air of reproof, the sword lay at his side. From the simplest ingredients, we had made a night of gaiety. It was ever thus in France.

215

The next morning, I put on the overalls and began showing François how to enamel the doors, which is to put a spot of paint on and another spot of paint immediately underneath it, and join the two before the edges of the preceding spot have dried. And you have to work fast enough to complete a stretch without slapping it on, for then it just runs and is impossible to paint in the direction of the panels.

All the other fellows were enjoying watching me, for all over the house I'd noticed bad paintwork, but François seemed mainly interested in his overalls. Over in the restaurant drinking a glass of rum before dinner-time, he told me in the hot weather he never wore anything under them and he hoped I wouldn't be minding. Now I didn't give a fiddler's fugh one way or another, except that I wished it was his sister. However, as Maurice Chevalier was known to remark, 'Vive la différence.'

Before the job was finished, François, ever without ambition in the painting line, announced he was taking a holiday with his girl friend, and we all subscribed heavily for the buying of two sleeping-bags. M. Monti, who was not out of his mind about his son's progress at work, remained aloof from the deal on the grounds that a double sleeping-bag would be cheaper. No harm to the boy. I would have joined him had the work been finished and the full amount in my pocket.

A few weeks later and the job done, and myself on a blue coach to the south, silent now as we drove on towards the sun, I fell to wondering how it is that the Parisian worker goes little on the beautiful Cote D'Azur on account of its being the playground of a gang of international millionaire loafers, for long before we came to Cannes I noticed, camped along the road, the tents of quite obviously ordinary French families.

I arrived in Cannes somewhat dazed and after stretching my legs and quenching my thirst at the Zanzi-Bar, I wished to go from that town to a place called Speracedes, A.M. There were no buses going at that hour, so I decided to do an auto-stop. The truck driver got out and had a look at me. He was a blocky, tough-looking man of the Midi, but smelt so strongly of expensive perfume that I thought he bathed in it. He invited me into a bistro while we discussed arrangements. He would take me in the cab with Albert. I was not anxious to go in the cab with Albert, for not alone was I a little taken aback by his beautiful odours, but to be smelling the two of them on the journey would be purgatory altogether.

'You are smelling me?' said the truck driver.

'I sure am.'

'Ah,' he smiled with satisfaction, 'I smell, yes?'

'Well, yes and no,' said I. 'I smell and you stink. A fair division of labour, like.'

He took me out to his truck. 'You must smell Albert,' he said.

There sat Albert, a hardened old geezer, who smelt like sweet Nellie Fowler, of whom it was said that young swells of the 'nineties used to pay her a fiver to put their handkerchiefs under her armpits for a night.

I looked round anxiously. 'It's not usual,' I said.

'No,' perhaps not, said the perfumed lorry driver, 'but sometimes that last twenty-five kilometres to Grasse is the longest and the loneliest. I must let you off before we arrive at the factory, of course.'

'The factory?' I said.

'Yes, the perfume factory at Grasse. That's why we smell like this.' He smiled with pride 'Albert has been retired ten years but he still has his smell. We don't require Union cards when we hold a general meeting. The delegate of the Confédération General de Travail just smells each man as he goes into the hall.'

I thought the lorry driver had not a bad job, but I did not fancy smelling like that. However, to cut a long story short, I got to Grasse all right and eventually to Speracedes, where I had the best of drink and the best of food and went down to Cannes each day by car and swam in the Mediterranean.

I was in Stockholm several years later where my first wife discovered the department stores. I would have put blinkers on her if such a thing were legal but contented myself with uttering appeals to her to remember the sterling area.

'You are getting very pro-British in your old age,' said she, savagely eyeing a fur cape for only seven hundred kroner.

'Well, Ireland is in it, too.'

She ignored that. 'It must be the change before death. All that *brandvin*.'

'Well, what do you want furs for, just now?'

'Fur—in the singular. That would cost two hundred pounds at home.'

'Look at all these healthy Swedish people out at Vaxholm wearing nothing but handkerchiefs—over their faces.'

'I don't wear a fur cape when I'm sunbathing, either.'

I met a Gaelic scholar too and he recited Gaelic to me. We were at this party, and he came over and did a Gaelic recitation.

'I'm sorry,' said I, 'but I don't understand it.'

'Well, you don't have much Gaelic if you can't understand a simple eleventh-century verse concerning the death of a pet elk.'

'How about moving on a bit to the eighteenth century,' said I, and gave him a verse from the Midnight Court:

> I saw, as I suddenly looked around,
> Approach from the bay with a horrible sound,
> A big-bellied bitch, and her bottom gigantic,
> Fierce, furious, fearless, formidable, frantic . . .

An elegant lady approached me and said, 'Wonderful, hur dur yur spik English?'

'Well, I open my mouth and I bring my lower jaw down up to my upper jaw and it comes out.'

'Ur, wonderful,' she smiled, discreetly waving her graceful arms and swelling her peerless orbs.

I sniffed. 'Voll da Newee,' said I.

'Oh, hur ever did yur know?'

'I once knew a French lorry driver smelt like that.'

My first wife rescued me and back in Ireland we complimented ourselves that we had paid no duty on the fur cape.

By 1951, this painter had wiped his pot clean down and fughed the brushes in, and apart from a few odd jobs here and there, never picked them up again. For the matter of that, I believe the last piece of organised work I was ever to do was the painting of the Hibernian Military School when it was being converted into a T.B. Hospital in 1952.

If I am anything at all, I am a man of letters. I'm a writer, a word which does not exactly mean anything in either the English, Irish or American language. But I have never seen myself as anything else, not even from the age of four when my mother says that when she sent me for a loaf of bread, I used to kick a piece of paper along the street in front of me so that I could read it. But she didn't approve of my literary efforts and echoed the sentiments of an aunt of mine, who was the widow of the author of the Irish National Anthem. 'May God preserve us from poets and playwrights,' she said. So I wrote silently, starkly, short stories, drafts of plays and many poems, and was the youngest writer included in 'Nuabheirciocht' (Modern Gaelic Poetry), an anthology of verse in the Irish language between 1900 and 1950.

I joined the Irish Press Association as a free-lance journalist, an occupation I was to enjoy until my retirement in 1956, following Joan Littlewood's direction, in a splendid cockney way, of *The Quare Fellow* and later *The Hostage*. She was the only producer I ever met with a spark of genius, but I also happen to remember that her theatre in the East End of London, the Theatre Royal in Stratford, would have shut were it not for me. Eaten bread is soon forgotten.

In addition to other extraordinary abilities, I'm a pretty good singer—or at least I was until my larynx gave in to too much of the gargle and too many cigarettes. And I had an extensive repertoire of songs, many of which I had learnt from my Uncle, Paedar, and from my mother who has never stopped singing, Not even the depression could stop her. I think if somebody mentioned China, she'd sing a song about China. No matter what anybody mentioned, she'd sing a song about it. And I was after doing the same, so when Michael OhAodha asked me to sing a few ballads professionally on the *Balladmakers' Saturday Night* programme on Radio Eireann, it seemed an easy way of lining the coffin. I even scripted the Dublin sections myself and had a number of my short stories broadcast, some of which I read, although I never enjoyed this part of it as I consider singing your own songs or reading your own work a form of mental incest. However, every cripple has his way of walking and I was in need of the readies, for my modest expenses in the journalistic line did not take into account my capacity for hoppin' and leepin' and skippin' in France, and indeed in that other island across the way where I was still *persona non grata*.

I often had reason to go into the office of the *Irish Times* in Fleet Street and glad of a place to sit in comfort, for I wouldn't be having more than a few pence in my pocket, and after having slept the night out in Hyde Park it was my feet that were needing the rest. And while waiting for the man I wanted to see, I would be entertained by the man who operated the telegraphic machine to Burgh Quay in Dublin. Amongst other things he told me was to be sure to see for myself the monument of love and gratitude erected by Queen Victoria to her consort, Albert, and in future be thankful for our own samples of British architecture in the way of memorials.

Now I was reared in the belief that the greatest disaster that ever befell mankind was the defeat of Napoleon at the battle of Waterloo, that it opened a century of unparalleled misery for the peoole of Ireland; and that the little corporal, even at his most cynical, was a more civilised figure than the licensed thug and the loud-mouthed bailiff whose victories on behalf of European reaction, and the privileges of landlords, are commemorated in the Phoenix Park.

Bonaparte's royalist pretentions and imperial lunacies were more worthy of a talentless, dull race of well-to-do nail and saucepan merchants, depending upon the revelations of homely native bodies about an imported royalty to give a bit of colour to their lives. And they ruined him, but at least he is remembered by the Code Napoleon and the straight roads he built. Wellington, the made-in-Brummagen Iron Duke, if he is remembered for any law, it is the Poor Law; if for any building, it is the workhouse. As for the obelisk in the Phoenix Park, it was put there by the enemies of the people of Ireland and should be shifted, now that they are no longer powerful enough to enforce its preservation. Neither has the Martyr of the Pillar any claim on our consideration. As Bernard Shaw said, he won victories he'd have been deservedly shot for losing, and anyway has nothing to do with us.

One occasionally hears about the attachment of the 'old Dubliner' to these objects, but in this context an 'old Dubliner' is usually some ignorant employee of the Castle or one of the banks, that came over as a trustworthy messenger or diligent hall-porter about fifty years ago and has only as much right as any other Irish citizen to debate this matter. The oldest Dubliners, the descendants of the native Irish that crept in and settled round Ballybough (an Baile Bocht—'the poor town') regarded the Wellington Monument and Nelson's Pillar as a gibe at their own helplessness in their own country.

I remember, as a very small child, travelling with a grand-aunt of mine. She was born and reared at Blessington Street, near the Basin, formerly the City Reservoir, and whose waters, she claimed, were cleaner and purer and better for making tea than the 'new stuff' from Roundwood: We sat in a tram and listened to an elderly gentleman inquire of the conductor whether the tram went to 'Kingstown.' The conductor replied in even tones that he did not know of the existence of any such place. The old gent, with some impatience, replied that the place, with the chopping and changing of modern times, was now called something else, 'er Done Lakery or some such.'

This bit of fencing, the old gent pretending he did not know how to pronounce Dún Laoire and the conductor pretending he had never heard of Kingstown, continued till at last, to cut a long story short, it was decided that he was on the right tram.

'Of course,' said the old gent, 'it was called Kingstown by the old people.'

'Excuse yourself,' said my grand-aunt, 'excuse yourself, sir. I don't know how old you are, but I'm nearly eighty and I never called it anything but Dún Laoire. I don't know how long you're in the city, sir, but my mother, who stayed with friends in Glasthule every summer, went to her grave without ever knowing it was called anything else.'

I was thinking about all this as I walked through Hyde Park. And sure enough, till I stood before Albert Memorial, I never knew how much we had to be thankful for in the matter of nineteenth century British memorials.

On a broad base, surrounded by stone elephants, stone mahouts, stone Red Indians and other inhabitants of the wife's Empire, there rises to a point, sixty or seventy feet above the lowest stone moccasin, a sort of shrine, the centre of which can best be described as a Gothic watch-box, where your man crouches, sheltering from the rain. His young wife stands waving to him from outside Kensington Palace, in sculpture executed by her daughter, a young German princess, who'd have been better advised to stick to her own business of kissing kangaroos and dancing with the Maoris.

It is a bit difficult to believe that the native language of this mortuary, could they but *speak*, would be German, and that after the Prussian victory at Sedan in 1870, the Royal Family assembled at the chapel in Windsor to give thanks for the Victory in a prayer composed by another artistic princess whose bent was for literature.

> Let's join our heart with cousin Bill,
> And praise the heavens, with a will.
> Ten thousand Frenchmen sent below—
> Praise God from whom all blessings flow.

The speakers at Marble Arch, at the other end of Hyde Park, I found extremely entertaining and many of them spoke a deal of common sense. I remember one, however, who was a preacher of Irish revolt. His following seemed more personal than organisational, but he did not lack support for all that. He was very fond of demanding: 'D'you think I done fifteen years in Maryborough Prison for nothing?'

This silenced all interrupters, including myself, until finally one man, with a similar accent to the speaker, replied with easy familiarity: 'You did not then, Tom. 'Twas for pushing a boy into the Shannon. You were a lucky man you weren't hung.'

By now I was becoming quite well-known as a writer and a broadcaster and stories of mine appeared at the one time in the *Catholic Standard* and the *People*. I think it was working for the *People* that I found the most satisfaction, for although the democratic paper I consider sometimes dirty, it is a big seller with a circulation of over four million copies, and I was always able to get a few bars from it.

Hanner Swaffer, the most popular writer on the *People*, was a very great man. At the beginning of the war, when he was over the age of sixty-five anyway, he'd taken a flat in Trafalgar Square and one of the conditions of the lease was that he had to do fire-watcher's duties. So Swaff did fire-watching duties but when the war ended the owner of the flat asked him to leave.

'I'm not leaving,' said Swaff. 'I didn't even know the war was over.' And to the best of my recollection he occupied the flat until the day he died.

Another very good man, in my opinion, was Robert Marie Smiley—the Lord have mercy on him—who was the editor of the *Irish Times* and whose London office provided me with the readies and preserved the soles of my feet in the true days.

And I thought a lot of him for this reason. He was from the County Sligo, the same as W. B. Yeats, and in the First World War he was interned in Berlin where he was a music student. As an Irishman he could have been released and gone into the German parlour, as the saying has it, but he preferred to remain a British citizen. And he stopped in prison for the whole four years of the war.

It was about W. B. Yeats that I remember Smiley getting into a bit of embarrassment. He had to ring up Yeats to inform him that he had won the Nobel prize.

'Senator Yeats,' said Smiley. 'Through you and to you a great honour has been paid to our country and to yourself . . . I have just received a cable from Stockholm telling me you've won the Nobel prize.'

And Yeats, with that fine practicality which is ever the mark of a real poet, replied: 'For Jesus' sake, Smiley, pull yourself together. How much?'

Nothing of any great consequence happened at this stage

of the game until this day when 1952 was beginning to feel its age. It was France versus Ireland in the football at Dalymount that year, and Smiley asked me would I ever write a colour article on the match? And I was to go to France—for it was not a description of the actual play that was needed, but a description of the attitude of the Frenchmen to the match. I was paid sufficient to take me from the *Irish Times* office out to Dublin Airport to Paris Airport and back.

'We'll get the tickets, Brendan,' said Smiley.

'Nonsense,' said I, and here is where Aughrim was lost, 'I'll get them myself.'

There was a sign of rain on the sky this morning as I walked the few steps along Westmoreland Road and into the nearest snug, thinking that those less fortunate than myself would be having it before the day was out. Not that it is to be implied that I thought lightly of the sufferings of any worker in bad weather, but it was the way I was looking out of the window and counting the blessings for myself.

Outside the window and looking in, was a friend of mine and our native defender in the boxing at the Olympics in 1932, Ernie Smith. God be good to him—he has since died of cancer. I beckoned to him and Ernie, being a North Dublin fellow, was in like a shot with him. And we had a few jars and eventually three days later I appeared with enough of the money for to get me to England only, where there was still a deportation order against me.

The boat was crowded and it was a diabolical journey, but I had the good fortune to get in with a fellow from some built-up bog of London who insisted on giving me a lift from Liverpool in his car, even if I did have to listen to him giving out the pay about the dangers of the Teddy Boys now inhabiting the place.

Like most people, I had seen reports in the papers of more or less inoffensive citizens being battered unconscious by Teddy Boys, teenaged boys whose uniform was an elaborate imitation of what the well-dressed man was wearing in the days of Edward the Seventh: drain-pipe trousers, long jacket with velvet collar, and what my father would call an All-for-Ireland-League M.P.'s overcoat.

That night I stood at a coffee stall nourishing myself with a cup of tea and a sandwich, and I watched half a dozen of these gentry devouring jellied eels. By the same token I am a great believer of sampling the local delicacies anywhere I may happen to be but I drew a very firm line at jellied eels. I remember Benedict Kiely telling me that they come from the bens and glens of County Antrim and that numerous canty bodies make a wheen of ha'pence on the export trade from Toomerbridge in that County to Waterloo Bridge in London. I will take his word for it that jellied eels are wholesome fare for man and beast and leave it at that.

Anyway I was at this stall at about one o'clock in the morning and these Teddy Boys seemed to be giving me searching looks. I am not notoriously a nervous type and was not reared in such a sheltered atmosphere as to feel I was slumming by going down the East End. But I was a long way from barracks and not in the humour to be asking the arm of the law for support, and while I was not less than twice the weight of any two of these anti-Parnellites I did not feel able for taking on six of them. Besides, from Sunday reading I had learned that the least offensive of the Edwardian armoury included a bicycle chain and a blunt instrument fashioned from the strap-hanging equipment of the London Transport Board.

The most velvety Teddy Boy looked over at me at last, and said: 'Eye.'

'Eye,' I said, learning the language apace.

'Yew Ahrish?'

I admitted as much and wondered which one of them I could drop before the belt on the back of the head. I could see the headstone in Glasnevin Cemetery, if they ever gathered up the bits and sent them home: 'Breandán O Beacháin. Coshálta chun báis ar Dhroichead Waterloo, 1952. His memory is an example to us all to keep away from jellied eel fanciers.'

The velvety Teddy Boy turned to his friends and said: 'Vere. Whe did eye sye?' He smiled at me and said: 'These geezers contradicted me. I knew you were Ahrish w'en I 'eard your browgue. We're all Ahrish 'ere.'

Proudly he pointed to his friends:' E's MacCarfy, en 'e's O'Leary, en 'Ealy, en 'Ogan, en Kelly, en my name is ... give a guess.'

'Murphy.'

225

'That's it,' said he delightedly,' and my mum is a Flanagan.'

'Gentlemen,' said I, 'I'm really pleased to hear this,' and I raised my cup of tea in salute.

I remember a young lady employee of the Irish Government in London who worked in her spare time for a Catholic Youth organisation telling me once of a dance they ran which was visited by Cardinal Griffin. The archiepiscopal party beamed on the young dancers who pranced round sedately till they left, and then went into the wildest and liveliest sort of jiving. My friend commented on this to one of them and on the rapidity with which they accelerated the pace of the light fantastic once the visitors were gone.

'Well,' asked the lad indignantly, 'what did you expect us to do? Be-bop in front of an archbishop? What do you take us for, 'eathens?'

Suddenly in the quiet of the early morning I fell to wondering what, in the name of the blessed Virgin Mary, was I going to do for the readies to get me across the Channel?

I have a sister, Carmel, who lives in Crawley, a new town in Sussex, and I got a loan from her and her Scots husband, Joe Paton, a very noble, kind man. And Joe came up to London and met me at Victoria with enough money for the trip and more beside. It was a Sunday morning—which to an alcoholic is hell—and I bought my favourite newspaper because I got a few quid from it occasionally. With heartfelt relief, I sat at the carriage window as the train pulled slowly out of the station.

The carriage was empty except for a purple shawl in the opposite corner, containing a woman of uncertain age, for it was not the season for the assmacrockery to be unloading their cats, dogs and small children on the beach and the perils of the grey sea. I opened my paper, and by the Lord Jesus, didn't I discover that Dick Timmons, the man I had helped get off a gaol sentence, had written his story of the escape?

With my eyes riveted on the print, I read: 'At last I got word from Liverpool. The old lady wrote to say that a man was coming to see me. When I saw who it was, I was amazed. For it was Brendan Behan, a friend who had served three years in Borstal for his part in the bombings and who had been expelled from England. He had travelled from Ireland with false papers to help me—and risked gaol to do so.' (Voice from Crumlin: 'Will you ever get out of the act?')

Be Jaysus, said I in my own mind, I would give back the Six Counties and go along with the singing to get out of this one. I put my hand in the inside pocket of my coat and felt the hardness of my passport—no longer false, albeit in the name of Francis Behan—and the purple shawl opposite moved and slumped forward.

And Dick Timmons, easy in his knowledge, was not in mind to be withholding any information this day. And I read on: 'We agreed to separate. The day after he went to Manchester, he was arrested and sentenced to three months imprisonment for illegal entry.'

Not all the sins of my past life crowded in front of me but as many as could get in the queue, and I wondered, with something approaching terror, whether I would ever get out of this one. I remembered too the puckered grin of the tough old Republican veteran from West Clare, who was asked whether his fight for Ireland had benefited him personally.

'What did you get now for it all?' said a Job's comforter of an artist that I am quite sure had never spent an hour out of his bed for anyone.

'I got,' and his hardy old face twisted in a grin, 'forty acres off this country. Forty acres—when the tide is out.'

And about the height of what I'd be getting was a further spell in the shovel and pick.

Under cover of the purple shawl I went through the barrier at Newhaven, but lost it on account of a young Irishman of the kind that would kill his mother for a spare ticket to a Radio Eireann symphony concert giving out the pay to me about the perils of losing all belonging to you on the Newhaven-Dieppe run. All I would be losing on the run would be the threat of the deportation order and several pounds in weight thinking about it.

God's help, they say, is never further than the door, for didn't this woman, with her young son, ask me if I was going to Paris and would I ever help her from the Gare Saint Lazare across to the Gare du Quai d'Austerlitz?

'Sure,' I said. 'We can go on a bus or in a taxi, but I'll take you anyway,' and I fell in alongside her while the immigration officer looked at the passports.

'Are you Francis Behan?' asked the immigration officer, and polite with it too.

'Yes,' I said, 'sure I am.'

'You say you are a journalist. For what papers or journals have you written?'

I felt my blood go to my scalp and heard my words stammering in the air as heavy as lead. 'Eerr. *Irish Times. Irish Press,* the *Irish Workers' Republic,* the *People,* and the *Fighting Carpenters' Gazette.*'

I swallowed some spit and looked into his face for the first time—a tallish man and with a good appearance. The thin lips of an Englishman and that was all right too—wasn't it his country to have any kind of lips he liked? If he would just stop the questioning and let me be easy in my mind. I lowered my eyes and tried to collect my utterence.

'I am on my way to France for the *Irish Times,*' I stuttered, 'to write a colour article on the attitude of the Frenchmen to the football at Dalymount Park.'

'Do you know Brendan Behan?' He spoke very reasonably, and I breathed more easily.

'Oh,' I said, 'a loud-mouthed bastard. I've seen him over in Dublin, but I don't know much about him.'

'You don't know much about him?' said the immigration officer. His indignation got the better of him and his voice grated and his accent changed. 'You are him,' he shouted into my face, grabbing me by the arm as he did so.

The woman and her son moved back a pace and both of them looked reproachfully at me.

228

I WAS taken into a little room where there was another well-dressed man, who smiled at me. Better again, he called me 'Francis'. Then he beckoned me to a table at the back of the room where there was a pile of photographs, and Jesus, Mary and Joseph, I nearly fell out of my standing for didn't my photograph stand very largely amongst the other ones?

It brought my blood back to my feet. 'For the love of God,' I said, 'would you ever get me a drink?'

The immigration officer grunted. 'No,' he said. 'But we'll give you a cup of tea.' He was fascinated with his capture which apparently was the big event of the day for him—but by Christ, not for me.

A sergeant came in carrying a tray containing a printed form, a bar of copper, a roller and a container of printing ink. The second well-dressed man spoke: 'We're going to take your finger-prints, but you probably know all about that.' He moved to the open door. 'Come on. Down for a wash.' I followed him out and he stood outside the door while I washed my hands and used the lavatory He chatted through the door, friendly, without caring much one way of the other, and in my own mind I decided to bluff it out and be easy in return.

Back in the room the sergeant took the form and laid it on the table and rolled ink on the bar. I gave him the index finger on my right hand and he took it and inked it and rolled it on the form, where it left an impression in the space marked 'Index Finger, Right Hand.' Then he took the middle finger, the ring finger and the little finger and the same on the left hand. I signed the form 'Francis Behan' on the bottom in the space provided, and the well-dressed man smiled again.

I was taken by car up to the County Headquarters of the Sussex Police at Lewes by my friend whom I subsequently discovered was called Johnston, and by another constable who said nothing to me one way or another. But I was treated with great politeness and Johnston put his hand in his pocket and took out a packet of cigarettes. He handed the constable one, took one himself and then passed them to me. 'Have one,' he said.

'Thank you,' I answered and the constable passed lights all round. I could see the driver looking in his mirror all the while, taking in every feature of my face for to tell the kids at home in the evening that he had driven the bastard that helped that prisoner to escape, and reading out bits of the *People* for to illustrate the point. And the children would listen with wide-eyed astonishment and give him great credit for his prowess and the smartness of the police.

By way of diversion we drove through Brighton. There was no beach, but a stony stretch of pebbles and the water, poised and angry, stretched away out in front of us, with no limit but the rim of the world. The car turned off past the Pavilion, built by the Prince Regent to house his mots and of no benefit to any, and we moseyed our way across the Downs to Lewes gaol. The gaol lay on the outskirts of the town itself, an ugly grey-flint and red-bricked building with warders' huts alongside overlooking the Downs. We went up the drive and the car eased to a halt at the main entrance.

Superintendent W. Britton came down the steps to meet us, followed by two guards who looked stern and strong as if physical assault was threatening the law and they'd be glad to die in its defence. Johnston was out of the car first and, after a hurried conversation, Supt. Britton turned to me, even smiling as he did so, and told me I was being held for questioning as they had reason to believe I was Brendan Behan. The guards stood one each side of me and I was escorted inside.

It wasn't a bad-looking room for all that and the wall-paper had got sea-shells all over it, though I must say it didn't do much for the improvement of my health, nor for the matter of that for the inhabitants inside.

I sat on a chair and swung my legs up on the table. 'Look,' I said. 'You're mad. I am not Brendan Behan.'

Supt. Britton rose from his side of the table and came round towards me and spoke in an even and gentle tone. 'Now, be sensible,' he said. 'We know you are. We know by your finger-prints and we know by your photograph.'

'All right, Superintendent, all right, I am,' and the Superintendent looked reproachfully at me and then lowered his eyes as I asked, in the name of the Blessed Virgin Mary, for a drink. He nodded to Johnstone and to a warder who went out and returned in very short order with tea and more tea. When the hips fail welcome the haws, for tea is not such a bad drink, particularly given in the spirit—I intend no pun—in which these gentlemen gave it.

And they fell to talking about Bentley, who had been charged that night with Craig, for the shooting of a policeman. Now I do not believe in the shooting of policemen, even indiscriminately, but I do not think Bentley should have been charged with murder, and certainly did not deserve the death penalty, but there was a great state of agreeing going on about the right to charge him between these two on this day and it wouldn't do to be giving out the pay at this stage of the game and downface the gentlemen, so I said: 'I suppose you're right, when you come to think of it.'

We went out to the top of the stairs and the turnkey came up and Britton smiled at me. 'Good night, men,' I said and I followed the turnkey up the landing until we came to the cell door. I took off my shoes and braces and went inside, and the door banged out behind me and I heard the key turn in the lock.

I looked up at the barred windows. I was there again in a concrete box. And the lavatory was there again, in the corner, in full view of the spy-hole and the John Bull bastard of a warder to look in. I lay down on the wooden bench in misery to await my doom. Monday would come soon enough.

Waking I lay for a while wondering when I would be for court. At Manchester the whore-melts of coppers had remanded me twice before sentencing me, but maybe this time they would only deport me and say: 'For the love of Jaysus, would you stop out of here in future,' and begod, I would and be thankful.

I heard noises of key-jangling and door-banging. I knew those noises. They were coming my way. The key turned in the lock and a thin-lipped warder told me there were some gentlemen to see me. I followed him out and he pointed to my shoes and socks and braces which were laid out in the passageway, and I eagerly put them on. Johnston was having a whispered conversation to another constable, but he stopped as soon as he saw me.

'There are some men to see you, Brendan,' he said, 'from M.I.5 of Scotland Yard. But first I'll take you down to the wash-house to get a clean-up and a shave.'

'I'm not so bad,' I said, rubbing my chin, but in my own mind, yes, we must be shipshape and Bristol fashion for those fugh-pigs of informers.

Afterwards I was taken to the Governor's office where we shook hands politely. The Governor was pleasant enough to me though by all accounts he wasn't very pleasant to the other prisoners. Somebody once said that a regular soldier is the scum of the earth, but by Christ, a warder is the scum of the scum, no matter from which place they come.

His two fellow-companions from Scotland Yard smiled the smiles of the professionally polite but their eyes remained hard with it. The one in the grey pin-striped suit offered me a cigarette, asking me at the same time what I did and all to that effect. I told him and then I put the cigarette into my mouth to take a draw of it, when the second man came round the table towards me. 'Listen Behan,' he said. 'I understand you have been in the I.R.A. organisation since you could walk and you know plenty about it, but you have made no mention of that.'

'What little I could tell you about the I.R.A.,' I said, 'would be of no interest to you at all,' and I hastily added, 'and a deal sight less that you already know,' for he looked the type of man who would sit up all night with a sick dog for the need of a few licks in the morning.

'That may very well be.' And he spoke very reasonably and I looked at him and something told me that neither of these bollockses of imitation policemen were as well briefed as perhaps they might have been.

Pin-stripe spoke again. 'This is a serious matter, Behan. More serious than perhaps you realise. What were you doing in 1947?' It was out, and the Governor settled comfortably in his chair as if he was in the front row of the stalls about to watch a film they had all been talking about.

The smiles faded from the professional lips of the M.I.5. as I gave them my eye-witness account of my three months in

232

Manchester gaol, and how I was a great attender of the shovel and pick. 'But,' I smiled, 'nothing else of any great interest happened in that year, unless of course you are referring to my coming to England on my way through to France as I was attempting to do now? That is all I was doing, and that's about the height of it.'

'You mean that that is all you're going to tell about it. And you can take the grin off your face.' Pin-stripe nodded to the other man and spoke in a quieter tone.

'You know, Behan, you can be of assistance to us over this matter.'

'I'm sorry,' I said. 'I can't help you.'

'Well, you've a few days to go before you come up for court. Think it over, and if you change your mind, let us know. One way or another, we'll find out anyway.'

The interview was over and although they let on to be unconcerned I could tell when I left the room that they were very huffed blokes indeed. I was glad of that. And I discovered for the first time in my life that there is a degree of professional jealousy existing amongst the police that you wouldn't be meeting everywhere. For the Sussex police were so happy that I had screwed up M.I.5., who had taken the job of interrogating me out of their hands, that their attitude towards me changed completely. Instead of taking me back to the cell, I was put in another room, where I was brought buckets of tea and smoked many cigarettes. And the coppers kept coming in and out the room to have a chat, and it was the happiest time I ever spent in the nick.

They told me about the Sussex Martyrs, and how they were burned at the stake in Lewes by Bloody Mary, and how they hoped I would be able to see the celebrations on November 5th which was in a few days time, for the town was great gas that night. They would take me round the district to each street and see the bonfires lit.

'You know, this is not a very popular night for Irishmen around here,' they said. 'We might even let you go.'

'If you give me a break, I'd soon show you,' I laughed, for damn it, I would have readily joined in.

It might interest those people who believe that the struggle for Irish Independence was mainly one of Catholics versus

Protestants to know that Bloody Mary, a Catholic, far from being pro-Irish, was the first person to expel the ancient inhabitants of Ireland and plant men of her own choosing in their place. Furthermore, she renamed two counties in Ireland, Leix and Offaly, King's County and Queen's County, and one of the main towns of Offaly was called Philipstown after her fancy man or husband, or whoever he was, Philip II of Spain. However, back in England, she sanctioned the wholesale persecution of Protestants, including the Sussex Martyrs which, I would say, contributed largely to the English being a Protestant people. On the whole, Mary I, Queen of England, was not a big deal.

It nearly drives me insane when I think of the opportunity I missed by not seeing Guy Fawkes night in Lewes, but maybe with the help of God and varied, I will yet.

I was on remand for about a week, and shared a police cell with a young Australian boy—not a bad kid at that—but he put years on me giving out the pay about having to use the lavatory in public. I was sorry for the chiseler, for he was only in on some minor charge and totally unused to hardships of this nature. For the matter of that I never got used to it either, but what can't be cured has to be endured and it was no good going on about it.

Although I had written an article about Borstal which was published in *The Bell* ten years before, I spent most of my time extending it, so that when the week got well under way I had more or less completed the rough draft of a book. This was later to appear as *Borstal Boy*, but I re-wrote it several times before the final version was published. I read bits of it to the Australian lad and his only comment, when he was not complaining about the sanitary arrangements, was, 'Cor, Paddy, did you write that?'

On the day before I was due to go to court, Jack Molloy, Counsellor at the Irish Embassy in London, came to see me. We had not met before and I found him a decent enough old skin. After he had asked me if there was anything he could do for me and all to that effect, he left, giving me forty Afton cigarettes. He told me he had arranged for a Mr. Carter to defend me the following day.

I went back to my cell in good humour. Digger was sitting

234

on the bench and I threw him the cigarettes. 'Thanks, Pad,' he said. 'I suppose you'll be out of this drum in the morning?'

'Your turn won't be long, kid,' I answered, and to cheer him up, 'You've got nothing to be frightened of. Just tell them your story and stick to it. It's your first offence. You'll be out and about before you know where you are.'

He said nothing, but took a cigarette and lit it, holding it in front of his nose, staring at it as if mesmerised, and the ash fell to the floor. He was still sitting there when I fell asleep.

In the morning I was brought away on my own and taken up to the charge-room by a policeman to sign for my property. Then I was out in a big cell along with the other remand blokes till the court opened. There were two rough-looking customers, caught on a warehouse roof, a man who had been taken off the Channel boat at Newhaven trying to avoid maintaining his wife, a young boy of about fifteen who had borrowed a bicycle to get to work in time after having it off with his mot, and a railwayman accused of raping male twins. He was weeping bitterly so I went over to him to try and console him.

'Look,' I said, 'for Christ's sake have a cigarette. You're not dead yet.' But the poor guy took the shame of it so much to heart, with all the pressure of the law against him, that he turned his head and moved away from me.

Two fresh-faced officious-looking bastards of policemen, who had been watching the proceedings, beckoned me over. The younger of them unlocked the cell and I was taken out. They explained that they had been sent down from London to take control of me, and yes, said I in my own mind, you'll not be wanting that poor old railwayman to be getting any comfort from me.

'I'd like to hear that case,' I said.

'It's a very unpleasant one and we don't think you should,' said the second man, who looked the type that wouldn't go away and leave the people die in peace in the time of the cholera.

'When I was sixteen you didn't mind my hearing unpleasant cases,' I snapped. 'I'm twenty-nine now,' and I walked away from these smart alecs, till I saw Johnston standing in the corridor.

'For the love of Jaysus,' I said, 'will you get me away from these fughs from the big smoke? They're too smart for me.'

'What's up, Brendan? Do you think they are going to get something out of you where we failed?' Johnston smiled.

'They'll get fugh-all out of Brendan Francis Behan, but to be honest with you I would like to hear the case against the railwayman, and they have it in mind that I shouldn't.'

And Johnston, to spite the London cops, for I don't think he intended for me to watch the proceedings, took me into the court.

The magistrate was a woman, a 'gentle English Tory', which, to me, is like talking about a tame cobra, dry water, a poor publican or a tame duck, and she had a face like Harris Tweed. When the prosecuting attorney said that he didn't think this was a nice case for a lady to hear, out like a shot with her she replied it was all right. 'In the line of duty,' she explained. Actually I think she was as anxious as myself to be hearing it.

Jesus, Mary and Joseph, they handed this poor unfortunate railwayman treatment that you would not be expecting if you were in Algeria under the paratroops, or a Jew under the Nazis. Quite obviously he could have been overwhelmed by the two kids he was accused of raping, but their stepfather put on a great act of indignation in the witness box and he was believed. If I had had my way the twins would have had their arses slapped and sent home. Instead of which the 'gentle English Tory' sent the railwayman up for trial.

I followed him into the dock and was charged with illegally entering England, which I must say was a bit much when, at the time, I was attempting to leave it. However I pleaded guilty, and then Superintendent Britton gave evidence that I had been expelled at Liverpool for being found with explosives in suspicious circumstances in 1941, and that later I had served four years of a fourteen-year sentence for attempting to murder Irish police officers. The old lady on the bench listened intently, but she was polite enough when she spoke.

Then Mr. Carter buttered her up with all sorts of nonsensical tales of how I had been led away by joining the I.R.A. at the age of fourteen, but now I was no longer concerned with subversive activities but a well-known writer and broadcaster on Radio Eireann, and was merely passing through England on my way to Paris where I had legitimate business. This softened her cough and she smiled at me, and so did other people in the court, and she fined me fifteen pounds, although I had to pay the costs as well. I could not complain about my treatment at Lewes.

On the heels of the reels I followed the sergeant into the car, for I was to be escorted to Newhaven, where I was to catch the cross-channel boat to France. On the way through Lewes I remarked on the buildings in that town, for they looked the height of good architecture to me. (Wasn't I set up in the intellectual line now?)

The sergeant greeted my account of metropolitan majesty from the High Street to Newhaven with 'Oh' and 'Ah' but for the best part he remained silent. No harm to him. A shut mouth catches no flies. I was taken through customs and if the tallish immigration officer with the thin lips of an Englishman recognised me, he too kept his mouth shut. At the gangway, I shook hands with the sergeant.

'Mind yourself, Brendan,' he said.

I turned round in astonishment. There was no mistaking the accent.

'You're a Dublin man,' I called after him, for although I had met plenty of Liverpool-Irish, and a more diabolical shower of bastards it would be hard to find, it was unusual for a man from my native city to join the British police, who for the most part are an ignorant body of men.

He ignored my remark but merely raised his hand and I walked up the gangway shouting, 'It's a pity you didn't learn more sense.' He was an Irishman, of the variety best known to me, who would be happily absorbed in the problem of seeing whom he could do next.

The boat was crowded but two light youths sitting together moved over a bit and invited me to sit down. I realised, with something approaching horror, that what with paying the fine and costs all I had left of the readies was an Irish threepenny piece.

It was France versus Ireland in the football at Dalymount the very next day, and if I was to write a colour article on the match I could hardly manage it with that class of money. Then I remembered Desmond.

Immediately on arrival in Paris I went up to Desmond's

pad, and he set me up at an hotel at the back of the Luxembourg Gardens. That night we sat outside a café and talked after dinner far into the soft November evening and past midnight, until the cold drove us indoors again.

The next day, in the bar of the hotel, I tried to listen to the match on the wireless, but it would have to be a linguist of a different variety to me to understand the French commentator's description of the match. The roar, the bawl, the yell, were the same in any language and hadn't I as a chiseler, and later too, given good account of myself from the sideline, and nobody I met ever begrudged the noise?

Now I wondered at the sour looks on the faces of the Frenchmen in the bar, and when their curses became directed at me I realised the match was over and Ireland had won. Naturally I was delighted but the reaction in the bar was to me completely incomprehensible. The following morning I read in a newspaper that 'the Dalymount roar frightened the French team so much that they lost their nerve and also the match.'

IT WAS late afternoon before I had recovered sufficiently enough to mosey round to the *Irish Times* office in Westmoreland Street to see Robert Smiley. I had decided, after I'd a few glasses of whiskey in me, to tell him the truth, for in the main I only told lies in the way of business—to get a drink and a feed or the price of my keep—to humble and simple souls, and Robert Smiley was neither of these.

'You'll kill yourself more with the drink than ever you will with the I.R.A., Brendan,' he said, as I walked into the room. I respected him greatly for this and the matter was discussed no further. Instead we fell to talking about a certain respectable member of the aristocracy who had spent a week trying to persuade W.B. Yeats to get out and fight in Easter Week, 1916. Legend had it that Yeats asked her what did she take him for, said he was too delicate a man, and threw her down the stairs two days after the fall of the General Post Office because he was going to write a poem about it.

At one time she had been on the Committee of International Red Aid, and she always insisted on giving this organisation its full name, in case it would be mistaken for the Irish Republican Army. She had fallen out with the I.R.A. in 1934 on the general question of the day-to-day struggle, and the particular one of their refusal to spare a dozen twelve-ounce sticks of gelignite for a parcel to be sent to the Secretary of the Employers' Federation during the coal strike.

Described by many as 'a champion of the downtrodden in every land, a fiery preacher for every good cause in her native land—the breaking-up of the big estates, the revival of the Irish language, and birth control—a splendid figure of revolting womanhood', she was believed to have been instrumental in getting Frank Harris and Charlie Chaplin to visit Jim Larkin in Sing Sing. She certainly used her influence with Governor

239

Al Smith to get him out. Smith had an almost feudal regard for her on account of her family having evicted his family out of their cottage in County Cavan back in the old days.

'I suppose you wouldn't know those parts, Brendan?' said Smiley.

I knew them well and have friends there and I knew Ballyjamesduff, and if I didn't know Lappanduff mountains I knew the song about it and heard it first sung in a bar on the Falls Road in Belfast.

> . . . on Cavan's mountain, Lappanduff,
> One fought with bravery,
> Until the English soldiers shot
> Brave Séan MacCartney . . .

Cavan of the little hills. For Cavan, the man said, you turn right at Navan. This happens to be true. I've done it.

We left the office together in the height of good humour and by way of no harm we called in at Michael's for a drink. But Smiley, ever an abstemious man, flew on the one wing and after a half of stout was off home. At the door, he turned and handed me an envelope.

I went into the 'jacks' and opened it. Inside was a blue ten-pound note and I put it in my pocket. Good man, I said to myself, but aloud, 'Now aren't you the great sport, Robert Marie Smiley!'

I went back to the bar.

'The same again, Michael,' said I, 'and a drink for yourself.'

'Thanks,' said Michael.

I threw down the tenner.

'A blue one, be Jaysus!' said Michael. 'You're blood's worth bottling.'

And there was great respect going on in the bar that evening for Brendan Behan. Doctor Crippen made room for me on the one side and McIntaggart the other side of me. Beside them I stood, like Christ between the two thieves.

McIntaggart's name in Irish was 'Mac an tsagairt', or 'son of the priest'. Some tease from Connemara told him this, and since then he'd gone round the gullible public with the tale that he was the son of a bloody priest. Not that anyone in this public house would believe the Lord's Prayer from his mouth. If you asked McIntaggart the time you'd check it on the telephone if you wanted the right time.

Doctor Crippen's real name I did not know. He got his nickname from the time he was a barman in a Free State Army canteen and was said to have poisoned the soldiers with bad drink. It was said that the man killed more that way than the I.R.A. whom they were fighting at the time.

Crippen in his day was a sergeant-major in the Free State Army and played Gaelic football for the Army Metro who were drawn from the barracks of the Dublin Metropolitan Garrison. Michael, the publican, respected him greatly for his former glory on the football field but Crippen did not know this. He was a gentle person and the only thing I knew him to boast about was his association with a literary magazine and his friendship with the associate editor.

The editor was a little left wing Republican from an island in the Atlantic Ocean off the coast of West Cork. He began writing when he came out of gaol in the 'twenties and Ireland had still the vogue amongst the English writing and reading class, on account of the Black and Tans putting Ireland on the Liberal conscience. Like all the other peasant writers he was an ex-schoolmaster and wrote lovingly about simple folk of his native place. I could make neither head nor tail of anything he wrote and this editor suspected as much. He did not like me for it, nor any of my bits of short stories would he publish.

But the associate editor, a big, hardy boy that boxed for Trinity College, was one of the gentlest people that I have ever met. He was a Protestant clergyman's son and had a mania for backing horses. This was shared by Crippen, who adored him, and Crippen was forever recalling the memory of his friend, now working for the B.B.C. in London.

As I had just come back from England, he asked me, as I knew he would, how his friend was ever since? I told the assembled company my story and for the most part I told the truth, at the same time giving good account of myself. Hours later, blinking into the night, I directed my gaze towards my kip, and as I made the long journey home, I fell to thinking that it was not every day in these weeks I get a bit of respect in this town. It might never happen again. A change is as good as a rest.

At this stage of the game, what readies I had, and there was not a deal of them, came from my bits of articles, short stories, poems and radio scripts. I originally wrote *The Quare Fellow* under the title *Casadh Sugáin Eile* (*The Twisting of Another Rope*) after Douglas Hyde's play, *The Twisting of the Rope*, and it was first written as a radio script. Later I turned it into a one-act play and submitted it to the Abbey Theatre who rejected it, saying that one day I might write a play. God damnit, you might as well be out of this world as out of the fashion, for didn't Joyce and O'Casey have their plays rejected one time? I extended it to three acts and wrote the same play in English, for although I didn't agree with him I remember a screw from Cork telling me in Liverpool that to read and speak Irish would not do you a deal of good in these times.

'What good is it anywhere outside a few in Ireland?' he said.

In English or Irish I knew I'd wait years to be read in Dublin, but I sent it back to the Abbey and this time the manager suggested that I meet the producer to see if it would be possible to make it stageable. He explained that as I had based the play on the twenty-four hours preceeding the execution of a man for carving up his brother, any one of the warders up in Mountjoy might choose to recognise himself and bring a libel action.

Fugh the producer, I said in my own mind, we don't speak the same language. I took it back, waited a few weeks, and submitted it again. Back like a shot it came, and prompt with it too. Like Joyce, I put it aside and went on with my other writing. By now I was well-known in the writing game and as the Irish have great *meas* for the traveller, I decided to write a detective story about Dublin's underworld, but using my knowledge of France, which was by now considerable, as the background. I wrote it under the phoney name of Emmet Street, which is the name of the street opposite the one I was reared in in North Dublin, partly because around the fashionable area of Grafton Street the Dublin intelligentsia still regarded me as a writer of pornography and partly because the district around Emmet Street is famous for another reason.

Beside Emmet Street is Rutland Street where formerly lived a man who was later President of the Irish Republic, Séan T. Kelly. But he lived in a whole Georgian house whereas the rest of the street was mostly tenements. In a back room in one of these lived Matt Talbot, and after his death there was a move on to make him a saint. But Séan O'Casey, who came from that area and lived only a couple of hundred yards from him, refers to him as 'Mad Talbot'. Not only in matters of the theatre, but also in matters appertaining to Dublin, do I bow to the expert.

Matt Talbot, the poor fellow, was some kind of a drunkard until he was about twenty, although I don't think he drank all that much. Amongst other things he did for to get the drink was as he said himself, to have stolen the fiddle from a blind fiddler. When he went off the drink and a big song and dance was made about his conversion from liquor, he got religion in a big way and for years he used to go to Mass every morning at five o'clock.

He worked in timber yards round the docks as a casual labourer and any time in the timber yards he was able, he would go through all sorts of religious exercises and slink off behind the pile of wood to say his prayers.

He also refused his overtime on the grounds that the time spent waiting for the lorries and trucks to come in for unloading should be set against his overtime, which was a fallacious piece of reasoning, because despite the fact that he wasn't actually unloading timber he wasn't exactly standing at the bar of the Shelbourne Hotel either when he was waiting in the cold and damp of a winter's day and the winds of the Liffey blowing through the shipyard.

And he starved himself too. It is said that he used to cook a herring each day and he would boil it up and give it to the cat, drinking the liquid himself.

In 1926, on his way to church, he fell and died and was taken into Jervis Street Hospital. When the nuns came to undress him in hospital they discovered that he had chains cutting into his bare flesh to mortify his passions, such as they were. I wouldn't be thinking you could work up a deal of passion on herring water.

However, he became something of a saint but not to the majority of the population in his own area around the north side. But he had a very saintly reputation amongst the middle and upper-classes and even a Presbyterian timber contractor said he was a great man. For the matter of that, I've no doubt that a Protestant timber contractor, or a Mohammedan, or a Jewish, or an atheist timber contractor, would all consider a man a saint if he refused his overtime. He was setting a good example to the rest of the men. However, the majority of his neighbours agreed that if Matt Talbot had had a wife and ten children he could not be affording to refuse his overtime. That was about the height of it.

There are two life stories written about him. One was written by Joseph Glyn who was a prominent Catholic layman and collaborator, and became Sir Joseph Glyn on account of his being one of the few Catholic members of the Dublin Corporation to join in a vote of welcome to King Edward VII when he came to visit Dublin. But he was regarded by a great many people as a 'Castle Catholic'—a particularly detested breed in Ireland—and was considered a very fortunate man to get through the War of Independence with his life.

At the time he wrote his life story of Matt Talbot unionism was still not respectable and he boasted how Matt Talbot was against the general strike of 1913 when the employers of Dublin were widely attacked, even at meetings in London at the Albert Hall by various intellectuals, including H. G. Wells and I will mention our own Bernard Shaw.

During the strike, William Martin Murphy, who was the biggest employer in the city and even owned the tramlines in Manchester and in Cape Town as well as the *Irish Independent* newspaper, incited the Dublin Metropolitan Police Force to go in and attack the people in the tenements on the north side.

There was one lady who said to me that she could never understand these men, the majority of whom were Catholics themselves and supposed to be very good ones at that, because they even smashed her little altar lamp, which is the little lamp that the people of the time put before the statue of the Blessed Virgin or the Sacred Heart. And not alone did they smash the lamps, but they smashed the people too, two of whom died during a baton charge in O'Connell Street. They were commonly known as the 'Dublin Cossacks' and the name has stuck to such an extent that even today the Dublin Police Force are referred to as this. Despite the Gaelic inscriptions they wear on their caps, they are as much hated on the north side as when they wore crowns on their caps.

But, according to Joseph Glyn, Matt Talbot held himself aloof from all this strife and averted his eyes from the placards that carried reports of the executions of the 1916 leaders. He certainly did not sympathise with his own people. However times change, and in his latest biography, written by a woman from the County Kilkenny—a school teacher and probably a farmer's daughter who could not possibly have known anything at all from family tradition about 1913 or 1916—it appears that Matt Talbot was a staunch trade unionist, trade unionism having become sort of respectable by now.

My father, who is President of the Painters' Union, was once asked in a television interview in Ireland whether he considered Matt Talbot a great trade unionist. 'He was a trade unionist,' he replied, 'when he had to be.'

So this unfortunate wretch, for that was all he was—he was like the dog that died; he never did anybody any good but he never did anybody much harm—was held up as an example to the Dublin worker. Whether the employers wanted all the Dublin workers to boil up herrings and give them to the cat and only drink the water and send their surplus wage, if any, to the foreign missions, I do not know. But in any event Matt Talbot in his own area was and is widely detested.

In 1932, the Catholic church granted Ireland the International Eucharistic Congress, which meant an influx of perhaps a million Catholics from all over the world into the city, and very good for business. And for once in a way, Ireland begets very little from the church. The French atheists have Lourdes and the Portuguese Fatima, where it is said that three little peasant girls saw the Blessed Virgin in 1917, and that she made numerous prophesies about Communism and told them a secret, which as far as I can see will never be revealed.

It is also alleged that on the first anniversary of this apparition, the sun shot out of its usual place and ran all over the sky. How this could happen and be observed by the thousands of people attending this religious ceremony and not be recorded in the observatories all over the world which have the sun watched twenty-four hours a day, I really don't know.

However, just before the start of the Congress in Dublin, there was great tidying up going on in Dublin, and housepainters could not be got for love nor money. And there was this contractor who was asked by Canon MacArgle (and for years I thought the man's name was Canon Gargle—the Dublin slang for drink) if he would ever do up Matt Talbot's room in Rutland Street and leave it exactly as it was when he was in it. So this contractor approaches my father, and knowing my father's rather sketchy ideas about religion he impresses on him the seriousness of the job, and my father agrees to do it. He moseyed round to Rutland Street, but after knocking a deal on the door of Matt's room in one of the tenements, he turned the handle and found it locked. But Aughrim was not lost, for didn't a woman, on hearing the noise, come to her door to find out if the devil himself was in the building?

My father asked her if she would ever be knowing how to get into Matt Talbot's room?

'For Jesus sake,' she said, 'I am trying to rear eight children in one room and my husband is unemployed. Do you think I've nothing better to worry me than Matt Talbot, that old *omadaun?*'

So my father explained that he had a job to do and that if he did up the room there'd be thousands coming to see it during the Eucharistic Congress, and that she'd be doing herself a good turn by setting up a little stall outside the door and selling holy pictures and other tokens of her religious respect.

Out like a shot with her, she gave him the name and address of the landlord.

'Don't mention that old bastard to me,' moaned the landlord. 'I can't let that fughing room because people are afraid he might appear like a ghost, clanking his chains.'

'You'll make enough of the readies and more beside,' said my ould one, 'if you stick a collection box in a prominent enough position in the room. Then all the people who come to pay homage to the unfortunate lunatic will think it's for the foreign missions or something and weigh out heavily. You needn't put anything on the box, so nobody can accuse you of lying or embezzling.'

So the landlord thought this was a good idea and my father the greatest of men and he gives him the key.

And my father, on finally opening the door of Matt's room, nearly passes out in a weakness on discovering that his bed, which is famous throughout the annals of Catholic hagiography, is missing.

'Oh, it's you again,' says the woman in the next door room and my father, after complimenting her on her eight fine children and all to that effect, asks about the missing bed.

'Ah, sure,' she replied, ''Twas only a block of timber. We burned it during the bad winter of 1931. Mr. Behan, jewel and darlin', 'twas either that or the hall door.'

'You'd better get some kind of a bed, Stephen,' said the contractor. He had gone with my father to the pub nearby for a sup or two of the plain porter and was glad of a few minutes' chat. 'The best thing you can do,' he said, 'is to go down to T. and C. Martin's (one of the timber yards where Matt Talbot worked) and see if they might sell you something that looks like his bed.'

In the heels of the reels, my father was down at the timber yard, and Jesus, Mary and Joseph, didn't he find a lot of railway sleepers off the Great Northern Railway which would exactly do the trick? He picked out one, and after arranging with the foreman to have four inches taken off the top of it for to remove the bolt holes he asked for it to be delivered up at Rutland Street.

The bed was duly delivered and the woman told him she would never be believing that it wasn't one and the same that had burned so beautiful in the bad cold of that winter, as she showed him where the poor bastard lay. And even my father was charmed with himself as he chose the most abominable-looking holy pictures from a little Catholic repository for to stick around the place. They were all printed in Belgium—mostly by Communists—and were of the Little Flower and the Little Lamp and the Holy Family and the like.

He locked up the room and forgot all about Matt Talbot and went off working round the city, and he worked so much overtime that he was able to pay the publican at the corner of Gardner Street, Thomas Hogan, the forty pounds that he owed him. Poor Hogan nearly dropped dead on seeing the readies; he nearly had a heart attack. But he gave my father a glass of whiskey on the head of paying the debt, and I think he had two for to revive himself.

My grandmother used to sit by the hour in Hogan's snug.

When she was in her cups, and she was seldom out of them, she would tell us chiselers at her feet the most fantastic stories. I remember this day when she was telling me about her times in Killarney.

'I never knew you were in Killarney,' I said. For the matter of that, I never knew she'd been outside Dublin in her life.

'Oh, yes,' she said. 'We walked from Killarney to the Giant's Causeway one time.'

Now Ireland is not a very big country, but it so happens the Lakes of Killarney are in the County Kerry, in south-west Ireland, and the Giant's Causeway is in the County Antrim, in the north-east of Ireland. It is a distance of at least three hundred and sixty miles, and even I, as a child, did not see how you could walk there.

'It's a long walk of course,' she continued, 'and it took over two hours. And then we saw the Cap of Dunloe and the meeting of the waters in County Wicklow.'

'Jesus,' I said, and it was out before I could stop it, 'you couldn't have seen these places on the one day, not even with an aeroplane, much less walk.'

'How dare you contradict your grandmother, me little man cut short,' she snapped. 'Of course I did.'

Years later I discovered there were twelve stained glass panels of the beauties of Erin in Hogan's snug, including the Lakes of Killarney, the Giant's Causeway, the meeting of the waters in County Wicklow, Galway Bay and the rest. Because there was only an inch dividing one panel from the other in the snug, my grandmother was under the impression that the places could not be very far from each other in actual fact.

The most elaborate preparations took place for the Eucharistic Congress and in our street was a banner showing St. Patrick with green whiskers on the one side and 'God Bless Our Lord' on the other, a theological complication if ever there was one. But I remember the Congress well because I sang in the choir of nine hundred at the children's Mass, as did John McCormack. And it was certainly good for trade and the pubs, which were full of foreigners of all descriptions, were open all night to the best of my recollection.

My father, like most Irish people, being over friendly with foreigners, though not to say nosey, spoke to many of them and there was this night in the local when a man who had a certain amount of English tells him that Dublin is a wonderful place and that he has just had a great experience.

'Is that so?' says my ould man. 'Were you in Becky Cooper's, or Nell Hayden's, or Harriet Butler's?'

'Are they convents?'

'Of a sort,' my father chuckled, and then he explained to him that they were brothels.

'Oh, no, no, no!' replied the visitor. 'Not that kind of experience! A spiritual experience, and I have here a relic to prove it.' And he proceeded to take out a clean white handkerchief from which fell a tiny chip of timber. And my father nearly fell out of his standing. 'A chip of timber? A relic?' he exclaimed.

'Yes,' said the foreigner in hushed tones. ' 'Tis from the Blessed Man's bed itself. Matt Talbot.'

'You, my friend, must be mad,' said my father. 'It's a piece of a railway sleeper and I wouldn't be minding only it's a Protestant railway sleeper off the Great Northern Railway!'

Luckily the foreigner did not understand so my old man decided not to press the point. After all, it was helping the country's economy.

However, I am digressing. I sent the first draft of the detective story, which I called *The Scarperer*, to Smiley and although he agreed to publish it in the *Irish Times*, he did not feel able at this stage of the game to pay me an advance on it. I went to Kilmurvey on the big Aran Island to finish it, and although I ran short of the readies and had to wire to Smiley to this effect—not without success—I was also privileged to attend one of the best hooleys I was at.

Máire Conghaile has guests of half a dozen European nationalities there, and I take the liberty of having been real proud of her cooking. German and French were united in praise of her art, delicate and lavish. As well they might, for I'm a fair judge, well used to the good grub and knacky manipulation of sauce and meat by my mother, who cooked at one time for Maud Gonne MacBride.

The first instalment of *The Scarperer* appeared on October 19th, 1953, and when the month had really begun to feel its age I was back in my native city moseying around the pubs in the fashionable area of Grafton Street. For God send, if you don't get down town you'd hear nothing. And it was the Dublin intelligentsia who fell to talking about Emmet Street, some of whom knew him, but the more didn't, and for once in a way I did not get in on the act. It was sufficient to know, although not out of their mind about me, they liked Emmet Street, and when pressed I will even drink with nobility.

E VERYBODY knows what they mean when they talk about a working man. It means someone that does things that are dirty, boring, dangerous, or all three. Talking about an artist working is like talking about a priest working, like they used to tell me when I was a kid. If it is so obvious that a priest is also a worker, why in the name of Jesus do they have to keep rubbing it in? You never heard anyone emphasizing the fact that a docker is a worker and you never heard anyone saying: 'Oh, a coal-miner is a worker too, you know.'

But we can't all be artists. Someone has to do the ordinary work of the world, and I have been known to lend a hand in the house-painting line. And not alone did I get paid for working but I also got paid 'wet time', which is the money you get when you are not able to work during the rain—a not infrequent occurrence in the British Islands. And I was discussing these things one time with some students in a bar.

'Surely you want to take part in the world's work?' they asked.

'No,' I replied truthfully. 'I've resigned till they get automation.'

So the ginger-haired youth of about twenty summers looked shocked. 'You're an anarchist,' he said.

'Excuse yourself,' I replied. 'Don't call me an anarchist. I won't be insulted. I have a brother who is an anarchist in London, which means singing red songs to the amused toleration of the police. And they get on the Third programme of the B.B.C. too. Revolutionary, romantic and respectable. That's London anarchism. You can get in with millionaire's daughters and all, but they are one breed of bastards I don't fancy. They remind me of the Salvation Army.'

'Maybe you like the Party?' said ginger-top.

'I like them well enough in Ireland, but I don't know would

251

I like them if I was in Russia. They're never done talking about work for the working-class and more production. Everyone wants the poor bloody working-class to work, the Russians included. They'd even make me work if I was there, I suppose. But I'm all for them here. They frighten the other craw-thumpers and the government. All the big-bellied bastards that I hate hate the Reds. Catholic, Protestant, Orange, Green, Trinity College, the National University, the Racing Board, the Committee for Civil Liberties, Ulster Conservatives, New Statesmen, Freemasons and the Knights of Columbus, all hate the Reds. But I also hate the Reds individually. They are snobbish and ill-mannered and if you haven't a job and aren't looking for one, they have no time for you.'

So this surprised the students. 'Snobbish?' they asked incredulously.

'Sure. They wouldn't give anyone a free trip to Russia except he had an education and owned an estate. The last Delegation they sent was three-quarters well-off Protestants, and the Chinese nearly shot them because they couldn't be kept out of the British Legation looking for tea and a read of the *Daily Mail*. And they are ill-mannered because if you mooch into a pub on the cripple and crutch—the touch—looking for a drink, they ignore you on account of your being a parasite.'

'You're an individualist,' said a long-haired youth disguised as a poet.

'Wasn't Christ?' I replied. 'But I don't really give a damn about Christ. Besides being the only man you've ever met that wouldn't take honest employment at Trade Union wages, I have another distinction. I'm the only person I've ever heard that is superstitious and not religious. I am a daylight atheist. Only in the night, or if I am very ill, do I favourably consider the claims of religion. In the daylight and in good health—in other words under the only circumstances where a man can give an honest answer to these things—I consider that Christ went in for a lot of rubbish. Why can't we just walk around enjoying ourselves and have a drink and a sit down and a feed and a bit of the other? A job is death without the dignity. Death always has dignity. Maybe dying hasn't much dignity but once dead man becomes defiant. You can no longer frighten him.'

There was this man standing at the bar and he came across to me. 'I have been listening to you,' he said, 'and I don't altogether know what some of your statements mean.'

'Neither do I,' I replied in all sincerity, 'but I had to say something to those bastards.'

So he insisted that we go to his home. Now I've always known that to take a person home when he's a little bit drunk is to indicate that you are the man responsible for his being drunk, so I was uneasy in my mind as we walked up to the door of his house in Morehampton Road.

We went into the front room and there was an old lady, whom I came to dearly love, listening to the B.B.C. Third programme, and another lady who didn't show any appreciation of my taking her husband home. There was a little girl doing her school homework, who was going to be my sister-in-law later on, and then there was a girl who walked out the door as we came in.

'Excuse me, miss,' I said, but she was out like a shot with never a word in reply.

'Goodnight, Miss,' I shouted at her. 'I don't know you, neither do I want to know you,' and ever nimble on my feet in those times I was back on the road again, breathing fresh air, but angry with it too.

A while later I was asked by some more civilized person to a party in Clontarf Castle, and it was a good hooley too, with plenty of the hard stuff and a bite to eat. And the night was well over age when this girl comes across to me. 'I'm Beatrice,' she said.

'No,' I said. 'I don't want to speak to you and I don't want to see you. You're a bourgeois swine and I don't like people like that,' but to tell the honest truth, I could have bitten off my tongue the moment I said it, for she turned away and someone told me she was in tears. Now I am not that much of a savage that I like to see anyone in tears so I went across to her.

'Look,' I said, 'I'm sorry if I upset you, but why are you in tears?'

'Why did you speak to me like that in front of everyone?' she asked sadly.

'And why did you behave to me the way you behaved up at your house in front of your family?'

253

She lowered her eyes. 'Because I was shy,' she said.

So I apologised again and said I did not mean to insult her and all to that effect and we made a date. And I remember on our very first date I asked her would she ever have the loan of a pound?

So we went to some pub on the outskirts of Dublin and we drank her pound and I suppose I tried to seduce her, when she tells me about this other fellow, Jim, whom she is thinking of marrying. Yes, said I in my own mind, but it won't be this day nor the next.

And we left it at that. And although I saw her from time to time afterwards, it was not until 1954 that we really saw a deal of each other. Alan Simpson and Carolyn Swift had started at the Pike, a tiny back lane theatre seating from sixty to seventy people, and I had sent them my play, *The Twisting of Another Rope*.

I was doing bits of articles by the week for the *Irish Press* at the time, a most healthy state of affairs, and as good a reason as ever for paying my respects to the city of London. It is diffi-cult to believe that that city is named after a Celtic god, Lud, whose name survives today, unchanged, in Ludgate Circus, near Saint Paul's, and in a public house called the 'King Lud', hidden beneath the towering bulk of Wren's masterpiece.

Lud's name is identified by Celtic mythologists with Lir, the Irish sea god, who brought the secret of the calendar alpha-bet to Ireland. In our alphabet, each letter represents a tree which is sacred to a certain month. I can only remember a few of them—*Ailm* (elm), *Beith* (birch), *Coll* (hazel), *Dair* (oak), but they can be found in *Dinneen*, the English-Irish dictionary. Incidentally, I cannot understand why they are not taught in the schools. Apart from anything else, it would give children the names of the trees.

Lir's principle home was the Isle of Man. Nearby Ludgate Circus is the church of Saint Bride, the most popular saint of all Celtic peoples, Britain, Scotland or Ireland, her home. How many of the thousands of Londoners, to whom these names are familiar, give thought to the common Celtic heritage of these islands from the days of antiquity?

Up to the middle of the last century, the Irish language was used extensively in the East End, and I was myself in the York

Road area of Leeds greeted with 'Kay kee will too?' by an elderly man who otherwise spoke the purest Yorkshire.

He told me, wistfully, that this was the way all the old people greeted each other, and with nostalgia he described the Saturday night scenes of his childhood when the old crowd gathered outside the 'Yorkshire Hussar' on the way home, while a 'fine hupstanding woman, she were, 'ad reared 'er family, after 'er man was killed in mine, upcountry, working twelve hours a day in mill,' threw back the shawl from off her head and sang up to the dark and alien sky, over the upturned toil-worn faces of the men and women listening to her, lost in memory and back, on a spring morn in Connacht, the song of the *Red Haired Man's* wife.

The Celt has many tracts on the banks of the Thames. Mananaan Mac Lir is commemorated in these parts, and Padraic O Conaire, Michael Collins, Sam Maguire and Doctor Mark Ryan, lived and worked there.

Tradition is the most persistent of man's creation. Pedants and scholars have often been proved wrong when some archaeologist takes the old myths and traditions seriously. Eighty years ago nobody believed that the Trojan War had ever been fought, except in Homer's imagination, until Schliemann actually dug up the flattened walls of Ilium and proved to the world that Homer's Trojan War was as real as Tolstoy's Battle of Austerlitz.

I was conducting an argument in English on these things with Joe and Kathy McGill, with whom I was staying in London at this stage of the game, when the phone rang and Joe called me over. It was Carolyn Swift. She and Alan had read my play and offered me a production of four weeks at the Pike.

'For God's sake, Carolyn, how much?' I asked, echoing Yeats' sentiments.

'Thirty Pounds,' she replied, 'but we want to change the title to *The Quare Fellow*.'

'For thirty pounds you can change the title to any bloody thing you like,' I laughed. I put down the receiver and far into the night the three of us lifted pints in the name of the Celtic god, Lud, and so far round they went, like a five-noggin bottle at a Wake, it was forgotten who first provided them.

In the morning I left for France. And she looked much the

same as usual, except for the fact that the Metro had gone up thirty francs and the Government of Mendès-France was getting a little less abuse than previous governments.

Thirty francs was about eightpence at the time, and for a short journey was rather dear. But once you bought your ticket you were at liberty to go anywhere the Metro went, and it would take you right from one end of the city to the other.

The first thing one learns on visiting Paris is that it is not what it was. I was told that some years ago, and for the first time was able to pass that remark to some Irish students half a generation younger than myself.

I did not really believe it, though things were a bit dearer. A hotel room was five hundred francs a night, which was about ten shillings, and not much if you think in terms of Galway race week, but twice as much as six or seven years ago.

Old Raymond Duncan, who ran the Akademia of Greek culture in the Rue Dauphine, was either dead or in America. Time was when I watched him and his disciples, and with what ecstasy I saw them trip over a wire thoughtfully provided by the boys of the Beaux Arts and stretched ankle high across the road. God be with the youth of us, the simple pleasures of the poor.

The Bonapartist who used to march along the Boulevard St.-Germain in his long coat and cocked hat was no longer in evidence; nor was Confucius, the old Chinaman, whom Jeus christened God.

But the Pergola was still open *jour et nuit*, and its proprietor still large and affable and very wide awake behind the bar, though he could hardly have got a sleep since the last time I was there.

He remembered me and shook me warmly by the hand when I went in. He asked me how long I expected to be around this time. I told him I was off to the Riveira in the morning and he smiled even more cordially and did not seem at all upset at the prospect of my departure after so short a visit. He remembered me all right.

In the south, I re-acquainted myself with Ralph Cusack, swam in the sea at Cannes, and acquainted myself with Sugar Ray Robinson, who was knocking up a bit in the Hollywood night-club at Juan les Pins. But time waits on no man and I wanted to be on that other island across the way for the rehearsals of *The Quare Fellow*.

I had to go back to Paris and be up early for the boat train in the morning, and I walked in sweet melancholy from the Avenue de l'Opera towards the Behan H.Q. situated in the Rue de Charenten and—not inappropriately, some may think—near the Place de la Bastille. My way lay through the edge of the Market districts, where I had spent many a happy sunrise and I joined some porters I knew in a cup of coffee. But British Railways wait on no man neither.

The journey, though, is not altogether to the advantage of that organisation, the profits and responsibility of the traffic being equally divided with the French Railways. This may account for the difference in comfort on the run, Victoria-Newhaven-Dieppe-Paris, and the horrors of travel between Dublin and London.

On the sea journey, the French ships, *Londres* and *Arromanches*, take it turn and turn about with the English ships. I cannot see why C.I.E. doesn't demand a similar arrangement on the run between Ireland and England and enforce better treatment for the passengers, most of whom are Irish people anyway.

At Saint Lazare Station, I need hardly say, I very nearly missed the train. I had lost the ticket of my luggage. You wouldn't get much for the lot in Cole's Lane, but my typewriter was amongst the scrap. I was arguing as best as I could to get it back before the train left, when a young clerk came up and asked me where I was from. I said Ireland and his face lit up as he bustled about.

'Syracusecque,' he muttered. 'Syracusecque,' and came back with the luggage and ten minutes to spare. 'Syracusecque,' he said in triumph, and shook my hand.

'The same to you,' said I, and was on the train and half way to Rouen when I figured out that this incantation referred to Cyril Cusack, latest hero of the theatre-going population of the city behind me.

'Twas the Playboy himself procured my release, mister honey.

I have been in the theatre business all my life, for one section of my family have been supplying costumes, running theatres and owning cinemas for generations. From the age of four, I had watched good old melodrama at the Queen's Theatre in Dublin:

'The O'Grady is as proud a title as any of your earls or dukes, and bedamned to you. I may be an English officer, but I'm also an Irish gentleman!' And with that, the hero of the play flung the scarlet coat, gold epaulettes and all, on the floor, and in a frenzy of fury, foaming at the mouth, to the cheers and shouts of 'Up the Republic!' and croaks of 'Up, Skin-the-Goat!' from the more venerable of the multitude, he leapt the high steps of a slip-jig on the cloth of scarlet and gold.

'God bless you, P.J.,' screeches an ould one from the gods. 'That's me dream out. You'll turn yet.'

Rory and Séan, my step-brothers, and I looked round the parterre in a weakness of adoration, wishing there was someone there to tell the people to point from us to the stage and at the centre, glorious against the lights, a strapping lad from Kildare in his lawn shirt and velvet breeches, and to say: 'See those three kids there, and see your man there, the O'Grady, the Colonel that's after telling off the other rat of an English officer on the courtmartial? Well, he's their uncle.' And at the Wicklow wedding he led the floor, and came out to face his fancy with a smart rap of his buckled shoes and his back hand holding up the tails of his homespun coat, and his impudent, lovely head to one side, in signal to her to take the floor with him. Shy enough she was, till the fiddler ran through the first bit of *Haste to the Wedding*, when she looked up from the floor, gazed proud and fearless at him, and away they went.

'Isn't he the fine man, God bless him,' you'd hear an ould one mutter, as they rapped their way, she firm and light and he easy and strong through the hornpipe, a murmur of one fiddle played by the old man in the corner of the kitchen, while the orchestra in the pit looked up in unbegrudging admiration. 'A fine, lovely man.'

So he was at that, and never lived to be anything less.

And if I say it, as one who shouldn't, *The Quare Fellow* got good notices, and was pretty well packed for the twenty-eight performances, and I stood there thinking of my uncle, Paddy J. Bourke, and the times I had watched him performing in his own melodramas and in the plays of Dion Boucioault.

On the last night of my play, Beatrice came to the show with

Jim and her father. I sang a stave or two off-stage, and afterwards I invited Jim and herself and her father, who had a car at the time, out for a few sups. And we went to a pub on the docks, where you could drink after hours, called Tommy English's, and we stayed there until about three o'clock in the morning. But it was a particularly lousy situation, because when Jim was after telling me that he thought my play was marvellous, I wanted to say that I thought his girl friend was marvellous.

Instead, when Jim was setting up a round I fixed myself up with her for the next Sunday, but her father got so jarred that night that when he drove us home I thought all I'd ever be getting was a kip of mud in the bottom of the Liffey.

After this, we went to race meetings and parties together and to a few shows. I remember on one occasion going to see Sam Beckett's *Waiting for Godot*, which Alan and Carolyn also produced at the Pike Theatre, and I, happy with my luck, had had a few jars. And when one of the tramps in the play shouts out, 'But when you're dead, who'll pull the rope?' I shouted back from the stalls, 'I will.' And there's much laughter going on in the audience in the middle of this deadly serious play.

'Look, Beatrice,' I said in a low voice, wondering what to say that wouldn't be embarrassing her further, 'you know, I'm really respectable.'

'I don't care whether you're respectable or not,' she whispered back. 'I just happen to like you.'

So we were married in the Church of the Sacred Heart at Donnybrook, on Wednesday, the fifteenth of February, nineteen hundred and fifty-five, and she has liked me from that day to this.

And I can only say, like, 'I've been faithful to thee, after my fashion.'

Arena

☐	The Gooseboy	A L Barker	£3.99
☐	The History Man	Malcolm Bradbury	£3.50
☐	Rates of Exchange	Malcolm Bradbury	£3.50
☐	Albert's Memorial	David Cook	£3.99
☐	Another Little Drink	Jane Ellison	£3.99
☐	Mother's Girl	Elaine Feinstein	£3.99
☐	Roots	Alex Haley	£5.95
☐	The March of the Long Shadows	Norman Lewis	£3.99
☐	After a Fashion	Stanley Middleton	£3.50
☐	Kiss of the Spiderwoman	Manuel Puig	£2.95
☐	Second Sight	Anne Redmon	£3.99
☐	Season of Anomy	Wole Soyinka	£3.99
☐	Nairn in Darkness and Light	David Thomson	£3.99
☐	The Clock Winder	Anne Tyler	£2.95
☐	The Rules of Life	Fay Weldon	£2.50

Prices and other details are liable to change

ARROW BOOKS, BOOKSERVICE BY POST, PO BOX 29, DOUGLAS, ISLE OF MAN, BRITISH ISLES

NAME...

ADDRESS...

....

....

Please enclose a cheque or postal order made out to Arrow Books Ltd. for the amount due and allow the following for postage and packing.

U.K. CUSTOMERS: Please allow 22p per book to a maximum of £3.00.

B.F.P.O. & EIRE: Please allow 22p per book to a maximum of £3.00.

OVERSEAS CUSTOMERS: Please allow 22p per book.

Whilst every effort is made to keep prices low it is sometimes necessary to increase cover prices at short notice. Arrow Books reserve the right to show new retail prices on covers which may differ from those previously advertised in the text or elsewhere.

Bestselling General Fiction

☐ No Enemy But Time	Evelyn Anthony	£2.95
☐ Skydancer	Geoffrey Archer	£3.50
☐ The Sisters	Pat Booth	£3.50
☐ Captives of Time	Malcolm Bosse	£2.99
☐ Saudi	Laurie Devine	£2.95
☐ Duncton Wood	William Horwood	£4.50
☐ Aztec	Gary Jennings	£3.95
☐ A World Apart	Marie Joseph	£3.50
☐ The Ladies of Missalonghi	Colleen McCullough	£2.50
☐ Lily Golightly	Pamela Oldfield	£3.50
☐ Sarum	Edward Rutherfurd	£4.99
☐ Communion	Whitley Strieber	£3.99

Prices and other details are liable to change

ARROW BOOKS, BOOKSERVICE BY POST, PO BOX 29, DOUGLAS, ISLE
OF MAN, BRITISH ISLES

NAME...

ADDRESS..

....

....

Please enclose a cheque or postal order made out to Arrow Books Ltd. for the amount
due and allow the following for postage and packing.

U.K. CUSTOMERS: Please allow 22p per book to a maximum of £3.00.

B.F.P.O. & EIRE: Please allow 22p per book to a maximum of £3.00.

OVERSEAS CUSTOMERS: Please allow 22p per book.

Whilst every effort is made to keep prices low it is sometimes necessary to increase cover
prices at short notice. Arrow Books reserve the right to show new retail prices on covers
which may differ from those previously advertised in the text or elsewhere.

A Selection of Arrow Books

☐	No Enemy But Time	Evelyn Anthony	£2.95
☐	The Lilac Bus	Maeve Binchy	£2.99
☐	Rates of Exchange	Malcolm Bradbury	£3.50
☐	Prime Time	Joan Collins	£3.50
☐	Rosemary Conley's Complete Hip and Thigh Diet	Rosemary Conley	£2.99
☐	Staying Off the Beaten Track	Elizabeth Gundrey	£6.99
☐	Duncton Wood	William Horwood	£4.50
☐	Duncton Quest	William Horwood	£4.50
☐	A World Apart	Marie Joseph	£3.50
☐	Erin's Child	Sheelagh Kelly	£3.99
☐	Colours Aloft	Alexander Kent	£2.99
☐	Gondar	Nicholas Luard	£4.50
☐	The Ladies of Missalonghi	Colleen McCullough	£2.50
☐	The Veiled One	Ruth Rendell	£3.50
☐	Sarum	Edward Rutherfurd	£4.99
☐	Communion	Whitley Strieber	£3.99

Prices and other details are liable to change

ARROW BOOKS, BOOKSERVICE BY POST, PO BOX 29, DOUGLAS, ISLE OF MAN, BRITISH ISLES

NAME...

ADDRESS...

....

....

Please enclose a cheque or postal order made out to Arrow Books Ltd. for the amount due and allow the following for postage and packing.

U.K. CUSTOMERS: Please allow 22p per book to a maximum of £3.00.

B.F.P.O. & EIRE: Please allow 22p per book to a maximum of £3.00.

OVERSEAS CUSTOMERS: Please allow 22p per book.

Whilst every effort is made to keep prices low it is sometimes necessary to increase cover prices at short notice. Arrow Books reserve the right to show new retail prices on covers which may differ from those previously advertised in the text or elsewhere.

Bestselling Fiction

☐ No Enemy But Time	Evelyn Anthony	£2.95
☐ The Lilac Bus	Maeve Binchy	£2.99
☐ Prime Time	Joan Collins	£3.50
☐ A World Apart	Marie Joseph	£3.50
☐ Erin's Child	Sheelagh Kelly	£3.99
☐ Colours Aloft	Alexander Kent	£2.99
☐ Gondar	Nicholas Luard	£4.50
☐ The Ladies of Missalonghi	Colleen McCullough	£2.50
☐ Lily Golightly	Pamela Oldfield	£3.50
☐ Talking to Strange Men	Ruth Rendell	£2.99
☐ The Veiled One	Ruth Rendell	£3.50
☐ Sarum	Edward Rutherfurd	£4.99
☐ The Heart of the Country	Fay Weldon	£2.50

Prices and other details are liable to change

ARROW BOOKS, BOOKSERVICE BY POST, PO BOX 29, DOUGLAS, ISLE OF MAN, BRITISH ISLES

NAME...

ADDRESS...

....

....

Please enclose a cheque or postal order made out to Arrow Books Ltd. for the amount due and allow the following for postage and packing.

U.K. CUSTOMERS: Please allow 22p per book to a maximum of £3.00.

B.F.P.O. & EIRE: Please allow 22p per book to a maximum of £3.00.

OVERSEAS CUSTOMERS: Please allow 22p per book.

Whilst every effort is made to keep prices low it is sometimes necessary to increase cover prices at short notice. Arrow Books reserve the right to show new retail prices on covers which may differ from those previously advertised in the text or elsewhere.

Bestselling Non-Fiction

☐ Complete Hip and Thigh Diet	Rosemary Conley	£2.99
☐ Staying off the Beaten Track	Elizabeth Gundrey	£6.99
☐ Raw Energy: Recipes	Leslie Kenton	£3.99
☐ The PM System	Dr J A Muir Gray	£5.99
☐ Women Who Love Too Much	Robin Norwood	£3.50
☐ Letters From Women Who Love Too Much	Robin Norwood	£3.50
☐ Fat is a Feminist Issue	Susie Orbach	£2.99
☐ Callanetics	Callan Pinckney	£6.99
☐ Elvis and Me	Priscilla Presley	£3.50
☐ Love, Medicine and Miracles	Bernie Siegel	£3.50
☐ Communion	Whitley Strieber	£3.50
☐ Trump: The Art of the Deal	Donald Trump	£3.99

Prices and other details are liable to change

ARROW BOOKS, BOOKSERVICE BY POST, PO BOX 29, DOUGLAS, ISLE
OF MAN, BRITISH ISLES

NAME..

ADDRESS ....

....

....

Please enclose a cheque or postal order made out to Arrow Books Ltd. for the amount
due and allow the following for postage and packing.

U.K. CUSTOMERS: Please allow 22p per book to a maximum of £3.00.

B.F.P.O. & EIRE: Please allow 22p per book to a maximum of £3.00.

OVERSEAS CUSTOMERS: Please allow 22p per book.

Whilst every effort is made to keep prices low it is sometimes necessary to increase cover
prices at short notice. Arrow Books reserve the right to show new retail prices on covers
which may differ from those previously advertised in the text or elsewhere.